THE WORLD'S CLASSICS

—

WILLIAM WORDSWORTH

Selected Poetry

—

Edited with an Introduction and Notes by
STEPHEN GILL and DUNCAN WU

Oxford   New York

OXFORD UNIVERSITY PRESS

1997

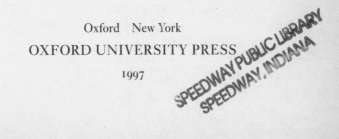

Oxford University Press, Great Clarendon Street, Oxford OX2 6DP

Oxford New York
Athens Auckland Bangkok Bogota Bombay Buenos Aires
Calcutta Cape Town Dar es Salaam Delhi Florence Hong Kong
Istanbul Karachi Kuala Lumpur Madras Madrid Melbourne
Mexico City Nairobi Paris Singapore Taipei Tokyo Toronto
and associated companies in
Berlin Ibadan

Oxford is a trade mark of Oxford University Press

British Library Cataloguing in Publication Data
Data available

Library of Congress Cataloging in Publication Data
Wordsworth, William, 1770–1850.
[Poems. Selections]
Selected poetry / William Wordsworth ; edited with an introduction
by Stephen Gill and Duncan Wu.
p. cm.—(The world's classics)
Includes bibliographical references (p.) and indexes.
I. Gill, Stephen Charles. II. Wu, Duncan. III. Title.
IV. Series.
PR5853.G54 1997 821.7—dc20 96–44123
ISBN 0–19–283280–8

1 3 5 7 9 10 8 6 4 2

Printed in Great Britain by
Biddles Ltd
Guildford and King's Lynn

W………………………………………………… in the
La………………………………………………… ol and
St………………………………………………… rance,
Lo………………………………………………… in his
wr………………………………………………… with
Co………………………………………………… ed his
voc………………………………………………… Here
he ………………………………………………… age in
1802, however, did not signal retreat. *Lyrical Ballads* (1798–1805) and
Poems in Two Volumes (1807) provoked much hostility and
Wordsworth had to fight to establish himself as the first poet of the
age. In 1843 he was appointed Poet Laureate, in public recognition of
the veneration in which he had long been held.

STEPHEN GILL is a Professor of English Literature in the University
of Oxford and a Fellow of Lincoln College. He has written *William
Wordsworth: A Life* (Oxford, 1989) and has edited *The Salisbury Plain
Poems of William Wordsworth* for the Cornell Wordsworth series.

DUNCAN WU is a Reader in English Literature at the University of
Glasgow. His publications include *Wordsworth's Reading 1770–1799*
(Cambridge, 1993); *Wordsworth's Reading 1800–1815* (Cambridge,
1995); *Romanticism: An Anthology* (Oxford, 1994); and *Romanticism:
A Critical Reader* (1995).

FRANK KERMODE, retired King Edward VII Professor of English
Literature at Cambridge, is the General Editor of The Oxford Authors
Series. He is the author of many books, including *Romantic Image,
The Sense of an Ending, The Classic, The Genesis of Secrecy, Forms of
Attention*, and *History and Value;* he is also co-editor with John
Hollander of *The Oxford Anthology of English Literature*.

Contents

Introduction

In June 1797 Coleridge arrived at Racedown Lodge in Dorset, where William and Dorothy Wordsworth had been living since 1795. 'We have both a distinct remembrance of his arrival', Wordsworth recalled in old age, 'He did not keep to the high road, but leapt over a gate and bounded down the pathless field, by which he cut off an angle. We both retain the liveliest possible image of his appearance at that moment.' It was the beginning of a unique relationship, which was to produce a revolution in literature. Throughout the 1790s Coleridge had responded more actively than Wordsworth to political events, even entering with Robert Southey into plans for an egalitarian society to be founded in America by a few like-minded idealists. After the collapse of that scheme he wrote, lectured, preached, drawing no line between religion and politics and bringing to bear on every subject the resources of a genuinely philosophic as well as a naturally poetic mind. Personal attraction between him and Wordsworth warmed to a love that, however tested by later misunderstandings, remained with both for their lifetimes.

To Coleridge, Wordsworth was 'a very great man—the only man to whom *at all times* and *in all modes of excellence* I feel myself inferior' (17 July 1797). To Wordsworth, Coleridge was always 'The rapt One, of the godlike forehead',[1] one of the two beings, he later declared, 'to whom my intellect is most indebted' (25 June 1832). It was a love that fused their minds during the *annus mirabilis* 1797–8 into a symbiotic creative power.[2] In summer 1798 Joseph Cottle was anxious to publish some of Wordsworth's longer poems, but Wordsworth resisted and it was a joint volume, *Lyrical Ballads*, which finally appeared.[3]

'The Ruined Cottage', 'Tintern Abbey', and other less obviously

---

[1] The phrase is from the tribute to Coleridge in 'Extempore Effusion . . .' (1835). Occasioned by the death of James Hogg, this, the most moving of Wordsworth's later verse, is a lament for a whole generation of friends.

[2] For an invaluable account, see Thomas McFarland, 'The Symbiosis of Coleridge and Wordsworth', *Studies in Romanticism*, 11 (1972), 263–303.

[3] The events which led to the publication of *Lyrical Ballads* are confusing. For the best unravelling see Mark L. Reed, 'Wordsworth, Coleridge, and the "Plan" of the *Lyrical Ballads*', *University of Toronto Quarterly*, 34 (1964–5), 238–53 and the introduction to Owen's edition of *Lyrical Ballads 1798*, (Oxford, 1967, 1969).

ambitious poems in *Lyrical Ballads* embody the convictions which
Wordsworth was struggling both to express in poetry and to live by.
What were they? The philosophical verse beginning 'Not useless
do I deem . . .' offers a sequential exposition: the universe is not
mechanical and dead, but alive and vitally connected with the
human mind; awakened consciousness leads to an awakened moral
sense and must lead to communion with the divine. In the
profoundest sense, love of nature leads to love of Man and
awareness of God. Such philosophical verse, however, was not
Wordsworth's real strength. The power of the other poems of
1797–8 is that they do not propose a chain of reasoning but draw
the reader to share Wordsworth's thought through lyrical utterance
and dramatic narrative which embody a sense of reverence for Man
and nature. They everywhere assert the vital significance of feeling
both as a bond between men and as a means of discovering truth
and declare as in 'Tintern Abbey' the unity of the individual
consciousness with the divine. Above all these poems declare by
their very form as poetry Wordsworth's newly confident belief in
poetry's special power to teach by incorporating 'itself with the
blood & vital juices of our minds'[4] and by appealing to the
imagination and to the 'grand elementary principle of pleasure, by
which man knows, and feels, and lives, and moves'. Much in these
poems, especially their emphasis on the inherent worth of simple
men, can be related to the political and social ferment of the times.
Hazlitt was not the only one to see that Wordsworth's poetry
'partakes of, and is carried along with, the revolutionary movement
of our age . . . His Muse . . . is a levelling one'.[5] Much of the
thought can be traced to eighteenth-century philosophy and psych-
ology. The particular nature of many of the poems is determined
by Wordsworth's quarrel with prevailing literary modes. But what
made the achievement of 1797–8 so great and, when all the
scholarly footnotes have been written, still a new beginning in
English poetry, is that the poems of whatever kind embodied a
coherent and unified vision of man and nature which had been
tested and found firm by a man searching not only for poetry but
for a basis to his life. Turbulent years of conflicting experience
brought, finally, not the somnolent peace of a closed mind, but

---

[4] From W's *Essay on Morals* (Prose, i. 103), in which he takes as impotent 'such
books as Mr Godwyn's, Mr Paley's, & those of the whole tribe of authors of that
class'.

[5] William Hazlitt, 'Mr Wordsworth', in *The Spirit of the Age* (1825).

certain calm assurances. It is not surprising that Wordsworth should have ended this first period with thanks for his 'more than Roman confidence' and hymns of praise to the Power that gave him 'A never-failing principle of joy | And purest passion'.

When Wordsworth entered Dove Cottage in December 1799 he began a new phase of life which was to be, in essentials, the pattern until he died. Financial uncertainty remained, but the years of wandering were over. Grasmere and then nearby Rydal was to be his home, and domestic life with an extended family which included Dorothy Wordsworth and his wife's sister Sara, was to be the secure personal base on which his creative life rested. Greater shocks than most families have to suffer tested them: the overwhelming blow of John Wordsworth's death by shipwreck in 1805; the deaths of two infant children in 1812; the bitter breach with Coleridge in 1810–12; the recurrent mental illness in later life of Dorothy; the death in 1847 of the beloved daughter named after the beloved sister. But it has always been clear from Dorothy's Journal and from Wordsworth's recorded tributes how strong the Dove Cottage community was, and the recent discovery of the letters which passed between William and Mary in 1810–12 has provided further evidence of the power of the love that united them.

Crossing the threshold of Dove Cottage marked a new phase in Wordsworth's creative life as well. From one point of view 1800–15 might be called the years of *The Recluse*. This philosophical poem was conceived in 1798. Wordsworth's announcement on 6 March that he has already 'written 1300 lines of a poem in which I contrive to convey most of the knowledge of which I am possessed. My object is to give pictures of Nature, Man, and Society. Indeed I know not any thing which will not come within the scope of my plan', suggests both the speed with which he embraced the idea of a comprehensive philosophic work and the grandeur of the conception which was, undoubtedly, Coleridge's. In later life he recalled the 'plan laid out, and, I believe, partly suggested by me', that 'Wordsworth should assume the station of a man in mental repose, one whose principles were made up, and so prepared to deliver upon authority a system of philosophy'.[6]

Wordsworth always suspected and resisted *systems* of any sort, however, and it is not surprising that after the summer at Alfoxden

---

[6] *Table Talk*, 21 July 1832. C's fascinating recollection, which is too long to quote here, is reprinted in *PW*, v. 364.

sustained composition towards *The Recluse* eluded him. First came the 1799 autobiographical poem—welcomed by Coleridge to whom it was addressed, but only if it were to be 'the tail-piece of "The Recluse!"', for of nothing but "The Recluse" can I hear patiently' (21 October 1799). Work on *Home at Grasmere* in 1800 included the lines 'On Man, on Nature, and on human Life', which give substance to what was only vague ambition in March 1798, 'I know not any thing that will not come within the scope of my plan'. But *Home at Grasmere* proved a false dawn at that time, as did extensive revision to 'The Ruined Cottage' and 'The Pedlar'. *The Prelude* itself reveals the poet's consciousness of a greater mission yet to be accomplished. In the opening section this consciousness is an 'awful burthen' from which the poet takes refuge, beguiling himself 'with trust | That mellower years will bring a riper mind | And clearer insight' (i. 235–8). At the end of the poem it has become a beacon, beckoning both Wordsworth and Coleridge, 'Prophets of Nature', to the fulfilment of their vocation. Only after *The Prelude* was completed did work on *The Recluse* take first place. But when *The Excursion* (the only part of *The Recluse* to be published) appeared in 1814 it fell far short of achieving what had been hoped for in 1798. The Preface announced the design of the whole work for the first time and offered the lines 'On Man, on Nature, and on human Life' as a 'kind of *Prospectus* of the design and scope of the whole Poem', but the poem only really lives in passages which Wordsworth had retrieved from poetry written long before in 1798. Though to Keats *The Excursion* was one of the 'three things to rejoice at in this Age', it disappointed Coleridge and remained for Wordsworth a life-long reminder of unrealized ambition.[7]

Looked at from another point of view, however, and judged not by what Coleridge wanted Wordsworth to achieve but on what he actually did achieve, the years 1800–15 are years of triumph. By 1815 the poet who had echoed in 1800 Milton's 'Fit audience let me find though few' had declared his purpose, won an audience, and demonstrated in his own way the rightness of Coleridge's perception that he was 'a thinking feeling Philosopher habitually— that your Poetry was your Philosophy under the action of strong winds of Feeling—a sea rolling high' (23 July 1803).

[7] References to *The Recluse* in progress crop up long after the project had in reality died. In November 1829, for example, Dora Wordsworth wrote of their mixed feelings about *On the Power of Sound*: 'We all think there is a grandeur in this Poem but it ought to have been in the "Recluse" . . .'

Most important of all, perhaps, these are the years of 'Resolution and Independence', Ode ('There was a time'), 'Ode to Duty', 'Elegiac Stanzas . . . Peele Castle', and *The Prelude*. In this series of poems—closely linked in origin to Coleridge's 'Dejection: An Ode'—Wordsworth explores both as private man and as Poet the dark passages of anxiety, self-doubt, and imaginative weakening. *The Prelude* explicitly traces the growth of the poet's mind from birth to that never-to-be forgotten summer of 1798 when 'on Quantock's grassy hills | Far ranging, and among the sylvan coombs' Wordsworth and Coleridge had 'Together wantoned in wild poesy' (xiii. 393–4, 414). But it is also implicitly a record of Wordsworth's intellectual journey between 1799 and 1805. In its growth from two, to five, to eight and finally to thirteen books it expands to include developing ideas about the nature and function of the creative imagination and about the powers and limitations of language, and becomes the triumphant embodiment of Wordsworth's 'last and favourite aspiration . . . some philosophic song | Of truth that cherishes our daily life' (i. 229–31). It was not *The Recluse* and so it remained unpublished in Wordsworth's lifetime, always anticipating the never-to-be-written work, but it was, as M. H. Abrams has said, a poem of 'radical novelty',[8] the first truly great achievement of a new era in English poetry.

[8] M. H. Abrams, *Natural Supernaturalism* (1971), 74.

Chronology

1770	W born 7 April at Cockermouth.
1771	Dorothy Wordsworth born 25 September at Cockermouth.
1778	Mother, Ann Wordsworth, dies c.8 March.
1779	W enters Hawkshead Grammar School, lodging with Hugh and Ann Tyson.
1783	Father, John Wordsworth, dies 30 December.
1787	W's first published poem, 'Sonnet, on Seeing Miss Helen Maria Williams Weep at a Tale of Distress' appears in *The European Magazine* in March. October: W enters St John's College, Cambridge.
1788–9	Composition of 'An Evening Walk', published 1793. Storming of the Bastille, 14 July 1789.
1790	Walking tour in France and Switzerland with Robert Jones, July–October.
1791–2	W in London. In November 1791 returns to France and sees Revolutionary fervour in Paris. Is influenced by Michel Beaupuy. Love affair with Annette Vallon and birth of their daughter, Caroline, 15 December 1792. Returns to England to seek a livelihood.
1793	Louis XVI executed in January. War declared between England and France in February. W feels an outcast in his own country. Writes, but does not publish, a seditious *Letter to the Bishop of Llandaff* and after wandering penniless across Salisbury Plain into Wales composes 'Salisbury Plain'. Sees Tintern Abbey. William Godwin's *Political Justice* published, as Government repression of dissent intensifies.
1794	W reunited with DW in stay at Windy Brow, Keswick. In August-September stays at Rampside and sees Peele Castle. Nurses Raisley Calvert, who leaves W £900 on his death in January 1795. Execution of Robespierre 28 July.
1795	C lectures in Bristol on politics and religion. W a familiar figure in radical circles in London in spring and summer and regularly visits Godwin. Meets C and Southey in Bristol in August. Settles with DW at Racedown in Dorset and rewrites 'Salisbury Plain'.
1797	Completes play, *The Borderers* and moves to Alfoxden to be nearer C, with whom period of greatest intimacy begins. First

version of 'The Ruined Cottage' and plans for joint composition with C.

1798   The *annus mirabilis*. W completes 'The Ruined Cottage' and composes the bulk of the verse published anonymously in September as *Lyrical Ballads*. Plans for *The Recluse* first mentioned. W, DW, and C go to Germany and over winter W writes autobiographical verse, the foundation of *The Prelude*.

1799   By end April W back in England. Move into Dove Cottage, Grasmere in December.

1800   Begins *Home at Grasmere* and probably composes lines printed in 1814 as a 'Prospectus' to *The Recluse*. Works on poems for second edition of *Lyrical Ballads*, published January 1801, and writes *Preface*.

1802   Much lyrical poetry composed. Publication in April of further edition of *Lyrical Ballads*, with revised *Preface*. Peace of Amiens enables Ws to visit Annette and Caroline in August. W marries Mary Hutchinson (b. 1770, d. 1859) 4 October.

1803   War begins again and fear of invasion grows. Birth of first son, John. W, DW, and C tour Scotland from mid-August. The Ws meet Sir Walter Scott 17 September. C ill and planning to leave for better climate.

1804   Much composition, especially on *The Prelude*, enlarged after March from planned five-book structure. 'Ode to Duty' and completion of Ode ('There was a time'). C sails to Malta.

1805   5–6 February: John Wordsworth (b. 1772), Captain of the *Earl of Abergavenny*, drowned. W circle very deeply affected. W completes *The Prelude*.

1806–7   Visits London. Sees Sir George Beaumont's picture of Peele Castle in a storm. C at last returns, much changed by ill-health. W reads *The Prelude* to him. *Poems in Two Volumes* published in 1807 and ridiculed in reviews.

1808–9   Ws leave Dove Cottage for larger house in Grasmere, Allan Bank.

1810   Son, William, born 12 May. Misunderstanding leads to breach with C—healed in 1812.

1811–12   Deaths of Children, Thomas (b. 1806) and Catherine (b. 1808). Ws move from Allan Bank to Rectory, Grasmere.

1813   Becomes Distributor of Stamps for Westmorland, a post in the revenue service. Moves to Rydal Mount, home for the rest of his life. Completes *The Excursion*.

1814   *The Excursion* published, prefaced by an account of the plan for *The Recluse*. Further attack by reviewers.

1815–20   First Collected Edition of Poems published, with Preface, in 1815. W moves more widely in London circles and meets Keats in 1817. For the General Election of 1818 W campaigned hard in the Tory interest to the distress of many admirers.

1820–8   Publishes *The River Duddon* sonnet sequence in 1820. Tours Europe and revisits places last seen in 1790. Enlarged Collected Editions published 1820 and 1827. Tours the Rhine with C and much loved daughter Dora (b. 1804).

1829–35   Catholic emancipation issue greatly troubles W. Tours Scotland again September–October 1831 and sees Sir Walter Scott (d. 1832) for last time. Further Collected Edition 1832. C dies 25 July 1834.

1836–43   Further Collected Edition, revised as always, 1836. Tours France and Italy 1837. In 1839 W revises *The Prelude* for the last time. Resigns Stamp distributorship in 1842 and becomes Poet Laureate on Southey's death in 1843. Dictates Fenwick Notes. W now a widely celebrated figure, receiving honorary degrees from Durham and Oxford. Steady increase in American reputation.

1844–50   Supervises with great care one-volume Collected Edition of 1845 and the final edition in six volumes of 1849–50. W deeply stricken by the death of Dora, 9 July 1847. W dies 23 April 1850. *The Prelude* published in July by his wife and executors.

Note on the Text

'A correct text is the first object of an editor,' Wordsworth declared to Sir Walter Scott (7 November 1805), and he is clearly right. Deciding on a 'correct text' and an order of presentation for Wordsworth's own poems, however, is not a straightforward matter. Stephen Gill has discussed the issues at length in 'Wordsworth's Poems: The Question of Text', *Review of English Studies*, NS 34 (1983), 172–90 and we can only outline them here.

The Collected Edition of 1849–50 must be regarded as the poet's final authorized text, and Wordsworth's view of such texts was stated firmly to Alexander Dyce: 'You know what importance I attach to following strictly the last copy text of an author' (*c*.19 April 1830).

For the reader interested in the development of Wordsworth's art, however, this last edition is most unsatisfactory. Many poems have been considerably revised from their first published state, altered moreover not in one creative burst of revision, but at various times throughout Wordsworth's lifetime. Some poems which were not published soon after composition only appear in a text which fundamentally changes the original conception. Others, such as 'The Ruined Cottage', are incorporated into other works or dismembered to make new ones. Some poems which were published are excised from the canon, while others, much excellent poetry which includes *The Prelude*, were not published by Wordsworth at all. The 1849–50 edition might have canonical status from some bibliographical points of view, but it does not present all of the poetry, nor the poems as they appeared to Wordsworth's first readers.

There is a further objection to the last authorized edition, namely that its organization deliberately prevents a chronological reading. From 1815 onwards Wordsworth arranged his poems in groupings designed to 'assist the attentive Reader in perceiving their connection with each other', as he explained in the *Preface*. New categories were added after *Poems* (1815) and poems were moved from one to another, but overall this remained Wordsworth's preferred arrangement. What determines the relation of poems within his classification is not chronology of composition, but the powers of mind predominant in their creation, or relationship of subject-matter.

In the belief that a chronological presentation can best reveal the growth of the poet's mind (the subject, after all, of his greatest poem, *The Prelude*) and the unfolding of his imagination, this volume is ordered according to date of composition. It follows—and here we break with all of the editorial pioneers, Dowden, Knight, Hutchinson, De Selincourt, Darbishire—that one *must* print a text which comes as close as possible to the state of a poem when it was first completed.

The decision to break with the poet's wishes both as to text and arrangement means that for the majority of the poems we have taken the text of the first appearance in a Wordsworth volume, i.e. not in a newspaper or magazine. When a significant time elapsed between the completion of a poem and its publication we have returned to the manuscript text. For poems which Wordsworth did not publish at all, a category which includes *Home at Grasmere* and *The Prelude*, our text is similarly drawn from the first completed manuscript. Obvious printing errors have been silently corrected. Ampersands and 'd have been expanded, but Wordsworth's spelling has been retained. The punctuation of published texts has only been altered when absolutely necessary and in texts taken from manuscript we have punctuated lightly, trying to follow our source wherever possible. [   ] indicates a word missing in the manuscript; [word] indicates material supplied by the editors.

The date of composition for many of the poems can be established quite accurately. Some, on the other hand—'Yew–Trees' or *Home at Grasmere* for example—pose problems, the major one being that surviving manuscripts are not contemporaneous with what seems a likely date for first composition. We have relied heavily and with immense gratitude on the scholarship of Mark L. Reed, Jonathan Wordsworth, and the editors of the individual volumes in the Cornell Wordsworth series.

The Prelude has been printed outside the chronological sequence to emphasize the fact that its composition spanned 1799–1805, Wordsworth's greatest years. The text is that of the first completed thirteen-book version of 1805, but to place it under 1805 would have been as misleading as to place *The Prelude* under 1799 or 1803–4. In this edition it stands apart, but it is, of course, closely related to all the poems in the chronological sequence 1799–1805.

ACKNOWLEDGEMENT

Duncan Wu wishes to thank the British Academy for its generous help during work on this volume.

Old Man Travelling

ANIMAL TRANQUILLITY AND DECAY, A SKETCH

      The little hedge-row birds,
That peck along the road, regard him not.
He travels on, and in his face, his step,
His gait, is one expression; every limb,
His look and bending figure, all bespeak
A man who does not move with pain, but moves
With thought—He is insensibly subdued
To settled quiet: he is one by whom
All effort seems forgotten, one to whom
Long patience has such mild composure given,   10
That patience now doth seem a thing, of which
He hath no need. He is by nature led
To peace so perfect, that the young behold
With envy, what the old man hardly feels.
—I asked him whither he was bound, and what
The object of his journey; he replied
'Sir! I am going many miles to take
A last leave of my son, a mariner,
Who from a sea-fight has been brought to Falmouth,
And there is dying in an hospital.'   20

The Ruined Cottage

'Twas summer and the sun was mounted high.
Along the south the uplands feebly glared
Through a pale steam, and all the northern downs
In clearer air ascending shewed far off
Their surfaces with shadows dappled o'er
Of deep embattled clouds: far as the sight
Could reach those many shadows lay in spots
Determined and unmoved, with steady beams
Of clear and pleasant sunshine interposed;
Pleasant to him who on the soft cool moss   10
Extends his careless limbs beside the root

Of some huge oak whose aged branches make
A twilight of their own, a dewy shade
Where the wren warbles while the dreaming man,
Half-conscious of that soothing melody,
With side-long eye looks out upon the scene,
By those impending branches made more soft,
More soft and distant. Other lot was mine.
Across a bare wide Common I had toiled
With languid feet which by the slipp'ry ground   20
Were baffled still, and when I stretched myself
On the brown earth my limbs from very heat
Could find no rest nor my weak arm disperse
The insect host which gathered round my face
And joined their murmurs to the tedious noise
Of seeds of bursting gorse that crackled round.
I rose and turned towards a group of trees
Which midway in that level stood alone,
And thither come at length, beneath a shade
Of clustering elms that sprang from the same root   30
I found a ruined house, four naked walls
That stared upon each other. I looked round
And near the door I saw an aged Man,
Alone, and stretched upon the cottage bench;
An iron-pointed staff lay at his side.
With instantaneous joy I recognized
That pride of nature and of lowly life,
The venerable Armytage, a friend
As dear to me as is the setting sun.
                    Two days before   40
We had been fellow-travellers. I knew
That he was in this neighbourhood and now
Delighted found him here in the cool shade.
He lay, his pack of rustic merchandize
Pillowing his head—I guess he had no thought
Of his way-wandering life. His eyes were shut;
The shadows of the breezy elms above
Dappled his face. With thirsty heat oppressed
At length I hailed him, glad to see his hat
Bedewed with water-drops, as if the brim   50
Had newly scooped a running stream. He rose
And pointing to a sun-flower bade me climb

The [   ] wall where that same gaudy flower
Looked out upon the road. It was a plot
Of garden-ground, now wild, its matted weeds
Marked with the steps of those whom as they passed,
The goose-berry trees that shot in long lank slips,
Or currants hanging from their leafless stems
In scanty strings, had tempted to o'erleap
The broken wall. Within that cheerless spot,   60
Where two tall hedgerows of thick willow boughs
Joined in a damp cold nook, I found a well
Half-choked [with willow flowers and weeds.]
I slaked my thirst and to the shady bench
Returned, and while I stood unbonneted
To catch the motion of the cooler air
The old Man said, 'I see around me here
Things which you cannot see: we die, my Friend,
Nor we alone, but that which each man loved
And prized in his peculiar nook of earth   70
Dies with him or is changed, and very soon
Even of the good is no memorial left.
The Poets in their elegies and songs
Lamenting the departed call the groves,
They call upon the hills and streams to mourn,
And senseless rocks, nor idly; for they speak
In these their invocations with a voice
Obedient to the strong creative power
Of human passion. Sympathies there are
More tranquil, yet perhaps of kindred birth,   80
That steal upon the meditative mind
And grow with thought. Beside yon spring I stood
And eyed its waters till we seemed to feel
One sadness, they and I. For them a bond
Of brotherhood is broken: time has been
When every day the touch of human hand
Disturbed their stillness, and they ministered
To human comfort. When I stooped to drink,
A spider's web hung to the water's edge,
And on the wet and slimy foot-stone lay   90
The useless fragment of a wooden bowl;
It moved my very heart. The day has been
When I could never pass this road but she

Who lived within these walls, when I appeared,
A daughter's welcome gave me, and I loved her
As my own child. O Sir! the good die first,
And they whose hearts are dry as summer dust
Burn to the socket. Many a passenger
Has blessed poor Margaret for her gentle looks
When she upheld the cool refreshment drawn   100
From that forsaken spring, and no one came
But he was welcome, no one went away
But that it seemed she loved him. She is dead,
The worm is on her cheek, and this poor hut,
Stripped of its outward garb of houshold flowers,
Of rose and sweet-briar, offers to the wind
A cold bare wall whose earthy top is tricked
With weeds and the rank spear-grass. She is dead,
And nettles rot and adders sun themselves
Where we have sate together while she nursed   110
Her infant at her breast. The unshod Colt,
The wandring heifer and the Potter's ass,
Find shelter now within the chimney-wall
Where I have seen her evening hearth-stone blaze
And through the window spread upon the road
Its chearful light.—You will forgive me, Sir,
But often on this cottage do I muse
As on a picture, till my wiser mind
Sinks, yielding to the foolishness of grief.

She had a husband, an industrious man,   120
Sober and steady; I have heard her say
That he was up and busy at his loom
In summer ere the mower's scythe had swept
The dewy grass, and in the early spring
Ere the last star had vanished. They who passed
At evening, from behind the garden-fence
Might hear his busy spade, which he would ply
After his daily work till the day-light
Was gone and every leaf and flower were lost
In the dark hedges. So they passed their days   130
In peace and comfort, and two pretty babes
Were their best hope next to the God in Heaven.
—You may remember, now some ten years gone,
Two blighting seasons when the fields were left

With half a harvest. It pleased heaven to add
A worse affliction in the plague of war:
A happy land was stricken to the heart;
'Twas a sad time of sorrow and distress:
A wanderer among the cottages,
I with my pack of winter raiment saw   140
The hardships of that season: many rich
Sunk down as in a dream among the poor,
And of the poor did many cease to be,
And their place knew them not. Meanwhile, abridged
Of daily comforts, gladly reconciled
To numerous self-denials, Margaret
Went struggling on through those calamitous years
With chearful hope: but ere the second autumn
A fever seized her husband. In disease
He lingered long, and when his strength returned   150
He found the little he had stored to meet
The hour of accident or crippling age
Was all consumed. As I have said, 'twas now
A time of trouble; shoals of artisans
Were from their daily labour turned away
To hang for bread on parish charity,
They and their wives and children—happier far
Could they have lived as do the little birds
That peck along the hedges or the kite
That makes her dwelling in the mountain rocks.   160
Ill fared it now with Robert, he who dwelt
In this poor cottage; at his door he stood
And whistled many a snatch of merry tunes
That had no mirth in them, or with his knife
Carved uncouth figures on the heads of sticks,
Then idly sought about through every nook
Of house or garden any casual task
Of use or ornament, and with a strange,
Amusing but uneasy novelty
He blended where he might the various tasks   170
Of summer, autumn, winter, and of spring.
But this endured not; his good-humour soon
Became a weight in which no pleasure was,
And poverty brought on a petted mood
And a sore temper: day by day he drooped,

And he would leave his home, and to the town
Without an errand would he turn his steps
Or wander here and there among the fields.
One while he would speak lightly of his babes
And with a cruel tongue: at other times 180
He played with them wild freaks of merriment:
And 'twas a piteous thing to see the looks
Of the poor innocent children. "Every smile,"
Said Margaret to me here beneath these trees,
"Made my heart bleed."' At this the old Man paused
And looking up to those enormous elms
He said, "Tis now the hour of deepest noon.
At this still season of repose and peace,
This hour when all things which are not at rest
Are chearful, while this multitude of flies 190
Fills all the air with happy melody,
Why should a tear be in an old man's eye?
Why should we thus with an untoward mind
And in the weakness of humanity
From natural wisdom turn our hearts away,
To natural comfort shut our eyes and ears,
And feeding on disquiet thus disturb
The calm of Nature with our restless thoughts?'

SECOND PART

He spake with somewhat of a solemn tone:
But when he ended there was in his face 200
Such easy chearfulness, a look so mild
That for a little time it stole away
All recollection, and that simple tale
Passed from my mind like a forgotten sound.
A while on trivial things we held discourse,
To me soon tasteless. In my own despite
I thought of that poor woman as of one
Whom I had known and loved. He had rehearsed
Her homely tale with such familiar power,
With such a[n active] countenance, an eye 210
So busy, that the things of which he spake
Seemed present, and, attention now relaxed,
There was a heartfelt chillness in my veins.

I rose, and turning from that breezy shade
Went out into the open air and stood
To drink the comfort of the warmer sun.
Long time I had not stayed ere, looking round
Upon that tranquil ruin, I returned
And begged of the old man that for my sake
He would resume his story. He replied,   220
'It were a wantonness and would demand
Severe reproof, if we were men whose hearts
Could hold vain dalliance with the misery
Even of the dead, contented thence to draw
A momentary pleasure never marked
By reason, barren of all future good.
But we have known that there is often found
In mournful thoughts, and always might be found,
A power to virtue friendly; were't not so,
I am a dreamer among men, indeed   230
An idle dreamer. 'Tis a common tale,
By moving accidents uncharactered,
A tale of silent suffering, hardly clothed
In bodily form, and to the grosser sense
But ill adapted, scarcely palpable
To him who does not think. But at your bidding
I will proceed.
                    While thus it fared with them
To whom this cottage till that hapless year
Had been a blessed home, it was my chance
To travel in a country far remote.   240
And glad I was when, halting by yon gate
That leads from the green lane, again I saw
These lofty elm-trees. Long I did not rest:
With many pleasant thoughts I cheered my way
O'er the flat common. At the door arrived,
I knocked, and when I entered with the hope
Of usual greeting, Margaret looked at me
A little while, then turned her head away
Speechless, and sitting down upon a chair
Wept bitterly. I wist not what to do   250
Or how to speak to her. Poor wretch! at last
She rose from off her seat—and then, oh Sir!
I cannot tell how she pronounced my name:

With fervent love, and with a face of grief
Unutterably helpless, and a look
That seemed to cling upon me, she enquired
If I had seen her husband. As she spake
A strange surprize and fear came to my heart,
Nor had I power to answer ere she told
That he had disappeared—just two months gone.   260
He left his house; two wretched days had passed,
And on the third by the first break of light,
Within her casement full in view she saw
A purse of gold. "I trembled at the sight,"
Said Margaret, "for I knew it was his hand
That placed it there, and on that very day
By one, a stranger, from my husband sent,
The tidings came that he had joined a troop
Of soldiers going to a distant land.
He left me thus—Poor Man! he had not heart   270
To take a farewell of me, and he feared
That I should follow with my babes, and sink
Beneath the misery of a soldier's life."
This tale did Margaret tell with many tears:
And when she ended I had little power
To give her comfort, and was glad to take
Such words of hope from her own mouth as served
To cheer us both: but long we had not talked
Ere we built up a pile of better thoughts,
And with a brighter eye she looked around   280
As if she had been shedding tears of joy.
We parted. It was then the early spring;
I left her busy with her garden tools;
And well remember, o'er that fence she looked,
And while I paced along the foot-way path
Called out, and sent a blessing after me
With tender chearfulness and with a voice
That seemed the very sound of happy thoughts.
    I roved o'er many a hill and many a dale
With this my weary load, in heat and cold,   290
Through many a wood, and many an open ground,
In sunshine or in shade, in wet or fair,
Now blithe, now drooping, as it might befal,
My best companions now the driving winds

And now the "trotting brooks" and whispering trees
And now the music of my own sad steps,
With many a short-lived thought that passed between
And disappeared. I came this way again
Towards the wane of summer, when the wheat
Was yellow, and the soft and bladed grass   300
Sprang up afresh and o'er the hay-field spread
Its tender green. When I had reached the door
I found that she was absent. In the shade
Where now we sit I waited her return.
Her cottage in its outward look appeared
As chearful as before; in any shew
Of neatness little changed, but that I thought
The honeysuckle crowded round the door
And from the wall hung down in heavier wreathes,
And knots of worthless stone-crop started out   310
Along the window's edge, and grew like weeds
Against the lower panes. I turned aside
And strolled into her garden.—It was changed:
The unprofitable bindweed spread his bells
From side to side and with unwieldy wreaths
Had dragged the rose from its sustaining wall
And bent it down to earth; the border-tufts—
Daisy and thrift and lowly camomile
And thyme—had straggled out into the paths
Which they were used to deck. Ere this an hour   320
Was wasted. Back I turned my restless steps,
And as I walked before the door it chanced
A stranger passed, and guessing whom I sought
He said that she was used to ramble far.
The sun was sinking in the west, and now
I sate with sad impatience. From within
Her solitary infant cried aloud.
The spot though fair seemed very desolate:
The longer I remained more desolate.
And, looking round, I saw the corner-stones,   330
Till then unmarked, on either side the door
With dull red stains discoloured and stuck o'er
With tufts and hairs of wool, as if the sheep
That feed upon the commons thither came
Familiarly and found a couching-place

Even at her threshold.—The house-clock struck eight;
I turned and saw her distant a few steps.
Her face was pale and thin, her figure too
Was changed. As she unlocked the door she said,
"It grieves me you have waited here so long,   340
But in good truth I've wandered much of late
And sometimes, to my shame I speak, have need
Of my best prayers to bring me back again."
While on the board she spread our evening meal
She told me she had lost her elder child,
That he for months had been a serving-boy
Apprenticed by the parish. "I perceive
You look at me, and you have cause. Today
I have been travelling far, and many days
About the fields I wander, knowing this   350
Only, that what I seek I cannot find.
And so I waste my time: for I am changed;
And to myself," said she, "have done much wrong,
And to this helpless infant. I have slept
Weeping, and weeping I have waked; my tears
Have flowed as if my body were not such
As others are, and I could never die.
But I am now in mind and in my heart
More easy, and I hope," said she, "that heaven
Will give me patience to endure the things   360
Which I behold at home." It would have grieved
Your very heart to see her. Sir, I feel
The story linger in my heart. I fear
'Tis long and tedious, but my spirit clings
To that poor woman: so familiarly
Do I perceive her manner, and her look
And presence, and so deeply do I feel
Her goodness, that not seldom in my walks
A momentary trance comes over me;
And to myself I seem to muse on one   370
By sorrow laid asleep or borne away,
A human being destined to awake
To human life, or something very near
To human life, when he shall come again
For whom she suffered. Sir, it would have grieved
Your very soul to see her: evermore

Her eye-lids drooped, her eyes were downward cast;
And when she at her table gave me food
She did not look at me. Her voice was low,
Her body was subdued. In every act   380
Pertaining to her house-affairs appeared
The careless stillness which a thinking mind
Gives to an idle matter—still she sighed,
But yet no motion of the breast was seen,
No heaving of the heart. While by the fire
We sate together, sighs came on my ear;
I knew not how, and hardly whence they came.
I took my staff, and when I kissed her babe
The tears stood in her eyes. I left her then
With the best hope and comfort I could give;   390
She thanked me for my will, but for my hope
It seemed she did not thank me.

                              I returned
And took my rounds along this road again
Ere on its sunny bank the primrose flower
Had chronicled the earliest day of spring.
I found her sad and drooping; she had learned
No tidings of her husband: if he lived
She knew not that he lived; if he were dead
She knew not he was dead. She seemed the same
In person [   ] appearance, but her house   400
Bespoke a sleepy hand of negligence;
The floor was neither dry nor neat, the hearth
Was comfortless [   ],
The windows too were dim, and her few books,
Which, one upon the other, heretofore
Had been piled up against the corner-panes
In seemly order, now with straggling leaves
Lay scattered here and there, open or shut
As they had chanced to fall. Her infant babe
Had from its mother caught the trick of grief   410
And sighed among its playthings. Once again
I turned towards the garden-gate and saw
More plainly still that poverty and grief
Were now come nearer to her: the earth was hard,
With weeds defaced and knots of withered grass;
No ridges there appeared of clear black mould,

No winter greenness: of her herbs and flowers
It seemed the better part were gnawed away
Or trampled on the earth; a chain of straw
Which had been twisted round the tender stem   420
Of a young apple-tree lay at its root;
The bark was nibbled round by truant sheep.
Margaret stood near, her infant in her arms,
And seeing that my eye was on the tree
She said, "I fear it will be dead and gone
Ere Robert come again." Towards the house
Together we returned, and she inquired
If I had any hope. But for her Babe
And for her little friendless Boy, she said,
She had no wish to live, that she must die   430
Of sorrow. Yet I saw the idle loom
Still in its place. His sunday garments hung
Upon the self-same nail, his very staff
Stood undisturbed behind the door. And when
I passed this way beaten by Autumn winds
She told me that her little babe was dead
And she was left alone. That very time,
I yet remember, through the miry lane
She walked with me a mile, when the bare trees
Trickled with foggy damps, and in such sort   440
That any heart had ached to hear her begged
That wheresoe'er I went I still would ask
For him whom she had lost. We parted then,
Our final parting, for from that time forth
Did many seasons pass ere I returned
Into this tract again.
                    Five tedious years
She lingered in unquiet widowhood,
A wife and widow. Needs must it have been
A sore heart-wasting. I have heard, my friend,
That in that broken arbour she would sit   450
The idle length of half a sabbath day—
There, where you see the toadstool's lazy head—
And when a dog passed by she still would quit
The shade and look abroad. On this old Bench
For hours she sate, and evermore her eye
Was busy in the distance, shaping things

Which made her heart beat quick. Seest thou that path?
(The green-sward now has broken its grey line)
There to and fro she paced through many a day
Of the warm summer, from a belt of flax   460
That girt her waist spinning the long-drawn thread
With backward steps.—Yet ever as there passed
A man whose garments shewed the Soldier's red,
Or crippled Mendicant in Sailor's garb,
The little child who sate to turn the wheel
Ceased from his toil, and she with faltering voice,
Expecting still to learn her husband's fate,
Made many a fond inquiry; and when they
Whose presence gave no comfort were gone by,
Her heart was still more sad. And by yon gate   470
Which bars the traveller's road she often stood
And when a stranger horseman came, the latch
Would lift, and in his face look wistfully,
Most happy if from aught discovered there
Of tender feeling she might dare repeat
The same sad question. Meanwhile her poor hut
Sunk to decay, for he was gone whose hand
At the first nippings of October frost
Closed up each chink and with fresh bands of straw
Chequered the green-grown thatch. And so she lived   480
Through the long winter, reckless and alone,
Till this reft house by frost, and thaw, and rain
Was sapped; and when she slept the nightly damps
Did chill her breast, and in the stormy day
Her tattered clothes were ruffled by the wind
Even at the side of her own fire. Yet still
She loved this wretched spot, nor would for worlds
Have parted hence; and still that length of road
And this rude bench one torturing hope endeared,
Fast rooted at her heart, and here, my friend,   490
In sickness she remained, and here she died,
Last human tenant of these ruined walls.'

    The old Man ceased: he saw that I was moved;
From that low Bench, rising instinctively,
I turned aside in weakness, nor had power
To thank him for the tale which he had told.
I stood, and leaning o'er the garden-gate

Reviewed that Woman's suff'rings, and it seemed
To comfort me while with a brother's love
I blessed her in the impotence of grief.   500
At length [   ] the [   ]
Fondly, and traced with milder interest
That secret spirit of humanity
Which, 'mid the calm oblivious tendencies
Of nature, 'mid her plants, her weeds, and flowers,
And silent overgrowings, still survived.
The old man, seeing this, resumed and said,
'My Friend, enough to sorrow have you given,
The purposes of wisdom ask no more;
Be wise and chearful, and no longer read   510
The forms of things with an unworthy eye.
She sleeps in the calm earth, and peace is here.
I well remember that those very plumes,
Those weeds, and the high spear-grass on that wall,
By mist and silent rain-drops silvered o'er,
As once I passed did to my heart convey
So still an image of tranquillity,
So calm and still, and looked so beautiful
Amid the uneasy thoughts which filled my mind,
That what we feel of sorrow and despair   520
From ruin and from change, and all the grief
The passing shews of being leave behind,
Appeared an idle dream that could not live
Where meditation was. I turned away
And walked along my road in happiness.'
    He ceased. By this the sun declining shot
A slant and mellow radiance which began
To fall upon us where beneath the trees
We sate on that low bench, and now we felt,
Admonished thus, the sweet hour coming on.   530
A linnet warbled from those lofty elms,
A thrush sang loud, and other melodies,
At distance heard, peopled the milder air.
The old man rose and hoisted up his load.
Together casting then a farewell look
Upon those silent walls, we left the shade
And ere the stars were visible attained
A rustic inn, our evening resting-place.

[A Night-Piece]

                    The sky is overspread
With a close veil of one continuous cloud
All whitened by the moon, that just appears,
A dim-seen orb, yet chequers not the ground
With any shadow—plant, or tower, or tree.
At last a pleasant instantaneous light
Startles the musing man whose eyes are bent
To earth. He looks around, the clouds are split
Asunder, and above his head he views
The clear moon and the glory of the heavens.   10
There in a black-blue vault she sails along
Followed by multitudes of stars, that small,
And bright, and sharp along the gloomy vault
Drive as she drives. How fast they wheel away!
Yet vanish not! The wind is in the trees;
But they are silent. Still they roll along
Immeasurably distant, and the vault
Built round by those white clouds, enormous clouds,
Still deepens its interminable depth.
At length the vision closes, and the mind   20
Not undisturbed by the deep joy it feels,
Which slowly settles into peaceful calm,
Is left to muse upon the solemn scene.

[The Discharged Soldier]

                         I love to walk
Along the public way when for the night,
Deserted in its silence, it assumes
A character of deeper quietness
Than pathless solitudes. At such a time
I slowly mounted up a steep ascent
Where the road's watry surface to the ridge
Of that sharp rising glittered in the moon
And seemed before my eyes another stream
Stealing with silent lapse to join the brook   10

That murmured in the valley. On I passed
Tranquil, receiving in my own despite
Amusement, as I slowly passed along,
From such near objects as from time to time
Perforce disturbed the slumber of the sense
Quiescent, and disposed to sympathy,
With an exhausted mind worn out by toil
And all unworthy of the deeper joy
Which waits on distant prospect, cliff or sea,
The dark blue vault, and universe of stars.   20
Thus did I steal along that silent road,
My body from the stillness drinking in
A restoration like the calm of sleep
But sweeter far. Above, before, behind,
Around me, all was peace and solitude:
I looked not round, nor did the solitude
Speak to my eye, but it was heard and felt.
Oh happy state! What beauteous pictures now
Rose in harmonious imagery—they rose
As from some distant region of my soul   30
And came along like dreams, yet such as left
Obscurely mingled with their passing forms
A consciousness of animal delight,
A self-possession felt in every pause
And every gentle movement of my frame.
    While thus I wandered, step by step led on,
It chanced a sudden turning of the road
Presented to my view an uncouth shape
So near that, stepping back into the shade
Of a thick hawthorn, I could mark him well,   40
Myself unseen. He was in stature tall,
A foot above man's common measure tall,
And lank, and upright. There was in his form
A meagre stiffness. You might almost think
That his bones wounded him. His legs were long,
So long and shapeless that I looked at them
Forgetful of the body they sustained.
His arms were long and lean; his hands were bare;
His visage, wasted though it seemed, was large
In feature; his cheeks sunken; and his mouth   50
Shewed ghastly in the moonlight. From behind

A mile-stone propped him, and his figure seemed
Half-sitting and half-standing. I could mark
That he was clad in military garb,
Though faded yet entire. His face was turned
Towards the road, yet not as if he sought
For any living thing. He appeared
Forlorn and desolate, a man cut off
From all his kind, and more than half detached
From his own nature.   60
                        He was alone,
Had no attendant, neither dog, nor staff,
Nor knapsack—in his very dress appeared
A desolation, a simplicity
That appertained to solitude. I think
If but a glove had dangled in his hand
It would have made him more akin to man.
Long time I scanned him with a mingled sense
Of fear and sorrow. From his lips meanwhile
There issued murmuring sounds as if of pain   70
Or of uneasy thought; yet still his form
Kept the same fearful steadiness. His shadow
Lay at his feet and moved not. In a glen
Hard by a village stood, whose silent doors
Were visible among the scattered trees,
Scarce distant from the spot an arrow's flight.
I wished to see him move, but he remained
Fixed to his place, and still from time to time
Sent forth a murmuring voice of dead complaint,
A groan scarce audible. Yet all the while   80
The chained mastiff in his wooden house
Was vexed, and from among the village trees
Howled never ceasing. Not without reproach
Had I prolonged my watch, and now confirmed,
And my heart's specious cowardice subdued,
I left the shady nook where I had stood
And hailed the Stranger. From his resting-place
He rose, and with his lean and wasted arm
In measured gesture lifted to his head
Returned my salutation. A short while   90
I held discourse on things indifferent
And casual matter. He meanwhile had ceased

From all complaint—his station had resumed,
Propped by the mile stone as before, and when erelong
I asked his history, he in reply
Was neither slow nor eager, but unmoved,
And with a quiet uncomplaining voice,
A stately air of mild indifference,
He told a simple fact: that he had been
A Soldier, to the tropic isles had gone,   100
Whence he had landed now some ten days past;
That on his landing he had been dismissed,
And with the little strength he yet had left
Was travelling to regain his native home.
At this I turned and through the trees looked down
Into the village—all were gone to rest,
Nor smoke nor any taper light appeared,
But every silent window to the moon
Shone with a yellow glitter. 'No one there,'
Said I, 'is waking; we must measure back   110
The way which we have come. Behind yon wood
A labourer dwells, an honest man and kind;
He will not murmur should we break his rest,
And he will give you food if food you need,
And lodging for the night.' At this he stooped,
And from the ground took up an oaken staff
By me yet unobserved, a traveller's staff,
Which I suppose from his slack hand had dropped,
And, such the languor of the weary man,
Had lain till now neglected in the grass,   120
But not forgotten. Back we turned and shaped
Our course toward the cottage. He appeared
To travel without pain, and I beheld
With ill-suppressed astonishment his tall
And ghostly figure moving at my side.
As we advanced I asked him for what cause
He tarried there, nor had demanded rest
At inn or cottage. He replied, 'In truth
My weakness made me loth to move, and here
I felt myself at ease and much relieved,   130
But that the village mastiff fretted me,
And every second moment rang a peal
Felt at my very heart. There was no noise,

Nor any foot abroad—I do not know
What ailed him, but it seemed as if the dog
Were howling to the murmur of the stream.'
While thus we travelled on I did not fail
To question him of what he had endured
From war and battle and the pestilence.
He all the while was in demeanor calm,   140
Concise in answer: solemn and sublime
He might have seemed, but that in all he said
There was a strange half-absence and a tone
Of weakness and indifference, as of one
Remembering the importance of his theme,
But feeling it no longer. We advanced
Slowly, and ere we to the wood were come
Discourse had ceased. Together on we passed
In silence through the shades gloomy and dark,
Then turning up along an open field   150
We gained the cottage. At the door I knocked,
And called aloud, 'My Friend, here is a man
By sickness overcome; beneath your roof
This night let him find rest, and give him food—
The service if need be I will requite.'
Assured that now my comrade would repose
In comfort, I entreated that henceforth
He would not linger in the public ways
But at the door of cottage or of inn
Demand the succour which his state required,   160
And told him, feeble as he was 'twere fit
He asked relief or alms. At this reproof
With the same ghastly mildness in his look
He said, 'My trust is in the God of heaven,
And in the eye of him that passes me.'
By this the labourer had unlocked the door,
And now my comrade touched his hat again
With his lean hand, and in a voice that seemed
To speak with a reviving interest
Till then unfelt, he thanked me. I returned   170
The blessing of the poor unhappy man,
And so we parted.

The Old Cumberland Beggar

A DESCRIPTION

The class of Beggars to which the old man here described belongs, will probably soon be extinct. It consisted of poor, and, mostly, old and infirm persons, who confined themselves to a stated round in their neighbourhood, and had certain fixed days, on which, at different houses, they regularly received charity; sometimes in money, but mostly in provisions.

I saw an aged Beggar in my walk,
And he was seated by the highway side
On a low structure of rude masonry
Built at the foot of a huge hill, that they
Who lead their horses down the steep rough road
May thence remount at ease. The aged man
Had placed his staff across the broad smooth stone
That overlays the pile, and from a bag
All white with flour the dole of village dames,
He drew his scraps and fragments, one by one,   10
And scanned them with a fixed and serious look
Of idle computation. In the sun,
Upon the second step of that small pile,
Surrounded by those wild unpeopled hills,
He sate, and eat his food in solitude;
And ever, scattered from his palsied hand,
That still attempting to prevent the waste,
Was baffled still, the crumbs in little showers
Fell on the ground, and the small mountain birds,
Not venturing yet to peck their destined meal,   20
Approached within the length of half his staff.

Him from my childhood have I known, and then
He was so old, he seems not older now;
He travels on, a solitary man,
So helpless in appearance, that for him
The sauntering horseman-traveller does not throw
With careless hands his alms upon the ground,
But stops, that he may safely lodge the coin
Within the old Man's hat; nor quits him so,
But still when he has given his horse the rein   30

Towards the aged Beggar turns a look,
Sidelong and half-reverted. She who tends
The toll-gate, when in summer at her door
She turns her wheel, if on the road she sees
The aged Beggar coming, quits her work,
And lifts the latch for him that he may pass.
The Post-boy when his rattling wheels o'ertake
The aged Beggar, in the woody lane,
Shouts to him from behind, and, if perchance
The old Man does not change his course, the Boy   40
Turns with less noisy wheels to the road-side,
And passes gently by, without a curse
Upon his lips, or anger at his heart.
He travels on, a solitary Man,
His age has no companion. On the ground
His eyes are turned, and, as he moves along,
They move along the ground; and evermore,
Instead of common and habitual sight
Of fields with rural works, of hill and dale,
And the blue sky, one little span of earth   50
Is all his prospect. Thus, from day to day,
Bowbent, his eyes for ever on the ground,
He plies his weary journey, seeing still,
And never knowing that he sees, some straw,
Some scattered leaf, or marks which, in one track,
The nails of cart or chariot wheel have left
Impressed on the white road, in the same line,
At distance still the same. Poor Traveller!
His staff trails with him, scarcely do his feet
Disturb the summer dust, he is so still   60
In look and motion that the cottage curs,
Ere he have passed the door, will turn away
Weary of barking at him. Boys and girls,
The vacant and the busy, maids and youths,
And urchins newly breeched all pass him by:
Him even the slow-paced waggon leaves behind.

But deem not this man useless.—Statesman! ye
Who are so restless in your wisdom, ye
Who have a broom still ready in your hands
To rid the world of nuisances; ye proud,   70

Heart-swoln, while in your pride ye contemplate
Your talents, power, and wisdom, deem him not
A burthen of the earth. 'Tis Nature's law
That none, the meanest of created things,
Of forms created the most vile and brute,
The dullest or most noxious, should exist
Divorced from good, a spirit and pulse of good,
A life and soul to every mode of being
Inseparably linked. While thus he creeps
From door to door, the Villagers in him   80
Behold a record which together binds
Past deeds and offices of charity
Else unremembered, and so keeps alive
The kindly mood in hearts which lapse of years,
And that half-wisdom half-experience gives
Make slow to feel, and by sure steps resign
To selfishness and cold oblivious cares.
Among the farms and solitary huts
Hamlets, and thinly-scattered villages,
Where'er the aged Beggar takes his rounds,   90
The mild necessity of use compels
To acts of love; and habit does the work
Of reason, yet prepares that after joy
Which reason cherishes. And thus the soul,
By that sweet taste of pleasure unpursued
Doth find itself insensibly disposed
To virtue and true goodness. Some there are,
By their good works exalted, lofty minds
And meditative, authors of delight
And happiness, which to the end of time   100
Will live, and spread, and kindle; minds like these,
In childhood, from this solitary being,
This helpless wanderer, have perchance received,
(A thing more precious far than all that books
Or the solicitudes of love can do!)
That first mild touch of sympathy and thought,
In which they found their kindred with a world
Where want and sorrow were. The easy man
Who sits at his own door, and like the pear
Which overhangs his head from the green wall,   110
Feeds in the sunshine; the robust and young,

The prosperous and unthinking, they who live
Sheltered, and flourish in a little grove
Of their own kindred, all behold in him
A silent monitor, which on their minds
Must needs impress a transitory thought
Of self-congratulation, to the heart
Of each recalling his peculiar boons,
His charters and exemptions; and perchance,
Though he to no one give the fortitude   120
And circumspection needful to preserve
His present blessings, and to husband up
The respite of the season, he, at least,
And 'tis no vulgar service, makes them felt.

Yet further.—Many, I believe, there are
Who live a life of virtuous decency,
Men who can hear the Decalogue and feel
No self-reproach, who of the moral law
Established in the land where they abide
Are strict observers, and not negligent,   130
Meanwhile, in any tenderness of heart
Or act of love to those with whom they dwell,
Their kindred, and the children of their blood.
Praise be to such, and to their slumbers peace!
—But of the poor man ask, the abject poor,
Go and demand of him, if there be here,
In this cold abstinence from evil deeds,
And these inevitable charities,
Wherewith to satisfy the human soul.
No—man is dear to man: the poorest poor   140
Long for some moments in a weary life
When they can know and feel that they have been
Themselves the fathers and the dealers out
Of some small blessings, have been kind to such
As needed kindness, for this single cause,
That we have all of us one human heart.
—Such pleasure is to one kind Being known,
My Neighbour, when with punctual care, each week
Duly as Friday comes, though pressed herself
By her own wants, she from her chest of meal   150
Takes one unsparing handful for the scrip

Of this old Mendicant, and, from her door
Returning with exhilarated heart,
Sits by her fire and builds her hope in heaven.

Then let him pass, a blessing on his head!
And while, in that vast solitude to which
The tide of things has led him, he appears
To breathe and live but for himself alone,
Unblamed, uninjured, let him bear about
The good which the benignant law of heaven　　160
Has hung around him, and, while life is his,
Still let him prompt the unlettered Villagers
To tender offices and pensive thoughts.
Then let him pass, a blessing on his head!
And, long as he can wander, let him breathe
The freshness of the vallies, let his blood
Struggle with frosty air and winter snows,
And let the chartered wind that sweeps the heath
Beat his grey locks against his withered face.
Reverence the hope whose vital anxiousness　　170
Gives the last human interest to his heart.
May never House, misnamed of industry,
Make him a captive; for that pent-up din,
Those life-consuming sounds that clog the air,
Be his the natural silence of old age.
Let him be free of mountain solitudes,
And have around him, whether heard or not,
The pleasant melody of woodland birds.
Few are his pleasures; if his eyes, which now
Have been so long familiar with the earth,　　180
No more behold the horizontal sun
Rising or setting, let the light at least
Find a free entrance to their languid orbs.
And let him, *where* and *when* he will, sit down
Beneath the trees, or by the grassy bank
Of high-way side, and with the little birds
Share his chance-gathered meal, and, finally,
As in the eye of Nature he has lived,
So in the eye of Nature let him die.

Lines

It is the first mild day of March:
Each minute sweeter than before,
The red-breast sings from the tall larch
That stands beside our door.

There is a blessing in the air,
Which seems a sense of joy to yield
To the bare trees, and mountains bare,
And grass in the green field.

My Sister! ('tis a wish of mine)
Now that our morning meal is done,   10
Make haste, your morning task resign;
Come forth and feel the sun.

Edward will come with you, and pray,
Put on with speed your woodland dress,
And bring no book, for this one day
We'll give to idleness.

No joyless forms shall regulate
Our living Calendar:
We from to-day, my friend, will date
The opening of the year.   20

Love, now an universal birth,
From heart to heart is stealing,
From earth to man, from man to earth,
—It is the hour of feeling.

One moment now may give us more
Than fifty years of reason;
Our minds shall drink at every pore
The spirit of the season.

Some silent laws our hearts may make,
Which they shall long obey;   30
We for the year to come may take
Our temper from to-day.

And from the blessed power that rolls
About, below, above;
We'll frame the measure of our souls,
They shall be tuned to love.

Then come, my sister! come, I pray,
With speed put on your woodland dress,
And bring no book; for this one day
We'll give to idleness.   40

Goody Blake and Harry Gill

A TRUE STORY

Oh! what's the matter? what's the matter?
What is't that ails young Harry Gill?
That evermore his teeth they chatter,
Chatter, chatter, chatter still.
Of waistcoats Harry has no lack,
Good duffle grey, and flannel fine;
He has a blanket on his back,
And coats enough to smother nine.

In March, December, and in July,
'Tis all the same with Harry Gill;   10
The neighbours tell, and tell you truly,
His teeth they chatter, chatter still.
At night, at morning, and at noon,
'Tis all the same with Harry Gill;
Beneath the sun, beneath the moon,
His teeth they chatter, chatter still.

Young Harry was a lusty drover,
And who so stout of limb as he?
His cheeks were red as ruddy clover,

His voice was like the voice of three. 20
Auld Goody Blake was old and poor,
Ill fed she was, and thinly clad;
And any man who passed her door,
Might see how poor a hut she had.

All day she spun in her poor dwelling,
And then her three hours' work at night!
Alas! 'twas hardly worth the telling,
It would not pay for candle-light.
—This woman dwelt in Dorsetshire,
Her hut was on a cold hill-side, 30
And in that country coals are dear,
For they come far by wind and tide.

By the same fire to boil their pottage,
Two poor old dames, as I have known,
Will often live in one small cottage,
But she, poor woman, dwelt alone.
'Twas well enough when summer came,
The long, warm, lightsome summer-day,
Then at her door the *canty* dame
Would sit, as any linnet gay. 40

But when the ice our streams did fetter,
Oh! then how her old bones would shake!
You would have said, if you had met her,
'Twas a hard time for Goody Blake.
Her evenings then were dull and dead;
Sad case it was, as you may think,
For very cold to go to bed,
And then for cold not sleep a wink.

Oh joy for her! when e'er in winter
The winds at night had made a rout, 50
And scattered many a lusty splinter,
And many a rotten bough about.
Yet never had she, well or sick,
As every man who knew her says,
A pile before-hand, wood or stick,
Enough to warm her for three days.

Now, when the frost was past enduring,
And made her poor old bones to ache,
Could any thing be more alluring,
Than an old hedge to Goody Blake?   60
And now and then, it must be said,
When her old bones were cold and chill,
She left her fire, or left her bed,
To seek the hedge of Harry Gill.

Now Harry he had long suspected
This trespass of old Goody Blake,
And vowed that she should be detected,
And he on her would vengeance take.
And oft from his warm fire he'd go,
And to the fields his road would take,   70
And there, at night, in frost and snow,
He watched to seize old Goody Blake.

And once, behind a rick of barley,
Thus looking out did Harry stand;
The moon was full and shining clearly,
And crisp with frost the stubble-land.
—He hears a noise—he's all awake—
Again?—on tip-toe down the hill
He softly creeps—'Tis Goody Blake,
She's at the hedge of Harry Gill.   80

Right glad was he when he beheld her:
Stick after stick did Goody pull,
He stood behind a bush of elder,
Till she had filled her apron full.
When with her load she turned about,
The bye-road back again to take,
He started forward with a shout,
And sprang upon poor Goody Blake.

And fiercely by the arm he took her,
And by the arm he held her fast,   90
And fiercely by the arm he shook her,
And cried, 'I've caught you then at last!'
Then Goody, who had nothing said,

Her bundle from her lap let fall;
And kneeling on the sticks, she prayed
To God that is the judge of all.

She prayed, her withered hand uprearing,
While Harry held her by the arm—
'God! who art never out of hearing,
Oh may he never more be warm!'   100
The cold, cold moon above her head,
Thus on her knees did Goody pray,
Young Harry heard what she had said,
And icy-cold he turned away.

He went complaining all the morrow
That he was cold and very chill:
His face was gloom, his heart was sorrow,
Alas! that day for Harry Gill!
That day he wore a riding-coat,
But not a whit the warmer he: 110
Another was on Thursday brought,
And ere the Sabbath he had three.

'Twas all in vain, a useless matter,
And blankets were about him pinned;
Yet still his jaws and teeth they clatter,
Like a loose casement in the wind.
And Harry's flesh it fell away;
And all who see him say 'tis plain,
That, live as long as live he may,
He never will be warm again.   120

No word to any man he utters,
A-bed or up, to young or old;
But ever to himself he mutters,
'Poor Harry Gill is very cold.'
A-bed or up, by night or day;
His teeth they chatter, chatter still.
Now think, ye farmers all, I pray,
Of Goody Blake and Harry Gill.

The Thorn

There is a thorn; it looks so old,
In truth you'd find it hard to say,
How it could ever have been young,
It looks so old and grey.
Not higher than a two-years' child,
It stands erect this aged thorn;
No leaves it has, no thorny points;
It is a mass of knotted joints,
A wretched thing forlorn.
It stands erect, and like a stone   10
With lichens it is overgrown.

Like rock or stone, it is o'ergrown
With lichens to the very top,
And hung with heavy tufts of moss,
A melancholy crop:
Up from the earth these mosses creep,
And this poor thorn they clasp it round
So close, you'd say that they were bent
With plain and manifest intent,
To drag it to the ground;   20
And all had joined in one endeavour
To bury this poor thorn for ever.

High on a mountain's highest ridge,
Where oft the stormy winter gale
Cuts like a scythe, while through the clouds
It sweeps from vale to vale;
Not five yards from the mountain-path,
This thorn you on your left espy;
And to the left, three yards beyond,
You see a little muddy pond   30
Of water, never dry;
I've measured it from side to side:
'Tis three feet long, and two feet wide.

And close beside this aged thorn,
There is a fresh and lovely sight,

A beauteous heap, a hill of moss,
Just half a foot in height.
All lovely colours there you see,
All colours that were ever seen,
And mossy network too is there,   40
As if by hand of lady fair
The work had woven been,
And cups, the darlings of the eye,
So deep is their vermilion dye.

Ah me! what lovely tints are there!
Of olive-green and scarlet bright,
In spikes, in branches, and in stars,
Green, red, and pearly white.
This heap of earth o'ergrown with moss,
Which close beside the thorn you see,   50
So fresh in all its beauteous dyes,
Is like an infant's grave in size
As like as like can be:
But never, never any where,
An infant's grave was half so fair.

Now would you see this aged thorn,
This pond and beauteous hill of moss,
You must take care and chuse your time
The mountain when to cross.
For oft there sits, between the heap   60
That's like an infant's grave in size,
And that same pond of which I spoke,
A woman in a scarlet cloak,
And to herself she cries,
'Oh misery! oh misery!
Oh woe is me! oh misery!'

At all times of the day and night
This wretched woman thither goes,
And she is known to every star,
And every wind that blows;   70
And there beside the thorn she sits
When the blue day-light's in the skies,
And when the whirlwind's on the hill,

Or frosty air is keen and still,
And to herself she cries,
'Oh misery! oh misery!
Oh woe is me! oh misery!'

'Now wherefore thus, by day and night,
In rain, in tempest, and in snow,
Thus to the dreary mountain-top   80
Does this poor woman go?
And why sits she beside the thorn
When the blue day-light's in the sky,
Or when the whirlwind's on the hill,
Or frosty air is keen and still,
And wherefore does she cry?—
Oh wherefore? wherefore? tell me why
Does she repeat that doleful cry?'

I cannot tell; I wish I could;
For the true reason no one knows,   90
But if you'd gladly view the spot,
The spot to which she goes;
The heap that's like an infant's grave,
The pond—and thorn, so old and grey,
Pass by her door—'tis seldom shut—
And if you see her in her hut,
Then to the spot away!—
I never heard of such as dare
Approach the spot when she is there.

'But wherefore to the mountain-top   100
Can this unhappy woman go,
Whatever star is in the skies,
Whatever wind may blow?'
Nay rack your brain—'tis all in vain,
I'll tell you every thing I know;
But to the thorn, and to the pond
Which is a little step beyond,
I wish that you would go:
Perhaps when you are at the place
You something of her tale may trace.   110

I'll give you the best help I can:
Before you up the mountain go,
Up to the dreary mountain-top,
I'll tell you all I know.
'Tis now some two and twenty years,
Since she (her name is Martha Ray)
Gave with a maiden's true good will
Her company to Stephen Hill;
And she was blithe and gay,
And she was happy, happy still   120
Whene'er she thought of Stephen Hill.

And they had fixed the wedding-day,
The morning that must wed them both;
But Stephen to another maid
Had sworn another oath;
And with this other maid to church
Unthinking Stephen went—
Poor Martha! on that woful day
A cruel, cruel fire, they say,
Into her bones was sent: 130
It dried her body like a cinder,
And almost turned her brain to tinder.

They say, full six months after this,
While yet the summer-leaves were green,
She to the mountain-top would go,
And there was often seen.
'Tis said, a child was in her womb,
As now to any eye was plain;
She was with child, and she was mad,
Yet often she was sober sad   140
From her exceeding pain.
Oh me! ten thousand times I'd rather
That he had died, that cruel father!

Sad case for such a brain to hold
Communion with a stirring child!
Sad case, as you may think, for one
Who had a brain so wild!
Last Christmas when we talked of this,

Old Farmer Simpson did maintain,
That in her womb the infant wrought   150
About its mother's heart, and brought
Her senses back again:
And when at last her time drew near,
Her looks were calm, her senses clear.

No more I know, I wish I did,
And I would tell it all to you;
For what became of this poor child
There's none that ever knew:
And if a child was born or no,
There's no one that could ever tell;   160
And if 'twas born alive or dead,
There's no one knows, as I have said,
But some remember well,
That Martha Ray about this time
Would up the mountain often climb.

And all that winter, when at night
The wind blew from the mountain-peak,
'Twas worth your while, though in the dark,
The church-yard path to seek:
For many a time and oft were heard   170
Cries coming from the mountain-head,
Some plainly living voices were,
And others, I've heard many swear,
Were voices of the dead:
I cannot think, whate'er they say,
They had to do with Martha Ray.

But that she goes to this old thorn,
The thorn which I've described to you,
And there sits in a scarlet cloak,
I will be sworn is true.   180
For one day with my telescope,
To view the ocean wide and bright,
When to this country first I came,
Ere I had heard of Martha's name,
I climbed the mountain's height:
A storm came on, and I could see
No object higher than my knee.

'Twas mist and rain, and storm and rain,
No screen, no fence could I discover,
And then the wind! in faith, it was   190
A wind full ten times over.
I looked around, I thought I saw
A jutting crag, and off I ran,
Head-foremost, through the driving rain,
The shelter of the crag to gain,
And, as I am a man,
Instead of jutting crag, I found
A woman seated on the ground.

I did not speak—I saw her face,
Her face it was enough for me;   200
I turned about and heard her cry,
'O misery! O misery!'
And there she sits, until the moon
Through half the clear blue sky will go,
And when the little breezes make
The waters of the pond to shake,
As all the country know,
She shudders and you hear her cry,
'Oh misery! oh misery!'

'But what's the thorn? and what's the pond?   210
And what's the hill of moss to her?
And what's the creeping breeze that comes
The little pond to stir?'
I cannot tell; but some will say
She hanged her baby on the tree,
Some say she drowned it in the pond,
Which is a little step beyond,
But all and each agree,
The little babe was buried there,
Beneath that hill of moss so fair.   220

I've heard the scarlet moss is red
With drops of that poor infant's blood;
But kill a new-born infant thus!
I do not think she could.
Some say, if to the pond you go,

And fix on it a steady view,
The shadow of a babe you trace,
A baby and a baby's face,
And that it looks at you;
Whene'er you look on it, 'tis plain   230
The baby looks at you again.

And some had sworn an oath that she
Should be to public justice brought;
And for the little infant's bones
With spades they would have sought.
But then the beauteous hill of moss
Before their eyes began to stir;
And for full fifty yards around,
The grass it shook upon the ground;
But all do still aver   240
The little babe is buried there,
Beneath that hill of moss so fair.

I cannot tell how this may be,
But plain it is, the thorn is bound
With heavy tufts of moss, that strive
To drag it to the ground.
And this I know, full many a time,
When she was on the mountain high,
By day, and in the silent night,
When all the stars shone clear and bright,   250
That I have heard her cry,
'Oh misery! oh misery!
O woe is me! oh misery!'

The Idiot Boy

'Tis eight o'clock,—a clear March night,
The moon is up—the sky is blue,
The owlet in the moonlight air,
He shouts from nobody knows where;
He lengthens out his lonely shout,
Halloo! halloo! a long halloo!

—Why bustle thus about your door,
What means this bustle, Betty Foy?
Why are you in this mighty fret?
And why on horseback have you set   10
Him whom you love, your idiot boy?

Beneath the moon that shines so bright,
Till she is tired, let Betty Foy
With girt and stirrup fiddle-faddle;
But wherefore set upon a saddle
Him whom she loves, her idiot boy?

There's scarce a soul that's out of bed;
Good Betty! put him down again;
His lips with joy they burr at you,
But, Betty! what has he to do   20
With stirrup, saddle, or with rein?

The world will say 'tis very idle,
Bethink you of the time of night;
There's not a mother, no not one,
But when she hears what you have done,
Oh! Betty she'll be in a fright.

But Betty's bent on her intent,
For her good neighbour, Susan Gale,
Old Susan, she who dwells alone,
Is sick, and makes a piteous moan,   30
As if her very life would fail.

There's not a house within a mile,
No hand to help them in distress:
Old Susan lies a bed in pain,
And sorely puzzled are the twain,
For what she ails they cannot guess.

And Betty's husband's at the wood,
Where by the week he doth abide,
A woodman in the distant vale;
There's none to help poor Susan Gale,   40
What must be done? what will betide?

And Betty from the lane has fetched
Her pony, that is mild and good,
Whether he be in joy or pain,
Feeding at will along the lane,
Or bringing faggots from the wood.

And he is all in travelling trim,
And by the moonlight, Betty Foy
Has up upon the saddle set,
The like was never heard of yet,   50
Him whom she loves, her idiot boy.

And he must post without delay
Across the bridge that's in the dale,
And by the church, and o'er the down,
To bring a doctor from the town,
Or she will die, old Susan Gale.

There is no need of boot or spur,
There is no need of whip or wand,
For Johnny has his holly-bough,
And with a hurly-burly now   60
He shakes the green bough in his hand.

And Betty o'er and o'er has told
The boy who is her best delight,
Both what to follow, what to shun,
What do, and what to leave undone,
How turn to left, and how to right.

And Betty's most especial charge,
Was, 'Johnny! Johnny! mind that you
Come home again, nor stop at all,
Come home again, whate'er befal,   70
My Johnny do, I pray you do.'

To this did Johnny answer make,
Both with his head, and with his hand,
And proudly shook the bridle too,
And then! his words were not a few,
Which Betty well could understand.

And now that Johnny is just going,
Though Betty's in a mighty flurry,
She gently pats the pony's side,
On which her idiot boy must ride,   80
And seems no longer in a hurry.

But when the pony moved his legs,
Oh! then for the poor idiot boy!
For joy he cannot hold the bridle,
For joy his head and heels are idle,
He's idle all for very joy.

And while the pony moves his legs,
In Johnny's left-hand you may see,
The green bough's motionless and dead;
The moon that shines above his head   90
Is not more still and mute than he.

His heart it was so full of glee,
That till full fifty yards were gone,
He quite forgot his holly whip,
And all his skill in horsemanship,
Oh! happy, happy, happy John.

And Betty's standing at the door,
And Betty's face with joy o'erflows,
Proud of herself, and proud of him,
She sees him in his travelling trim;   100
How quietly her Johnny goes.

The silence of her idiot boy,
What hopes it sends to Betty's heart!
He's at the guide-post—he turns right,
She watches till he's out of sight,
And Betty will not then depart.

Burr, burr—now Johnny's lips they burr,
As loud as any mill, or near it,
Meek as a lamb the pony moves,
And Johnny makes the noise he loves,   110
And Betty listens, glad to hear it.

Away she hies to Susan Gale:
And Johnny's in a merry tune,
The owlets hoot, the owlets curr,
And Johnny's lips they burr, burr, burr,
And on he goes beneath the moon.

His steed and he right well agree,
For of this pony there's a rumour,
That should he lose his eyes and ears,
And should he live a thousand years,   120
He never will be out of humour.

But then he is a horse that thinks!
And when he thinks his pace is slack;
Now, though he knows poor Johnny well,
Yet for his life he cannot tell
What he has got upon his back.

So through the moonlight lanes they go,
And far into the moonlight dale,
And by the church, and o'er the down,
To bring a doctor from the town,   130
To comfort poor old Susan Gale.

And Betty, now at Susan's side,
Is in the middle of her story,
What comfort Johnny soon will bring,
With many a most diverting thing,
Of Johnny's wit and Johnny's glory.

And Betty's still at Susan's side:
By this time she's not quite so flurried;
Demure with porringer and plate
She sits, as if in Susan's fate   140
Her life and soul were buried.

But Betty, poor good woman! she,
You plainly in her face may read it,
Could lend out of that moment's store
Five years of happiness or more,
To any that might need it.

But yet I guess that now and then
With Betty all was not so well,
And to the road she turns her ears,
And thence full many a sound she hears,   150
Which she to Susan will not tell.

Poor Susan moans, poor Susan groans,
'As sure as there's a moon in heaven,'
Cries Betty, 'he'll be back again;
They'll both be here, 'tis almost ten,
They'll both be here before eleven.'

Poor Susan moans, poor Susan groans,
The clock gives warning for eleven;
'Tis on the stroke—'If Johnny's near,'
Quoth Betty 'he will soon be here,   160
As sure as there's a moon in heaven.'

The clock is on the stroke of twelve,
And Johnny is not yet in sight,
The moon's in heaven, as Betty sees,
But Betty is not quite at ease;
And Susan has a dreadful night.

And Betty, half an hour ago,
On Johnny vile reflections cast;
'A little idle sauntering thing!'
With other names, an endless string,   170
But now that time is gone and past.

And Betty's drooping at the heart,
That happy time all past and gone,
'How can it be he is so late?
The doctor he has made him wait,
Susan! they'll both be here anon.'

And Susan's growing worse and worse,
And Betty's in a sad quandary;
And then there's nobody to say
If she must go or she must stay: 180
—She's in a sad quandary.

The clock is on the stroke of one;
But neither Doctor nor his guide
Appear along the moonlight road,
There's neither horse nor man abroad,
And Betty's still at Susan's side.

And Susan she begins to fear
Of sad mischances not a few,
That Johnny may perhaps be drowned,
Or lost perhaps, and never found;   190
Which they must both for ever rue.

She prefaced half a hint of this
With, 'God forbid it should be true!'
At the first word that Susan said
Cried Betty, rising from the bed,
'Susan, I'd gladly stay with you.

I must be gone, I must away,
Consider, Johnny's but half-wise;
Susan, we must take care of him,
If he is hurt in life or limb'—   200
'Oh God forbid!' poor Susan cries.

'What can I do?' says Betty, going,
'What can I do to ease your pain?
Good Susan tell me, and I'll stay;
I fear you're in a dreadful way,
But I shall soon be back again.'

'Good Betty go, good Betty go,
There's nothing that can ease my pain.'
Then off she hies, but with a prayer
That God poor Susan's life would spare,   210
Till she comes back again.

So, through the moonlight lane she goes,
And far into the moonlight dale;
And how she ran, and how she walked,
And all that to herself she talked,
Would surely be a tedious tale.

In high and low, above, below,
In great and small, in round and square,
In tree and tower was Johnny seen,
In bush and brake, in black and green,   220
'Twas Johnny, Johnny, every where.

She's past the bridge that's in the dale,
And now the thought torments her sore,
Johnny perhaps his horse forsook,
To hunt the moon that's in the brook,
And never will be heard of more.

And now she's high upon the down,
Alone amid a prospect wide;
There's neither Johnny nor his horse,
Among the fern or in the gorse;   230
There's neither doctor nor his guide.

'Oh saints! what is become of him?
Perhaps he's climbed into an oak,
Where he will stay till he is dead;
Or sadly he has been misled,
And joined the wandering gypsey-folk.

Or him that wicked pony's carried
To the dark cave, the goblins' hall,
Or in the castle he's pursuing,
Among the ghosts, his own undoing;   240
Or playing with the waterfall.'

At poor old Susan then she railed,
While to the town she posts away;
'If Susan had not been so ill,
Alas! I should have had him still,
My Johnny, till my dying day.'

Poor Betty! in this sad distemper,
The doctor's self would hardly spare,
Unworthy things she talked and wild,
Even he, of cattle of the most mild,   250
The pony had his share.

And now she's got into the town,
And to the doctor's door she hies;
'Tis silence all on every side;
The town so long, the town so wide,
Is silent as the skies.

And now she's at the doctor's door,
She lifts the knocker, rap, rap, rap,
The doctor at the casement shews,
His glimmering eyes that peep and doze;   260
And one hand rubs his old night-cap.

'Oh Doctor! Doctor! where's my Johnny?'
'I'm here, what is't you want with me?'
'Oh Sir! you know I'm Betty Foy,
And I have lost my poor dear boy,
You know him—him you often see;

He's not so wise as some folks be,'
'The devil take his wisdom!' said
The Doctor, looking somewhat grim,
'What, woman! should I know of him?'   270
And, grumbling, he went back to bed.

'O woe is me! O woe is me!
Here will I die; here will I die;
I thought to find my Johnny here,
But he is neither far nor near,
Oh! what a wretched mother I!'

She stops, she stands, she looks about,
Which way to turn she cannot tell.
Poor Betty! it would ease her pain
If she had heart to knock again;   280
—The clock strikes three—a dismal knell!

Then up along the town she hies,
No wonder if her senses fail,
This piteous news so much it shocked her,
She quite forgot to send the Doctor,
To comfort poor old Susan Gale.

And now she's high upon the down,
And she can see a mile of road,
'Oh cruel! I'm almost three-score;
Such night as this was ne'er before, 290
There's not a single soul abroad.'

She listens, but she cannot hear
The foot of horse, the voice of man;
The streams with softest sound are flowing,
The grass you almost hear it growing,
You hear it now if e'er you can.

The owlets through the long blue night
Are shouting to each other still:
Fond lovers, yet not quite hob nob,
They lengthen out the tremulous sob 300
That echoes far from hill to hill.

Poor Betty now has lost all hope,
Her thoughts are bent on deadly sin;
A green-grown pond she just has passed,
And from the brink she hurries fast,
Lest she should drown herself therein.

And now she sits her down and weeps;
Such tears she never shed before;
'O dear, dear pony! my sweet joy!
Oh carry back my idiot boy! 310
And we will ne'er o'erload thee more.'

A thought is come into her head;
'The pony he is mild and good,
And we have always used him well;
Perhaps he's gone along the dell,
And carried Johnny to the wood.'

Then up she springs as if on wings;
She thinks no more of deadly sin;
If Betty fifty ponds should see,
The last of all her thoughts would be, 320
To drown herself therein.

Oh reader! now that I might tell
What Johnny and his horse are doing!
What they've been doing all this time,
Oh could I put it into rhyme,
A most delightful tale pursuing!

Perhaps, and no unlikely thought!
He with his pony now doth roam
The cliffs and peaks so high that are,
To lay his hands upon a star,   330
And in his pocket bring it home.

Perhaps he's turned himself about,
His face unto his horse's tail,
And still and mute, in wonder lost,
All like a silent horseman-ghost,
He travels on along the vale.

And now, perhaps, he's hunting sheep,
A fierce and dreadful hunter he!
Yon valley, that's so trim and green,
In five months' time, should he be seen,   340
A desart wilderness will be.

Perhaps, with head and heels on fire,
And like the very soul of evil,
He's galloping away, away,
And so he'll gallop on for aye,
The bane of all that dread the devil.

I to the muses have been bound,
These fourteen years, by strong indentures;
Oh gentle muses! let me tell
But half of what to him befel.   350
For sure he met with strange adventures.

Oh gentle muses! is this kind?
Why will ye thus my suit repel?
Why of your further aid bereave me?
And can ye thus unfriended leave me?
Ye muses! whom I love so well.

Who's yon, that, near the waterfall,
Which thunders down with headlong force,
Beneath the moon, yet shining fair,
As careless as if nothing were, 360
Sits upright on a feeding horse?

Unto his horse, that's feeding free,
He seems, I think, the rein to give;
Of moon or stars he takes no heed;
Of such we in romances read,
—'Tis Johnny! Johnny! as I live.

And that's the very pony too.
Where is she, where is Betty Foy?
She hardly can sustain her fears;
The roaring water-fall she hears, 370
And cannot find her idiot boy.

Your pony's worth his weight in gold,
Then calm your terrors, Betty Foy!
She's coming from among the trees,
And now, all full in view, she sees
Him whom she loves, her idiot boy.

And Betty sees the pony too:
Why stand you thus Good Betty Foy?
It is not goblin, 'tis no ghost,
'Tis he whom you so long have lost, 380
He whom you love, your idiot boy.

She looks again—her arms are up—
She screams—she cannot move for joy;
She darts as with a torrent's force,
She almost has o'erturned the horse,
And fast she holds her idiot boy.

And Johnny burrs and laughs aloud,
Whether in cunning or in joy,
I cannot tell; but while he laughs,
Betty a drunken pleasure quaffs, 390
To hear again her idiot boy.

And now she's at the pony's tail,
And now she's at the pony's head,
On that side now, and now on this,
And almost stifled with her bliss,
A few sad tears does Betty shed.

She kisses o'er and o'er again,
Him whom she loves, her idiot boy,
She's happy here, she's happy there,
She is uneasy every where;   400
Her limbs are all alive with joy.

She pats the pony, where or when
She knows not, happy Betty Foy!
The little pony glad may be,
But he is milder far than she,
You hardly can perceive his joy.

'Oh! Johnny, never mind the Doctor;
You've done your best, and that is all.'
She took the reins, when this was said,
And gently turned the pony's head   410
From the loud water-fall.

By this the stars were almost gone,
The moon was setting on the hill,
So pale you scarcely looked at her:
The little birds began to stir,
Though yet their tongues were still.

The pony, Betty, and her boy,
Wind slowly through the woody dale:
And who is she, be-times abroad,
That hobbles up the steep rough road?   420
Who is it, but old Susan Gale?

Long Susan lay deep lost in thought,
And many dreadful fears beset her,
Both for her messenger and nurse;
And as her mind grew worse and worse,
Her body it grew better.

She turned, she tossed herself in bed,
On all sides doubts and terrors met her;
Point after point did she discuss;
And while her mind was fighting thus,   430
Her body still grew better.

'Alas! what is become of them?
These fears can never be endured,
I'll to the wood.'—The word scarce said,
Did Susan rise up from her bed,
As if by magic cured.

Away she posts up hill and down,
And to the wood at length is come,
She spies her friends, she shouts a greeting;
Oh me! it is a merry meeting,   440
As ever was in Christendom.

The owls have hardly sung their last,
While our four travellers homeward wend;
The owls have hooted all night long,
And with the owls began my song,
And with the owls must end.

For while they all were travelling home,
Cried Betty, 'Tell us Johnny, do,
Where all this long night you have been,
What you have heard, what you have seen,   450
And Johnny, mind you tell us true.'

Now Johnny all night long had heard
The owls in tuneful concert strive;
No doubt too he the moon had seen;
For in the moonlight he had been
From eight o'clock till five.

And thus to Betty's question, he
Made answer, like a traveller bold,
(His very words I give to you,)
'The cocks did crow to-whoo, to-whoo,   460
And the sun did shine so cold.'
—Thus answered Johnny in his glory,
And that was all his travel's story.

Lines written in Early Spring

I heard a thousand blended notes,
While in a grove I sate reclined,
In that sweet mood when pleasant thoughts
Bring sad thoughts to the mind.

To her fair works did nature link
The human soul that through me ran;
And much it grieved my heart to think
What man has made of man.

Through primrose-tufts, in that sweet bower,
The periwinkle trailed its wreathes;   10
And 'tis my faith that every flower
Enjoys the air it breathes.

The birds around me hopped and played:
Their thoughts I cannot measure,
But the least motion which they made,
It seemed a thrill of pleasure.

The budding twigs spread out their fan,
To catch the breezy air;
And I must think, do all I can,
That there was pleasure there.   20

If I these thoughts may not prevent,
If such be of my creed the plan,
Have I not reason to lament
What man has made of man?

Anecdote for Fathers

SHEWING HOW THE ART OF LYING MAY BE TAUGHT

I have a boy of five years old,
His face is fair and fresh to see;
His limbs are cast in beauty's mould,
And dearly he loves me.

One morn we strolled on our dry walk,
Our quiet house all full in view,
And held such intermitted talk
As we are wont to do.

My thoughts on former pleasures ran;
I thought of Kilve's delightful shore,
My pleasant home, when spring began,
A long, long year before.

A day it was when I could bear
To think, and think, and think again;
With so much happiness to spare,
I could not feel a pain.

My boy was by my side, so slim
And graceful in his rustic dress!
And oftentimes I talked to him,
In very idleness.

The young lambs ran a pretty race;
The morning sun shone bright and warm;
'Kilve,' said I, 'was a pleasant place,
And so is Liswyn farm.

My little boy, which like you more,'
I said and took him by the arm—
'Our home by Kilve's delightful shore,
Or here at Liswyn farm?'

'And tell me, had you rather be,'
I said and held him by the arm,
'At Kilve's smooth shore by the green sea,
Or here at Liswyn farm?'

In careless mood he looked at me,
While still I held him by the arm,
And said, 'At Kilve I'd rather be
Than here at Liswyn farm.'

'Now, little Edward, say why so;
My little Edward, tell me why;'
'I cannot tell, I do not know.'
'Why this is strange,' said I.   40

'For, here are woods and green-hills warm;
There surely must some reason be
Why you would change sweet Liswyn farm
For Kilve by the green sea.'

At this, my boy, so fair and slim,
Hung down his head, nor made reply;
And five times did I say to him,
'Why? Edward, tell me why?'

His head he raised—there was in sight,
It caught his eye, he saw it plain—   50
Upon the house-top, glittering bright,
A broad and gilded vane.

Then did the boy his tongue unlock,
And thus to me he made reply;
'At Kilve there was no weather-cock,
And that's the reason why.'

O dearest, dearest boy! my heart
For better lore would seldom yearn,
Could I but teach the hundredth part
Of what from thee I learn.   60

We Are Seven

A simple child, dear brother Jim,
That lightly draws its breath,
And feels its life in every limb,
What should it know of death?

I met a little cottage girl,
She was eight years old, she said;
Her hair was thick with many a curl
That clustered round her head.

She had a rustic, woodland air,
And she was wildly clad;
Her eyes were fair, and very fair,
—Her beauty made me glad.

'Sisters and brothers, little maid,
How many may you be?'
'How many? seven in all,' she said,
And wondering looked at me.

'And where are they, I pray you tell?'
She answered, 'Seven are we,
And two of us at Conway dwell,
And two are gone to sea.

Two of us in the church-yard lie,
My sister and my brother,
And in the church-yard cottage, I
Dwell near them with my mother.'

'You say that two at Conway dwell,
And two are gone to sea,
Yet you are seven; I pray you tell
Sweet Maid, how this may be?'

Then did the little Maid reply,
'Seven boys and girls are we;
Two of us in the church-yard lie,
Beneath the church-yard tree.'

'You run about, my little maid,
Your limbs they are alive;
If two are in the church-yard laid,
Then ye are only five.'

'Their graves are green, they may be seen,'
The little Maid replied,
'Twelve steps or more from my mother's door,
And they are side by side.

'My stockings there I often knit,
My 'kerchief there I hem;
And there upon the ground I sit—
I sit and sing to them.

And often after sunset, Sir,
When it is light and fair,
I take my little porringer,
And eat my supper there.

The first that died was little Jane;
In bed she moaning lay,   50
Till God released her of her pain,
And then she went away.

So in the church-yard she was laid,
And all the summer dry,
Together round her grave we played,
My brother John and I.

And when the ground was white with snow,
And I could run and slide,
My brother John was forced to go,
And he lies by her side.'   60

'How many are you then,' said I,
'If they two are in Heaven?'
The little Maiden did reply,
'O Master! we are seven.'

'But they are dead; those two are dead!
Their spirits are in heaven!'
'Twas throwing words away; for still
The little Maid would have her will,
And said, 'Nay, we are seven!'

Expostulation and Reply

'Why William, on that old grey stone,
Thus for the length of half a day,
Why William, sit you thus alone,
And dream your time away?

Where are your books? that light bequeathed
To beings else forlorn and blind!
Up! Up! and drink the spirit breathed
From dead men to their kind.

You look round on your mother earth,
As if she for no purpose bore you;   10
As if you were her first-born birth,
And none had lived before you!'

One morning thus, by Esthwaite lake,
When life was sweet I knew not why,
To me my good friend Matthew spake,
And thus I made reply.

'The eye it cannot chuse but see,
We cannot bid the ear be still;
Our bodies feel, where'er they be,
Against, or with our will.   20

Nor less I deem that there are powers,
Which of themselves our minds impress,
That we can feed this mind of ours,
In a wise passiveness.

Think you, 'mid all this mighty sum
Of things for ever speaking,
That nothing of itself will come,
But we must still be seeking?

—Then ask not wherefore, here, alone,
Conversing as I may,   30
I sit upon this old grey stone,
And dream my time away.'

The Tables Turned

AN EVENING SCENE, ON THE SAME SUBJECT

Up! up! my friend, and clear your looks,
Why all this toil and trouble?
Up! up! my friend, and quit your books,
Or surely you'll grow double.

The sun above the mountain's head,
A freshening lustre mellow,
Through all the long green fields has spread,
His first sweet evening yellow.

Books! 'tis a dull and endless strife,
Come, hear the woodland linnet,   10
How sweet his music; on my life
There's more of wisdom in it.

And hark! how blithe the throstle sings!
And he is no mean preacher;
Come forth into the light of things,
Let Nature be your teacher.

She has a world of ready wealth,
Our minds and hearts to bless—
Spontaneous wisdom breathed by health,
Truth breathed by chearfulness.   20

One impulse from a vernal wood
May teach you more of man;
Of moral evil and of good,
Than all the sages can.

Sweet is the lore which nature brings;
Our meddling intellect
Mis-shapes the beauteous forms of things;
—We murder to dissect.

Enough of science and of art;
Close up these barren leaves; 30
Come forth, and bring with you a heart
That watches and receives.

Lines written a few miles above Tintern Abbey

ON REVISITING THE BANKS OF THE WYE DURING A TOUR,
JULY 13, 1798

Five years have passed; five summers, with the length
Of five long winters! and again I hear
These waters, rolling from their mountain-springs
With a sweet inland murmur.—Once again
Do I behold these steep and lofty cliffs,
Which on a wild secluded scene impress
Thoughts of more deep seclusion; and connect
The landscape with the quiet of the sky.
The day is come when I again repose
Here, under this dark sycamore, and view 10
These plots of cottage-ground, these orchard-tufts,
Which, at this season, with their unripe fruits,
Among the woods and copses lose themselves,
Nor, with their green and simple hue, disturb
The wild green landscape. Once again I see
These hedge-rows, hardly hedge-rows, little lines
Of sportive wood run wild; these pastoral farms
Green to the very door; and wreathes of smoke
Sent up, in silence, from among the trees,
With some uncertain notice, as might seem, 20
Of vagrant dwellers in the houseless woods,
Or of some hermit's cave, where by his fire
The hermit sits alone.

                    Though absent long,
These forms of beauty have not been to me,
As is a landscape to a blind man's eye:
But oft, in lonely rooms, and mid the din
Of towns and cities, I have owed to them,

In hours of weariness, sensations sweet,
Felt in the blood, and felt along the heart,
And passing even into my purer mind   30
With tranquil restoration:—feelings too
Of unremembered pleasure; such, perhaps,
As may have had no trivial influence
On that best portion of a good man's life;
His little, nameless, unremembered acts
Of kindness and of love. Nor less, I trust,
To them I may have owed another gift,
Of aspect more sublime; that blessed mood,
In which the burthen of the mystery,
In which the heavy and the weary weight   40
Of all this unintelligible world
Is lightened:—that serene and blessed mood,
In which the affections gently lead us on,
Until, the breath of this corporeal frame,
And even the motion of our human blood
Almost suspended, we are laid asleep
In body, and become a living soul:
While with an eye made quiet by the power
Of harmony, and the deep power of joy,
We see into the life of things.

       If this   50
Be but a vain belief, yet, oh! how oft,
In darkness, and amid the many shapes
Of joyless day-light; when the fretful stir
Unprofitable, and the fever of the world,
Have hung upon the beatings of my heart,
How oft, in spirit, have I turned to thee
O sylvan Wye! Thou wanderer through the woods,
How often has my spirit turned to thee!

And now, with gleams of half-extinguished thought,
With many recognitions dim and faint,   60
And somewhat of a sad perplexity,
The picture of the mind revives again:
While here I stand, not only with the sense
Of present pleasure, but with pleasing thoughts
That in this moment there is life and food

For future years. And so I dare to hope
Though changed, no doubt, from what I was, when first
I came among these hills; when like a roe
I bounded o'er the mountains, by the sides
Of the deep rivers, and the lonely streams,   70
Wherever nature led; more like a man
Flying from something that he dreads, than one
Who sought the thing he loved. For nature then
(The coarser pleasures of my boyish days,
And their glad animal movements all gone by,)
To me was all in all.—I cannot paint
What then I was. The sounding cataract
Haunted me like a passion: the tall rock,
The mountain, and the deep and gloomy wood,
Their colours and their forms, were then to me   80
An appetite: a feeling and a love,
That had no need of a remoter charm,
By thought supplied, or any interest
Unborrowed from the eye.—That time is past,
And all its aching joys are now no more,
And all its dizzy raptures. Not for this
Faint I, nor mourn nor murmur: other gifts
Have followed, for such loss, I would believe,
Abundant recompence. For I have learned
To look on nature, not as in the hour   90
Of thoughtless youth, but hearing oftentimes
The still, sad music of humanity,
Not harsh nor grating, though of ample power
To chasten and subdue. And I have felt
A presence that disturbs me with the joy
Of elevated thoughts; a sense sublime
Of something far more deeply interfused,
Whose dwelling is the light of setting suns,
And the round ocean, and the living air,
And the blue sky, and in the mind of man,   100
A motion and a spirit, that impels
All thinking things, all objects of all thought,
And rolls through all things. Therefore am I still
A lover of the meadows and the woods,
And mountains; and of all that we behold
From this green earth; of all the mighty world

Of eye and ear, both what they half-create,
And what perceive; well pleased to recognize
In nature and the language of the sense,
The anchor of my purest thoughts, the nurse,   110
The guide, the guardian of my heart, and soul
Of all my moral being.

               Nor, perchance,
If I were not thus taught, should I the more
Suffer my genial spirits to decay:
For thou art with me, here, upon the banks
Of this fair river; thou, my dearest Friend,
My dear, dear Friend, and in thy voice I catch
The language of my former heart, and read
My former pleasures in the shooting lights
Of thy wild eyes. Oh! yet a little while   120
May I behold in thee what I was once,
My dear, dear Sister! And this prayer I make,
Knowing that Nature never did betray
The heart that loved her; 'tis her privilege,
Through all the years of this our life, to lead
From joy to joy: for she can so inform
The mind that is within us, so impress
With quietness and beauty, and so feed
With lofty thoughts, that neither evil tongues,
Rash judgments, nor the sneers of selfish men,   130
Nor greetings where no kindness is, nor all
The dreary intercourse of daily life,
Shall e'er prevail against us, or disturb
Our chearful faith that all which we behold
Is full of blessings. Therefore let the moon
Shine on thee in thy solitary walk;
And let the misty mountain winds be free
To blow against thee: and in after years,
When these wild ecstasies shall be matured
Into a sober pleasure, when thy mind   140
Shall be a mansion for all lovely forms,
Thy memory be as a dwelling-place
For all sweet sounds and harmonies; Oh! then,
If solitude, or fear, or pain, or grief,
Should be thy portion, with what healing thoughts

Of tender joy wilt thou remember me,
And these my exhortations! Nor, perchance,
If I should be, where I no more can hear
Thy voice, nor catch from thy wild eyes these gleams
Of past existence, wilt thou then forget 150
That on the banks of this delightful stream
We stood together; and that I, so long
A worshipper of Nature, hither came,
Unwearied in that service: rather say
With warmer love, oh! with far deeper zeal
Of holier love. Nor wilt thou then forget,
That after many wanderings, many years
Of absence, these steep woods and lofty cliffs,
And this green pastoral landscape, were to me
More dear, both for themselves, and for thy sake. 160

The Fountain

A CONVERSATION

We talked with open heart, and tongue
Affectionate and true,
A pair of Friends, though I was young,
And Matthew seventy-two.

We lay beneath a spreading oak,
Beside a mossy seat,
And from the turf a fountain broke,
And gurgled at our feet.

Now, Matthew, let us try to match
This water's pleasant tune 10
With some old Border-song, or catch
That suits a summer's noon.

Or of the Church-clock and the chimes
Sing here beneath the shade,
That half-mad thing of witty rhymes
Which you last April made!

In silence Matthew lay, and eyed
The spring beneath the tree;
And thus the dear old Man replied,
The grey-haired Man of glee.   20

'Down to the vale this water steers,
How merrily it goes!
'Twill murmur on a thousand years,
And flow as now it flows.

And here, on this delightful day,
I cannot chuse but think
How oft, a vigorous Man, I lay
Beside this Fountain's brink.

My eyes are dim with childish tears,
My heart is idly stirred,   30
For the same sound is in my ears,
Which in those days I heard.

Thus fares it still in our decay:
And yet the wiser mind
Mourns less for what age takes away
Than what it leaves behind.

The blackbird in the summer trees,
The lark upon the hill,
Let loose their carols when they please,
Are quiet when they will.   40

With Nature never do *they* wage
A foolish strife; they see
A happy youth, and their old age
Is beautiful and free:

But we are pressed by heavy laws,
And often, glad no more,
We wear a face of joy, because
We have been glad of yore.

If there is one who need bemoan
His kindred laid in earth,　　　　　　50
The household hearts that were his own,
It is the man of mirth.

My days, my Friend, are almost gone,
My life has been approved,
And many love me, but by none
Am I enough beloved.'

'Now both himself and me he wrongs,
The man who thus complains!
I live and sing my idle songs
Upon these happy plains,　　　　　　60

And, Matthew, for thy Children dead
I'll be a son to thee!'
At this he grasped his hands, and said,
'Alas! that cannot be.'

We rose up from the fountain-side,
And down the smooth descent
Of the green sheep-track did we glide,
And through the wood we went,

And, ere we came to Leonard's Rock,
He sang those witty rhymes　　　　　　70
About the crazy old church-clock
And the bewildered chimes.

The Two April Mornings

We walked along, while bright and red
Uprose the morning sun,
And Matthew stopped, he looked, and said,
'The will of God be done!'

A village Schoolmaster was he,
With hair of glittering grey;
As blithe a man as you could see
On a spring holiday.

And on that morning, through the grass,
And by the steaming rills,   10
We travelled merrily to pass
A day among the hills.

'Our work,' said I, 'was well begun;
Then, from thy breast what thought,
Beneath so beautiful a sun,
So sad a sigh has brought?'

A second time did Matthew stop,
And fixing still his eye
Upon the eastern mountain-top
To me he made reply.   20

'Yon cloud with that long purple cleft
Brings fresh into my mind
A day like this which I have left
Full thirty years behind.

And on that slope of springing corn
The self-same crimson hue
Fell from the sky that April morn,
The same which now I view!

With rod and line my silent sport
I plied by Derwent's wave,   30
And, coming to the church, stopped short
Beside my Daughter's grave.

Nine summers had she scarcely seen
The pride of all the vale;
And then she sang!—she would have been
A very nightingale.

Six feet in earth my Emma lay,
And yet I loved her more,
For so it seemed, than till that day
I e'er had loved before.   40

And, turning from her grave, I met
Beside the church-yard Yew
A blooming Girl, whose hair was wet
With points of morning dew.

A basket on her head she bare,
Her brow was smooth and white,
To see a Child so very fair,
It was a pure delight!

No fountain from its rocky cave
E'er tripped with foot so free, 50
She seemed as happy as a wave
That dances on the sea.

There came from me a sigh of pain
Which I could ill confine;
I looked at her and looked again;
—And did not wish her mine.'

Matthew is in his grave, yet now
Methinks I see him stand,
As at that moment, with his bough
Of wilding in his hand. 60

'A slumber did my spirit seal'

A slumber did my spirit seal;
    I had no human fears:
She seemed a thing that could not feel
    The touch of earthly years.

No motion has she now, no force;
    She neither hears nor sees,
Rolled round in earth's diurnal course
    With rocks and stones and trees.

Song

She dwelt among th' untrodden ways
    Beside the springs of Dove,
A Maid whom there were none to praise
    And very few to love.

A Violet by a mossy stone
    Half-hidden from the Eye!
—Fair, as a star when only one
    Is shining in the sky!

She *lived* unknown, and few could know
    When Lucy ceased to be;   10
But she is in her Grave, and Oh!
    The difference to me.

'Strange fits of passion I have known'

Strange fits of passion I have known,
And I will dare to tell,
But in the lover's ear alone,
What once to me befel.

When she I loved, was strong and gay
And like a rose in June,
I to her cottage bent my way,
Beneath the evening moon.

Upon the moon I fixed my eye
All over the wide lea;   10
My horse trudged on, and we drew nigh
Those paths so dear to me.

And now we reached the orchard plot,
And, as we climbed the hill,
Towards the roof of Lucy's cot
The moon descended still.

In one of those sweet dreams I slept,
Kind Nature's gentlest boon!
And, all the while, my eyes I kept
On the descending moon.   20

My horse moved on; hoof after hoof
He raised and never stopped:
When down behind the cottage roof
At once the planet dropped.

What fond and wayward thoughts will slide
Into a Lover's head—
'O mercy!' to myself I cried,
'If Lucy should be dead!'

Lucy Gray

Oft had I heard of Lucy Gray,
And when I crossed the Wild,
I chanced to see at break of day
The solitary Child.

No Mate, no comrade Lucy knew;
She dwelt on a wide Moor,
The sweetest Thing that ever grew
Beside a human door!

You yet may spy the Fawn at play,
The Hare upon the Green;   10
But the sweet face of Lucy Gray
Will never more be seen.

'To-night will be a stormy night,
You to the Town must go,
And take a lantern, Child, to light
Your Mother thro' the snow.'

'That, Father! will I gladly do;
'Tis scarcely afternoon—
The Minster-clock has just struck two,
And yonder is the Moon.'   20

At this the Father raised his hook
And snapped a faggot-band;
He plied his work, and Lucy took
The lantern in her hand.

Not blither is the mountain roe,
With many a wanton stroke
Her feet disperse the powd'ry snow
That rises up like smoke.

The storm came on before its time,
She wandered up and down,   30
And many a hill did Lucy climb
But never reached the Town.

The wretched Parents all that night
Went shouting far and wide;
But there was neither sound nor sight
To serve them for a guide.

At day-break on a hill they stood
That overlooked the Moor;
And thence they saw the Bridge of Wood
A furlong from their door.   40

And now they homeward turned, and cried
'In Heaven we all shall meet!'
When in the snow the Mother spied
The print of Lucy's feet.

Then downward from the steep hill's edge
They tracked the footmarks small;
And through the broken hawthorn-hedge,
And by the long stone-wall;

And then an open field they crossed,
The marks were still the same;   50
They tracked them on, nor ever lost,
And to the Bridge they came.

They followed from the snowy bank
The footmarks, one by one,
Into the middle of the plank,
And further there were none.

Yet some maintain that to this day
She is a living Child,
That you may see sweet Lucy Gray
Upon the lonesome Wild.   60

O'er rough and smooth she trips along,
And never looks behind;
And sings a solitary song
That whistles in the wind.

Nutting

————————It seems a day,
One of those heavenly days which cannot die,
When forth I sallied from our cottage-door,
And with a wallet o'er my shoulder slung,
A nutting crook in hand, I turned my steps
Towards the distant woods, a Figure quaint,
Tricked out in proud disguise of Beggar's weeds
Put on for the occasion, by advice
And exhortation of my frugal Dame.
Motley accoutrements! of power to smile   10
At thorns, and brakes, and brambles, and, in truth,
More ragged than need was. Among the woods,
And o'er the pathless rocks, I forced my way
Until, at length, I came to one dear nook
Unvisited, where not a broken bough
Drooped with its withered leaves, ungracious sign
Of devastation, but the hazels rose
Tall and erect, with milk-white clusters hung,
A virgin scene!—A little while I stood,
Breathing with such suppression of the heart   20
As joy delights in; and with wise restraint
Voluptuous, fearless of a rival, eyed

The banquet, or beneath the trees I sate
Among the flowers, and with the flowers I played;
A temper known to those, who, after long
And weary expectation, have been blessed
With sudden happiness beyond all hope.—
—Perhaps it was a bower beneath whose leaves
The violets of five seasons re-appear
And fade, unseen by any human eye,   30
Where fairy water-breaks do murmur on
For ever, and I saw the sparkling foam,
And with my cheek on one of those green stones
That, fleeced with moss, beneath the shady trees,
Lay round me scattered like a flock of sheep,
I heard the murmur and the murmuring sound,
In that sweet mood when pleasure loves to pay
Tribute to ease, and, of its joy secure
The heart luxuriates with indifferent things,
Wasting its kindliness on stocks and stones,
And on the vacant air. Then up I rose,   40
And dragged to earth both branch and bough, with crash
And merciless ravage; and the shady nook
Of hazels, and the green and mossy bower,
Deformed and sullied, patiently gave up
Their quiet being: and unless I now
Confound my present feelings with the past,
Even then, when from the bower I turned away,
Exulting, rich beyond the wealth of kings
I felt a sense of pain when I beheld   50
The silent trees and the intruding sky.—

Then, dearest Maiden! move along these shades
In gentleness of heart; with gentle hand
Touch,—for there is a Spirit in the woods.

'Three years she grew in sun and shower'

Three years she grew in sun and shower,
Then Nature said, 'A lovelier flower
On earth was never sown;
This Child I to myself will take,

She shall be mine, and I will make
A Lady of my own.

Myself will to my darling be
Both law and impulse, and with me
The Girl in rock and plain,
In earth and heaven, in glade and bower,   10
Shall feel an overseeing power
To kindle or restrain.

She shall be sportive as the fawn
That wild with glee across the lawn
Or up the mountain springs,
And hers shall be the breathing balm,
And hers the silence and the calm
Of mute insensate things.

The floating clouds their state shall lend
To her, for her the willow bend,   20
Nor shall she fail to see
Even in the motions of the storm
A beauty that shall mould her form
By silent sympathy.

The stars of midnight shall be dear
To her, and she shall lean her ear
In many a secret place
Where rivulets dance their wayward round,
And beauty born of murmuring sound
Shall pass into her face   30

And vital feelings of delight
Shall rear her form to stately height,
Her virgin bosom swell,
Such thoughts to Lucy I will give
While she and I together live
Here in this happy dell.'

Thus Nature spake—The work was done—
How soon my Lucy's race was run!

She died and left to me
This heath, this calm and quiet scene,   40
The memory of what has been,
And never more will be.

The Brothers

These Tourists, Heaven preserve us! needs must live
A profitable life: some glance along,
Rapid and gay, as if the earth were air,
And they were butterflies to wheel about
Long as their summer lasted; some, as wise,
Upon the forehead of a jutting crag
Sit perched with book and pencil on their knee,
And look and scribble, scribble on and look,
Until a man might travel twelve stout miles,
Or reap an acre of his neighbour's corn.   10
But, for that moping son of Idleness
Why can he tarry *yonder?*—In our church-yard
Is neither epitaph nor monument,
Tomb-stone nor name, only the turf we tread,
And a few natural graves. To Jane, his Wife,
Thus spake the homely Priest of Ennerdale.
It was a July evening, and he sate
Upon the long stone-seat beneath the eaves
Of his old cottage, as it chanced that day,
Employed in winter's work. Upon the stone   20
His Wife sate near him, teasing matted wool,
While, from the twin cards toothed with glittering wire,
He fed the spindle of his youngest child,
Who turned her large round wheel in the open air
With back and forward steps. Towards the field
In which the parish chapel stood alone,
Girt round with a bare ring of mossy wall,
While half an hour went by, the Priest had sent
Many a long look of wonder, and at last,
Risen from his seat, beside the snowy ridge   30
Of carded wool which the old Man had piled
He laid his implements with gentle care,

Each in the other locked; and, down the path
Which from his cottage to the church-yard led,
He took his way, impatient to accost
The Stranger, whom he saw still lingering there.

'Twas one well known to him in former days,
A Shepherd-lad: who ere his thirteenth year
Had changed his calling, with the mariners
A fellow-mariner, and so had fared   40
Through twenty seasons; but he had been reared
Among the mountains, and he in his heart
Was half a Shepherd on the stormy seas.
Oft in the piping shrouds had Leonard heard
The tones of waterfalls, and inland sounds
Of caves and trees; and when the regular wind
Between the tropics filled the steady sail
And blew with the same breath through days and weeks,
Lengthening invisibly its weary line
Along the cloudless main, he, in those hours   50
Of tiresome indolence would often hang
Over the vessel's side, and gaze and gaze,
And, while the broad green wave and sparkling foam
Flashed round him images and hues, that wrought
In union with the employment of his heart,
He, thus by feverish passion overcome,
Even with the organs of his bodily eye,
Below him, in the bosom of the deep,
Saw mountains, saw the forms of sheep that grazed
On verdant hills, with dwellings among trees,   60
And Shepherds clad in the same country grey
Which he himself had worn.
                 And now at length,
From perils manifold, with some small wealth
Acquired by traffic in the Indian Isles,
To his paternal home he is returned,
With a determined purpose to resume
The life which he lived there, both for the sake
Of many darling pleasures, and the love
Which to an only brother he has borne
In all his hardships, since that happy time   70
When, whether it blew foul or fair, they two

Were brother Shepherds on their native hills.
—They were the last of all their race; and now,
When Leonard had approached his home, his heart
Failed in him, and, not venturing to inquire
Tidings of one whom he so dearly loved,
Towards the church-yard he had turned aside,
That, as he knew in what particular spot
His family were laid, he thence might learn
If still his Brother lived, or to the file   80
Another grave was added.—He had found
Another grave, near which a full half hour
He had remained, but, as he gazed, there grew
Such a confusion in his memory,
That he began to doubt, and he had hopes
That he had seen this heap of turf before,
That it was not another grave, but one,
He had forgotten. He had lost his path,
As up the vale he came that afternoon,
Through fields which once had been well known to him.   90
And Oh! what joy the recollection now
Sent to his heart! he lifted up his eyes,
And looking round he thought that he perceived
Strange alteration wrought on every side
Among the woods and fields, and that the rocks,
And the eternal hills, themselves were changed.

  By this the Priest who down the field had come
Unseen by Leonard, at the church-yard gate
Stopped short, and thence, at leisure, limb by limb
He scanned him with a gay complacency.   100
Aye, thought the Vicar, smiling to himself,
'Tis one of those who needs must leave the path
Of the world's business, to go wild alone:
His arms have a perpetual holiday,
The happy man will creep about the fields
Following his fancies by the hour, to bring
Tears down his cheek, or solitary smiles
Into his face, until the setting sun
Write Fool upon his forehead. Planted thus
Beneath a shed that overarched the gate   110
Of this rude church-yard, till the stars appeared

The good man might have communed with himself
But that the Stranger, who had left the grave,
Approached; he recognized the Priest at once,
And after greetings interchanged, and given
By Leonard to the Vicar as to one
Unknown to him, this dialogue ensued.

LEONARD

You live, Sir, in these dales, a quiet life:
Your years make up one peaceful family;
And who would grieve and fret, if, welcome come   120
And welcome gone, they are so like each other,
They cannot be remembered. Scarce a funeral
Comes to this church-yard once in eighteen months;
And yet, some changes must take place among you:
And you, who dwell here, even among these rocks
Can trace the finger of mortality,
And see, that with our threescore years and ten
We are not all that perish.—I remember,
For many years ago I passed this road,
There was a foot-way all along the fields   130
By the brook-side—'tis gone—and that dark cleft!
To me it does not seem to wear the face
Which then it had.

PRIEST
                Why, Sir, for aught I know,
That chasm is much the same—

LEONARD
                            But, surely, yonder—

PRIEST
Aye, there indeed, your memory is a friend
That does not play you false.—On that tall pike,
(It is the loneliest place of all these hills)
There were two Springs which bubbled side by side
As if they had been made that they might be
Companions for each other: ten years back,   140
Close to those brother fountains, the huge crag
Was rent with lightning—one is dead and gone,
The other, left behind, is flowing still.—
For accidents and changes such as these,

Why we have store of them! a water-spout
Will bring down half a mountain; what a feast
For folks that wander up and down like you,
To see an acre's breadth of that wide cliff
One roaring cataract—a sharp May storm
Will come with loads of January snow,   150
And in one night send twenty score of sheep
To feed the ravens, or a Shepherd dies
By some untoward death among the rocks:
The ice breaks up and sweeps away a bridge—
A wood is felled:—and then for our own homes!
A child is born or christened, a field ploughed,
A daughter sent to service, a web spun,
The old house clock is decked with a new face;
And hence, so far from wanting facts or dates
To chronicle the time, we all have here   160
A pair of diaries, one serving, Sir,
For the whole dale, and one for each fire-side—
Your's was a stranger's judgment; for historians
Commend me to these vallies.

LEONARD
                              Yet your church-yard
Seems, if such freedom may be used with you,
To say that you are heedless of the past.
Here's neither head nor foot-stone, plate of brass,
Cross-bones or skull, type of our earthly state
Or emblem of our hopes: the dead man's home
Is but a fellow to that pasture field.   170

PRIEST
Why there, Sir, is a thought that's new to me.
The Stone-cutters, 'tis true, might beg their bread
If every English church-yard were like ours:
Yet your conclusion wanders from the truth.
We have no need of names and epitaphs,
We talk about the dead by our fire-sides.
And then for our immortal part, *we* want
No symbols, Sir, to tell us that plain tale:
The thought of death sits easy on the man
Who has been born and dies among the mountains: 180

LEONARD

Your dalesmen, then, do in each other's thoughts
Possess a kind of second life: no doubt
You, Sir, could help me to the history
Of half these Graves?

PRIEST

With what I've witnessed, and with what I've heard,
Perhaps I might, and, on a winter's evening,
If you were seated at my chimney's nook
By turning o'er these hillocks one by one,
We two could travel, Sir, through a strange round,
Yet all in the broad high-way of the world.   190
Now there's a grave—your foot is half upon it,
It looks just like the rest, and yet that man
Died broken hearted.

LEONARD

                    'Tis a common case,
We'll take another: who is he that lies
Beneath yon ridge, the last of those three graves,
It touches on that piece of native rock
Left in the church-yard wall.

PRIEST

                    That's Walter Ewbank.
He had as white a head and fresh a cheek
As ever were produced by youth and age
Engendering in the blood of hale fourscore.   200
For five long generations had the heart
Of Walter's forefathers o'erflowed the bounds
Of their inheritance, that single cottage,
You see it yonder, and those few green fields.
They toiled and wrought, and still, from sire to son
Each struggled, and each yielded as before
A little—yet a little—and old Walter,
They left to him the family heart, and land
With other burthens than the crop it bore.
Year after year the old man still preserved   210
A chearful mind, and buffeted with bond,
Interest and mortgages; at last he sank,
And went into his grave before his time.

Poor Walter! whether it was care that spurred him
God only knows, but to the very last
He had the lightest foot in Ennerdale:
His pace was never that of an old man:
I almost see him tripping down the path
With his two Grandsons after him—but you,
Unless our Landlord be your host to-night,   220
Have far to travel, and in these rough paths
Even in the longest day of midsummer—

LEONARD
But these two Orphans!

PRIEST
              Orphans! such they were—
Yet not while Walter lived—for, though their Parents
Lay buried side by side as now they lie,
The old Man was a father to the boys,
Two fathers in one father: and if tears
Shed, when he talked of them where they were not,
And hauntings from the infirmity of love,
Are aught of what makes up a mother's heart,   230
This old Man in the day of his old age
Was half a mother to them.—If you weep, Sir,
To hear a stranger talking about strangers,
Heaven bless you when you are among your kindred!
Aye. You may turn that way—it is a grave
Which will bear looking at.

LEONARD
              These Boys I hope
They loved this good old Man—

PRIEST
              They did—and truly,
But that was what we almost overlooked,
They were such darlings of each other. For
Though from their cradles they had lived with Walter,   240
The only kinsman near them in the house,
Yet he being old, they had much love to spare,
And it all went into each other's hearts.
Leonard, the elder by just eighteen months,
Was two years taller: 'twas a joy to see,

To hear, to meet them! from their house the School
Was distant three short miles, and in the time
Of storm and thaw, when every water-course
And unbridged stream, such as you may have noticed
Crossing our roads at every hundred steps,   250
Was swoln into a noisy rivulet,
Would Leonard then, when elder boys perhaps
Remained at home, go staggering through the fords
Bearing his Brother on his back.—I've seen him,
On windy days, in one of those stray brooks,
Aye, more than once I've seen him mid-leg deep,
Their two books lying both on a dry stone
Upon the hither side:—and once I said,
As I remember, looking round these rocks
And hills on which we all of us were born,   260
That God who made the great book of the world
Would bless such piety—

                    LEONARD
            It may be then—

                    PRIEST
Never did worthier lads break English bread:
The finest Sunday that the Autumn saw,
With all its mealy clusters of ripe nuts,
Could never keep these boys away from church,
Or tempt them to an hour of sabbath breach.
Leonard and James! I warrant, every corner
Among these rocks and every hollow place
Where foot could come, to one or both of them   270
Was known as well as to the flowers that grew there.
Like roe-bucks they went bounding o'er the hills:
They played like two young ravens on the crags:
Then they could write, aye and speak too, as well
As many of their betters—and for Leonard!
The very night before he went away,
In my own house I put into his hand
A Bible, and I'd wager twenty pounds,
That, if he is alive, he has it yet.

                    LEONARD
It seems, these Brothers have not lived to be   280
A comfort to each other.—

PRIEST

That they might
Live to that end, is what both old and young
In this our valley all of us have wished,
And what, for my part, I have often prayed:
But Leonard—

LEONARD

Then James still is left among you—

PRIEST

'Tis of the elder Brother I am speaking:
They had an Uncle, he was at that time
A thriving man, and trafficked on the seas:
And, but for this same Uncle, to this hour
Leonard had never handled rope or shroud.   290
For the Boy loved the life which we lead here;
And, though a very Stripling, twelve years old;
His soul was knit to this his native soil.
But, as I said, old Walter was too weak
To strive with such a torrent; when he died,
The estate and house were sold, and all their sheep,
A pretty flock, and which, for aught I know,
Had clothed the Ewbanks for a thousand years.
Well—all was gone, and they were destitute.
And Leonard, chiefly for his brother's sake,   300
Resolved to try his fortune on the seas.
'Tis now twelve years since we had tidings from him.
If there was one among us who had heard
That Leonard Ewbank was come home again,
From the great Gavel, down by Leeza's Banks,
And down the Enna, far as Egremont,
The day would be a very festival,
And those two bells of ours, which there you see
Hanging in the open air—but, O good Sir!
This is sad talk—they'll never sound for him   310
Living or dead—When last we heard of him
He was in slavery among the Moors
Upon the Barbary Coast—'Twas not a little
That would bring down his spirit, and, no doubt,
Before it ended in his death, the Lad
Was sadly crossed—Poor Leonard! when we parted,

He took me by the hand and said to me,
If ever the day came when he was rich,
He would return, and on his Father's Land
He would grow old among us.

LEONARD
                    If that day   320
Should come, 'twould needs be a glad day for him;
He would himself, no doubt, be as happy then
As any that should meet him—

PRIEST
                    Happy, Sir—

LEONARD
You said his kindred all were in their graves,
And that he had one Brother—

PRIEST
                    That is but
A fellow tale of sorrow. From his youth
James, though not sickly, yet was delicate,
And Leonard being always by his side
Had done so many offices about him,
That, though he was not of a timid nature,   330
Yet still the spirit of a mountain boy
In him was somewhat checked, and when his Brother
Was gone to sea and he was left alone
The little colour that he had was soon
Stolen from his cheek, he drooped, and pined and pined:

LEONARD
But these are all the graves of full grown men!

PRIEST
Aye, Sir, that passed away: we took him to us.
He was the child of all the dale—he lived
Three months with one, and six months with another:
And wanted neither food, nor clothes, nor love,   340
And many, many happy days were his.
But, whether blithe or sad, 'tis my belief
His absent Brother still was at his heart.
And, when he lived beneath our roof, we found
(A practice till this time unknown to him)

That often, rising from his bed at night,
He in his sleep would walk about, and sleeping
He sought his Brother Leonard—You are moved!
Forgive me, Sir: before I spoke to you,
I judged you most unkindly.

LEONARD

But this youth,   350
How did he die at last?

PRIEST

One sweet May morning,
It will be twelve years since, when Spring returns,
He had gone forth among the new-dropped lambs,
With two or three companions whom it chanced
Some further business summoned to a house
Which stands at the Dale-head. James, tired perhaps,
Or from some other cause remained behind.
You see yon precipice—it almost looks
Like some vast building made of many crags,
And in the midst is one particular rock   360
That rises like a column from the vale,
Whence by our Shepherds it is called, the Pillar.
James, pointing to its summit, over which
They all had purposed to return together,
Informed them that he there would wait for them:
They parted, and his comrades passed that way
Some two hours after, but they did not find him
At the appointed place, a circumstance
Of which they took no heed: but one of them,
Going by chance, at night, into the house   370
Which at this time was James's home, there learned
That nobody had seen him all that day:
The morning came, and still, he was unheard of:
The neighbours were alarmed, and to the Brook
Some went, and some towards the Lake; ere noon
They found him at the foot of that same Rock
Dead, and with mangled limbs. The third day after
I buried him, poor lad, and there he lies.

LEONARD

And that then *is* his grave!—Before his death
You said that he saw many happy years?   380

PRIEST

Aye, that he did—

LEONARD

And all went well with him—

PRIEST

If he had one, the Lad had twenty homes.

LEONARD

And you believe then, that his mind was easy—

PRIEST

Yes, long before he died, he found that time
Is a true friend to sorrow, and unless
His thoughts were turned on Leonard's luckless fortune,
He talked about him with a chearful love.

LEONARD

He could not come to an unhallowed end!

PRIEST

Nay, God forbid! You recollect I mentioned
A habit which disquietude and grief   390
Had brought upon him, and we all conjectured
That, as the day was warm, he had lain down
Upon the grass, and, waiting for his comrades
He there had fallen asleep, that in his sleep
He to the margin of the precipice
Had walked, and from the summit had fallen head-long,
And so no doubt he perished: at the time,
We guess, that in his hands he must have had
His Shepherd's staff; for midway in the cliff
It had been caught, and there for many years   400
It hung—and mouldered there.
                       The Priest here ended.
The Stranger would have thanked him, but he felt
Tears rushing in; both left the spot in silence,
And Leonard, when they reached the church-yard gate,
As the Priest lifted up the latch, turned round,
And, looking at the grave, he said, 'My Brother'.
The Vicar did not hear the words: and now,
Pointing towards the Cottage, he entreated
That Leonard would partake his homely fare:

The other thanked him with a fervent voice,   410
But added, that, the evening being calm,
He would pursue his journey. So they parted.

It was not long ere Leonard reached a grove
That overhung the road: he there stopped short,
And, sitting down beneath the trees, reviewed
All that the Priest had said: his early years
Were with him in his heart: his cherished hopes,
And thoughts which had been his an hour before,
All pressed on him with such a weight, that now,
This vale, where he had been so happy, seemed   420
A place in which he could not bear to live:
So he relinquished all his purposes.
He travelled on to Egremont; and thence,
That night, addressed a letter to the Priest
Reminding him of what had passed between them;
And adding, with a hope to be forgiven,
That it was from the weakness of his heart,
He had not dared to tell him, who he was.

This done, he went on shipboard, and is now
A Seaman, a grey headed Mariner.   430

Hart-Leap Well

Hart-Leap Well is a small spring of water, about five miles from Richmond
in Yorkshire, and near the side of the road which leads from Richmond
to Askrigg. Its name is derived from a remarkable chace, the memory of
which is preserved by the monuments spoken of in the second Part of the
following Poem, which monuments do now exist as I have there described
them.

The Knight had ridden down from Wensley moor
With the slow motion of a summer's cloud;
He turned aside towards a Vassal's door,
And, 'Bring another Horse!' he cried aloud.

'Another Horse!'—That shout the Vassal heard,
And saddled his best steed, a comely Grey;

Sir Walter mounted him; he was the third
Which he had mounted on that glorious day.

Joy sparkled in the prancing Courser's eyes,
The horse and horseman are a happy pair;   10
But, though Sir Walter like a falcon flies,
There is a doleful silence in the air.

A rout this morning left Sir Walter's Hall,
That as they galloped made the echoes roar;
But horse and man are vanished, one and all;
Such race, I think, was never seen before.

Sir Walter, restless as a veering wind,
Calls to the few tired dogs that yet remain:
Brach, Swift and Music, noblest of their kind,
Follow, and weary up the mountain strain.   20

The Knight hallooed, he chid and cheered them on
With suppliant gestures and upbraidings stern;
But breath and eye-sight fail, and, one by one,
The dogs are stretched among the mountain fern.

Where is the throng, the tumult of the chace?
The bugles that so joyfully were blown?
—This race it looks not like an earthly race;
Sir Walter and the Hart are left alone.

The poor Hart toils along the mountain side;
I will not stop to tell how far he fled,   30
Nor will I mention by what death he died;
But now the Knight beholds him lying dead.

Dismounting then, he leaned against a thorn;
He had no follower, dog, nor man, nor boy:
He neither smacked his whip, nor blew his horn,
But gazed upon the spoil with silent joy.

Close to the thorn on which Sir Walter leaned,
Stood his dumb partner in this glorious act;
Weak as a lamb the hour that it is yeaned,
And foaming like a mountain cataract.   40

Upon his side the Hart was lying stretched:
His nose half-touched a spring beneath a hill,
And with the last deep groan his breath had fetched
The waters of the spring were trembling still.

And now, too happy for repose or rest,
Was never man in such a joyful case,
Sir Walter walked all around, north, south and west,
And gazed, and gazed upon that darling place.

And turning up the hill, it was at least
Nine roods of sheer ascent, Sir Walter found   50
Three several marks which with his hoofs the beast
Had left imprinted on the verdant ground.

Sir Walter wiped his face, and cried, 'Till now
Such sight was never seen by living eyes:
Three leaps have borne him from this lofty brow,
Down to the very fountain where he lies.

I'll build a Pleasure-house upon this spot,
And a small Arbour, made for rural joy;
'Twill be the traveller's shed, the pilgrim's cot
A place of love for damsels that are coy.   60

A cunning Artist will I have to frame
A bason for that fountain in the dell;
And they, who do make mention of the same,
From this day forth, shall call it Hart-leap Well.

And, gallant brute, to make thy praises known,
Another monument shall here be raised;
Three several pillars, each a rough hewn stone,
And planted where thy hoofs the turf have grazed.

And in the summer-time when days are long,
I will come hither with my paramour,   70
And with the dancers, and the minstrel's song,
We will make merry in that pleasant bower.

Till the foundations of the mountains fail
My mansion with its arbour shall endure,
—The joy of them who till the fields of Swale,
And them who dwell among the woods of Ure.'

Then home he went, and left the Hart, stone-dead,
With breathless nostrils stretched above the spring.
And soon the Knight performed what he had said,
The fame whereof through many a land did ring.   80

Ere thrice the moon into her port had steered,
A cup of stone received the living well;
Three pillars of rude stone Sir Walter reared,
And built a house of pleasure in the dell.

And near the fountain, flowers of stature tall,
With trailing plants and trees were intertwined,
Which soon composed a little sylvan hall,
A leafy shelter from the sun and wind.

And thither, when the summer days were long,
Sir Walter journeyed with his paramour;   90
And with the dancers and the minstrel's song
Made merriment within that pleasant bower.

The Knight, Sir Walter, died in course of time,
And his bones lie in his paternal vale.
But there is matter for a second rhyme,
And I to this would add another tale.

PART SECOND

The moving accident is not my trade,
To curl the blood I have no ready arts;
'Tis my delight, alone in summer shade,
To pipe a simple song to thinking hearts.   100

As I from Hawes to Richmond did repair,
It chanced that I saw standing in a dell
Three aspins at three corners of a square,
And one, not four yards distant, near a well.

What this imported I could ill divine,
And, pulling now the rein my horse to stop,
I saw three pillars standing in a line,
The last stone pillar on a dark hill-top.

The trees were grey, with neither arms nor head;
Half-wasted the square mound of tawny green;   110
So that you just might say, as then I said,
'Here in old time the hand of man has been.'

I looked upon the hills both far and near;
More doleful place did never eye survey;
It seemed as if the spring-time came not here,
And Nature here were willing to decay.

I stood in various thoughts and fancies lost,
When one who was in Shepherd's garb attired,
Came up the hollow. Him did I accost,
And what this place might be I then inquired.

The Shepherd stopped, and that same story told
Which in my former rhyme I have rehearsed.
'A jolly place,' said he, 'in times of old,
But something ails it now; the spot is cursed.   120

You see these lifeless stumps of aspin wood,
Some say that they are beeches, others elms,
These were the Bower; and here a Mansion stood,
The finest palace of a hundred realms.

The arbour does its own condition tell,
You see the stones, the fountain, and the stream,
But as to the great Lodge, you might as well
Hunt half a day for a forgotten dream.

There's neither dog nor heifer, horse nor sheep,
Will wet his lips within that cup of stone;   130
And, oftentimes, when all are fast asleep,
This water doth send forth a dolorous groan.

Some say that here a murder has been done,
And blood cries out for blood: but, for my part,
I've guessed, when I've been sitting in the sun,
That it was all for that unhappy Hart.

What thoughts must through the creature's brain have
   passed!
To this place from the stone upon the steep
Are but three bounds, and look, Sir, at this last!
O Master! it has been a cruel leap. 140

For thirteen hours he ran a desperate race;
And in my simple mind we cannot tell
What cause the Hart might have to love this place,
And come and make his death-bed near the well.

Here on the grass perhaps asleep he sank,
Lulled by this fountain in the summer-tide;
This water was perhaps the first he drank
When he had wandered from his mother's side.

In April here beneath the scented thorn
He heard the birds their morning carols sing, 150
And he, perhaps, for aught we know, was born
Not half a furlong from that self-same spring.

But now here's neither grass nor pleasant shade;
The sun on drearier hollow never shone:
So will it be, as I have often said,
Till trees, and stones, and fountain all are gone.'

'Grey-headed Shepherd, thou hast spoken well;
Small difference lies between thy creed and mine;
This beast not unobserved by Nature fell,
His death was mourned by sympathy divine. 160

The Being, that is in the clouds and air,
That is in the green leaves among the groves,
Maintains a deep and reverential care
For them the quiet creatures whom he loves.

The Pleasure-house is dust:—behind, before,
This is no common waste, no common gloom;
But Nature, in due course of time, once more
Shall here put on her beauty and her bloom.

She leaves these objects to a slow decay
That what we are, and have been, may be known;   170
But, at the coming of the milder day,
These monuments shall all be overgrown.

One lesson, Shepherd, let us two divide,
Taught both by what she shews, and what conceals,
Never to blend our pleasure or our pride
With sorrow of the meanest thing that feels.'

from *Home at Grasmere*

Once on the brow of yonder Hill I stopped
While I was yet a School-boy (of what age
I cannot well remember, but the hour
I well remember though the year be gone),
And, with a sudden influx overcome
At sight of this seclusion, I forgot
My haste, for hasty had my footsteps been
As boyish my pursuits; and sighing said,
'What happy fortune were it here to live!
And if I thought of dying, if a thought   10
Of mortal separation could come in
With paradise before me, here to die.'
I was no Prophet, nor had even a hope,
Scarcely a wish, but one bright pleasing thought,
A fancy in the heart of what might be
The lot of others, never could be mine.
   The place from which I looked was soft and green,
Not giddy yet aerial, with a depth
Of Vale below, a height of Hills above.
Long did I halt; I could have made it even   20
My business and my errand so to halt.
For rest of body 'twas a perfect place,

All that luxurious nature could desire,
But tempting to the Spirit; who could look
And not feel motions there? I thought of clouds
That sail on winds; of breezes that delight
To play on water, or in endless chase
Pursue each other through the liquid depths
Of grass or corn, over and through and through,
In billow after billow, evermore;   30
Of Sunbeams, Shadows, Butterflies and Birds,
Angels and winged Creatures that are Lords
Without restraint of all which they behold.
I sate and stirred in Spirit as I looked,
I seemed to feel such liberty was mine,
Such power and joy; but only for this end,
To flit from field to rock, from rock to field,
From shore to island, and from isle to shore,
From open place to covert, from a bed
Of meadow-flowers into a tuft of wood,   40
From high to low, from low to high, yet still
Within the bounds of this huge Concave; here
Should be my home, this Valley be my World.

    From that time forward was the place to me
As beautiful in thought, as it had been
When present to my bodily eyes; a haunt
Of my affections, oftentimes in joy
A brighter joy, in sorrow (but of that
I have known little) in such gloom, at least,
Such damp of the gay mind as stood to me   50
In place of sorrow, 'twas a gleam of light.
And now 'tis mine for life: dear Vale,
One of thy lowly dwellings is my home!
    .   .   .   .

                        What wonder if I speak
With fervour, am exalted with the thought
Of my possessions, of my genuine wealth   90
Inward and outward? What I keep, have gained,
Shall gain, must gain, if sound be my belief
From past and present, rightly understood,
That in my day of childhood I was less
The mind of Nature, less, take all in all,
Whatever may be lost, than I am now.

For proof behold this Valley, and behold
Yon Cottage, where with me my Emma dwells.
   Aye, think on that, my Heart, and cease to stir,
Pause upon that, and let the breathing frame   100
No longer breathe, but all be satisfied.
Oh, if such silence be not thanks to God
For what hath been bestowed, then where, where then
Shall gratitude find rest? Mine eyes did ne'er
Rest on a lovely object, nor my mind
Take pleasure in the midst of happy thoughts,
But either She whom now I have, who now
Divides with me this loved abode, was there,
Or not far off. Where'er my footsteps turned,
Her Voice was like a hidden Bird that sang;   110
The thought of her was like a flash of light
Or an unseen companionship, a breath
Or fragrance independent of the wind;
In all my goings, in the new and old
Of all my meditations, and in this
Favorite of all, in this the most of all.
What Being, therefore, since the birth of Man
Had ever more abundant cause to speak
Thanks, and if music and the power of song
Make him more thankful, then to call on these   120
To aid him, and with these resound his joy.
The boon is absolute; surpassing grace
To me hath been vouchsafed; among the bowers
Of blissful Eden this was neither given,
Nor could be given, possession of the good
Which had been sighed for, antient thought fulfilled
And dear Imaginations realized,
Up to their highest measure, yea, and more.
   Embrace me, then, ye Hills, and close me in,
Now in the clear and open day I feel   130
Your guardianship; I take it to my heart;
'Tis like the solemn shelter of the night.
But I would call thee beautiful, for mild,
And soft, and gay, and beautiful thou art,
Dear Valley, having in thy face a smile
Though peaceful, full of gladness. Thou art pleased,
Pleased with thy crags, and woody steeps, thy Lake,

Its one green Island and its winding shores,
The multitude of little rocky hills,
Thy Church and Cottages of mountain stone—   140
Clustered like stars, some few, but single most,
And lurking dimly in their shy retreats,
Or glancing at each other chearful looks,
Like separated stars with clouds between.
What want we? Have we not perpetual streams,
Warm woods, and sunny hills, and fresh green fields,
And mountains not less green, and flocks and herds,
And thickets full of songsters, and the voice
Of lordly birds—an unexpected sound
Heard now and then from morn to latest eve,   150
Admonishing the man who walks below
Of solitude and silence in the sky?
These have we, and a thousand nooks of earth
Have also these, but no where else is found—
No where (or is it fancy?) can be found—
The one sensation that is here; 'tis here,
Here as it found its way into my heart
In childhood, here as it abides by day,
By night, here only; or in chosen minds
That take it with them hence, where'er they go.   160
'Tis (but I cannot name it) 'tis the sense
Of majesty, and beauty, and repose,
A blended holiness of earth and sky,
Something that makes this individual Spot,
This small abiding-place of many men,
A termination, and a last retreat,
A Centre, come from wheresoe'er you will,
A Whole without dependence or defect,
Made for itself, and happy in itself,
Perfect Contentment, Unity entire.   170

·   ·   ·   ·   ·   ·   ·

                    But the gates of Spring
Are opened; churlish Winter hath giv'n leave
That she should entertain for this one day,
Perhaps for many genial days to come,   280
His guests, and make them happy. They are pleased,
But most of all the birds that haunt the flood,
With the mild summons; inmates though they be

Of Winter's household: they are jubilant
This day, who drooped, or seemed to droop, so long;
They shew their pleasure, and shall I do less?
Happier of happy though I be, like them
I cannot take possession of the sky,
Mount with a thoughtless impulse and wheel there
One of a mighty multitude, whose way   290
And motion is a harmony and dance
Magnificent. Behold them, how they shape
Orb after orb their course still round and round
Above the area of the Lake, their own
Adopted region, girding it about
In wanton repetition, yet therewith
With that large circle evermore renewed:
Hundreds of curves and circlets high and low,
Backwards and forwards, progress intricate,
As if one spirit was in all and swayed   300
Their indefatigable flight. 'Tis done,
Ten times or more I fancied it had ceased,
And lo! the vanished company again
Ascending,—list again—I hear their wings
Faint, faint at first; and then an eager sound
Passed in a moment—and as faint again!
They tempt the sun to sport among their plumes;
They tempt the water, and the gleaming ice,
To shew them a fair image,—'tis themselves,
Their own fair forms, upon the glimm'ring plain,   310
Painted more soft and fair as they descend,
Almost to touch,—then up again aloft,
Up with a sally and a flash of speed,
As if they scorned both resting-place and rest.
Spring! for this day belongs to thee, rejoice!
Not upon me alone hath been bestowed,
Me blessed with many onward-looking thoughts,
The sunshine and mild air; oh surely these
Are grateful, not the happy Quires of love,
Thine own peculiar family, Sweet Spring,   320
That sport among green leaves so blithe a train.
    But two are missing—two, a lonely pair
Of milk-white Swans—ah, why are they not here?
These above all, ah, why are they not here

To share in this day's pleasure? From afar
They came, like Emma and myself, to live
Together here in peace and solitude,
Chusing this Valley, they who had the choice
Of the whole world. We saw them day by day,
Through those two months of unrelenting storm,   330
Conspicuous in the centre of the Lake,
Their safe retreat; we knew them well—I guess
That the whole Valley knew them—but to us
They were more dear than may be well believed,
Not only for their beauty and their still
And placid way of life and faithful love
Inseparable, not for these alone,
But that their state so much resembled ours,
They also having chosen this abode;
They strangers, and we strangers; they a pair,   340
And we a solitary pair like them.
They should not have departed; many days
I've looked for them in vain, nor on the wing
Have seen them, nor in that small open space
Of blue unfrozen water, where they lodged,
And lived so long in quiet, side by side.
Companions, brethren, consecrated friends,
Shall we behold them yet another year
Surviving, they for us, and we for them,
And neither pair be broken?—nay, perchance   350
It is too late already for such hope;
The Shepherd may have seized the deadly tube,
And parted them, incited by the prize
Which, for the sake of those he loves at home
And for the Lamb upon the mountain tops,
He should have spared; or haply both are gone,
One death, and that were mercy giv'n to both.

      ·   ·   ·   ·   ·   ·   ·

                      An awful voice,
'Tis true, I in my walks have often heard,
Sent from the mountains or the sheltered fields,
Shout after shout—reiterated whoop   410
In manner of a bird that takes delight
In answering to itself, or like a hound
Single at chace among the lonely woods—

A human voice, how awful in the gloom
Of coming night, when sky is dark, and earth
Not dark, nor yet enlightened, but by snow
Made visible, amid the noise of winds
And bleatings manifold of sheep that know
Their summons, and are gathering round for food—
That voice, the same, the very same, that breath   420
Which was an utterance awful as the wind,
Or any sound the mountains ever heard.

   That Shepherd's voice, it may have reached mine ear
Debased and under prophanation, made
An organ for the sounds articulate
Of ribaldry and blasphemy and wrath,
Where drunkenness hath kindled senseless frays.
I came not dreaming of unruffled life,
Untainted manners; born among the hills,
Bred also there, I wanted not a scale   430
To regulate my hopes; pleased with the good,
I shrink not from the evil in disgust,
Or with immoderate pain. I look for man,
The common Creature of the brotherhood,
But little differing from the man elsewhere,
For selfishness and envy and revenge,
Ill neighbourhood—pity that this should be—
Flattery and double-dealing, strife and wrong.

  ·   ·   ·   ·   ·   ·   ·   ·

  No, We are not alone, we do not stand,
My Emma, here misplaced and desolate,
Loving what no one cares for but ourselves.
We shall not scatter through the plains and rocks
Of this fair Vale, and o'er its spatious heights,   650
Unprofitable kindliness, bestowed
On Objects unaccustomed to the gifts
Of feeling, that were cheerless and forlorn
But few weeks past, and would be so again
If we were not; we do not tend a lamp
Whose lustre we alone participate,
Which is dependent upon us alone,
Mortal though bright, a dying, dying flame.
Look where we will, some human heart has been
Before us with its offering; not a tree   660

Sprinkles these little pastures, but the same
Hath furnished matter for a thought; perchance
To some one is as a familiar Friend.
Joy spreads and sorrow spreads; and this whole Vale,
Home of untutored Shepherds as it is,
Swarms with sensation, as with gleams of sunshine,
Shadows or breezes, scents or sounds.

.   .   .   .   .   .

  On Man, on Nature, and on human Life,
Thinking in solitude, from time to time   960
I feel sweet passions traversing my Soul
Like Music; unto these, where'er I may,
I would give utterance in numerous verse.
Of truth, of grandeur, beauty, love, and hope—
Hope for this earth and hope beyond the grave;
Of virtue and of intellectual power;
Of blessed consolations in distress;
Of joy in widest commonalty spread;
Of the individual mind that keeps its own
Inviolate retirement, and consists   970
With being limitless, the one great Life;
I sing: fit audience let me find though few.
  'Fit audience find though few'—thus prayed the Bard,
Holiest of Men. Urania, I shall need
Thy guidance, or a greater Muse, if such
Descend to earth or dwell in highest heaven.
For I must tread on shadowy ground, must sink
Deep, and, aloft ascending, breathe in worlds
To which the Heaven of heavens is but a veil.
All strength, all terror, single or in bands,   980
That ever was put forth in personal form—
Jehovah, with his thunder, and the quire
Of shouting angels, and the empyreal thrones—
I pass them unalarmed. The darkest Pit
Of the profoundest Hell, chaos, night,
Nor aught of [   ] vacancy scooped out
By help of dreams can breed such fear and awe
As fall upon us often when we look
Into our minds, into the mind of Man,
My haunt, and the main region of my song.   990
Beauty, whose living home is the green earth,

Surpassing the most fair ideal Forms
The craft of delicate spirits hath composed
From earth's materials, waits upon my steps,
Pitches her tents before me where I move,
An hourly Neighbour. Paradise, and groves
Elysian, fortunate islands, fields like those of old
In the deep ocean, wherefore should they be
A History, or but a dream, when minds
Once wedded to this outward frame of things   1000
In love, find these the growth of common day?
I, long before the blessèd hour arrives,
Would sing in solitude the spousal verse
Of this great consummation, would proclaim—
Speaking of nothing more than what we are—
How exquisitely the individual Mind
(And the progressive powers perhaps no less
Of the whole species) to the external world
Is fitted; and how exquisitely too—
Theme this but little heard of among men—   1010
The external world is fitted to the mind;
And the creation (by no lower name
Can it be called) which they with blended might
Accomplish: this is my great argument.
Such [   ] foregoing, if I oft
Must turn elsewhere, and travel near the tribes
And fellowships of men, and see ill sights
Of passions ravenous from each other's rage,
Must hear humanity in fields and groves
Pipe solitary anguish, or must hang   1020
Brooding above the fierce confederate Storm
Of Sorrow, barricadoed evermore
Within the walls of Cities—may these sounds
Have their authentic comment, that even these
Hearing, I be not heartless or forlorn!
Come, thou prophetic Spirit, Soul of Man,
Thou human Soul of the wide earth that hast
Thy metropolitan Temple in the hearts
Of mighty Poets: unto me vouchsafe
Thy guidance, teach me to discern and part   1030
Inherent things from casual, what is fixed
From fleeting, that my verse may live, and be

Even as a light hung up in heaven to chear
Mankind in times to come! And if with this
I blend more lowly matter—with the thing
Contemplated describe the mind and man
Contemplating, and who and what he was,
The transitory Being that beheld
This vision, when and where and how he lived,
His joys and sorrows and his hopes and fears,   1040
With all his little realities of life—
Be not this labour useless. If such theme
With highest things may [   ], then Great God,
Thou who art breath and being, way and guide,
And power and understanding, may my life
Express the image of a better time,
More wise desires and simple manners; nurse
My heart in genuine freedom; all pure thoughts
Be with me and uphold me to the end!

from *Poems on the Naming of Places*

II

To Joanna

Amid the smoke of cities did you pass
Your time of early youth, and there you learned,
From years of quiet industry, to love
The living Beings by your own fire-side,
With such a strong devotion, that your heart
Is slow towards the sympathies of them
Who look upon the hills with tenderness,
And made dear friendships with the streams and groves.
Yet we who are transgressors in this kind,
Dwelling retired in our simplicity   10
Among the woods and fields, we love you well,
Joanna! and I guess, since you have been
So distant from us now for two long years,
That you will gladly listen to discourse
However trivial, if you thence are taught

That they, with whom you once were happy, talk
Familiarly of you and of old times.
While I was seated, now some ten days past,
Beneath those lofty firs, that overtop
Their ancient neighbour, the old Steeple tower,   20
The Vicar from his gloomy house hard by
Came forth to greet me, and when he had asked,
'How fares Joanna, that wild-hearted Maid!
And when will she return to us?' he paused,
And after short exchange of village news,
He with grave looks demanded, for what cause,
Reviving obsolete Idolatry,
I like a Runic Priest, in characters
Of formidable size, had chiseled out
Some uncouth name upon the native rock,   30
Above the Rotha, by the forest side.
—Now, by those dear immunities of heart
Engendered betwixt malice and true love,
I was not loth to be so catechized,
And this was my reply.—'As it befel,
One summer morning we had walked abroad
At break of day, Joanna and myself.
—'Twas that delightful season, when the broom,
Full flowered, and visible on every steep,
Along the copses runs in veins of gold.   40
Our pathway led us on to Rotha's banks,
And when we came in front of that tall rock
Which looks towards the East, I there stopped short,
And traced the lofty barrier with my eye
From base to summit; such delight I found
To note in shrub and tree, in stone and flower,
That intermixture of delicious hues,
Along so vast a surface, all at once,
In one impression, by connecting force
Of their own beauty, imaged in the heart.   50
—When I had gazed perhaps two minutes' space,
Joanna, looking in my eyes, beheld
That ravishment of mine, and laughed aloud.
The rock, like something starting from a sleep,
Took up the Lady's voice, and laughed again:
That ancient Woman seated on Helm-crag

Was ready with her cavern; Hammar-Scar,
And the tall Steep of Silver-How sent forth
A noise of laughter; southern Loughrigg heard,
And Fairfield answered with a mountain tone: 60
Helvellyn far into the clear blue sky
Carried the Lady's voice,—old Skiddaw blew
His speaking trumpet;—back out of the clouds
Of Glaramara southward came the voice;
And Kirkstone tossed it from his misty head.
Now whether, (said I to our cordial Friend
Who in the hey-day of astonishment
Smiled in my face) this were in simple truth
A work accomplished by the brotherhood
Of ancient mountains, or my ear was touched   70
With dreams and visionary impulses,
Is not for me to tell; but sure I am
That there was a loud uproar in the hills.
And, while we both were listening, to my side
The fair Joanna drew, as if she wished
To shelter from some object of her fear.
—And hence, long afterwards, when eighteen moons
Were wasted, as I chanced to walk alone
Beneath this rock, at sun-rise, on a calm
And silent morning, I sate down, and there,   80
In memory of affections old and true,
I chiseled out in those rude characters
Joanna's name upon the living stone.
And I, and all who dwell by my fire-side
Have called the lovely rock, Joanna's Rock.'

IV

'A narrow girdle of rough stones and crags'

A narrow girdle of rough stones and crags,
A rude and natural causeway, interposed
Between the water and a winding slope
Of copse and thicket, leaves the eastern shore
Of Grasmere safe in its own privacy.
And there, myself and two beloved Friends,
One calm September morning, ere the mist
Had altogether yielded to the sun,

Sauntered on this retired and difficult way.
—Ill suits the road with one in haste, but we   10
Played with our time; and, as we strolled along,
It was our occupation to observe
Such objects as the waves had tossed ashore,
Feather, or leaf, or weed, or withered bough,
Each on the other heaped along the line
Of the dry wreck. And in our vacant mood,
Not seldom did we stop to watch some tuft
Of dandelion seed or thistle's beard,
Which, seeming lifeless half, and half impelled
By some internal feeling, skimmed along   20
Close to the surface of the lake that lay
Asleep in a dead calm, ran closely on
Along the dead calm lake, now here, now there,
In all its sportive wanderings all the while
Making report of an invisible breeze
That was its wings, its chariot, and its horse,
Its very playmate, and its moving soul.
—And often, trifling with a privilege
Alike indulged to all, we paused, one now,
And now the other, to point out, perchance   30
To pluck, some flower or water-weed, too fair
Either to be divided from the place
On which it grew, or to be left alone
To its own beauty. Many such there are,
Fair ferns and flowers, and chiefly that tall plant
So stately, of the Queen Osmunda named,
Plant lovelier in its own retired abode
On Grasmere's beach, than Naiad by the side
Of Grecian brook, or Lady of the Mere
Sole-sitting by the shores of old Romance.   40
—So fared we that sweet morning: from the fields
Meanwhile, a noise was heard, the busy mirth
Of Reapers, Men and Women, Boys and Girls.
Delighted much to listen to those sounds,
And in the fashion which I have described,
Feeding unthinking fancies, we advanced
Along the indented shore; when suddenly,
Through a thin veil of glittering haze, we saw
Before us on a point of jutting land

The tall and upright figure of a Man 50
Attired in peasant's garb, who stood alone
Angling beside the margin of the lake.
That way we turned our steps; nor was it long,
Ere making ready comments on the sight
Which then we saw, with one and the same voice
We all cried out, that he must be indeed
An idle man, who thus could lose a day
Of the mid harvest, when the labourer's hire
Is ample, and some little might be stored
Wherewith to chear him in the winter time. 60
Thus talking of that Peasant we approached
Close to the spot where with his rod and line
He stood alone; whereat he turned his head
To greet us—and we saw a man worn down
By sickness, gaunt and lean, with sunken cheeks
And wasted limbs, his legs so long and lean
That for my single self I looked at them,
Forgetful of the body they sustained.—
Too weak to labour in the harvest field,
The man was using his best skill to gain 70
A pittance from the dead unfeeling lake
That knew not of his wants. I will not say
What thoughts immediately were ours, nor how
The happy idleness of that sweet morn,
With all its lovely images, was changed
To serious musing and to self-reproach.
Nor did we fail to see within ourselves
What need there is to be reserved in speech,
And temper all our thoughts with charity.
—Therefore, unwilling to forget that day, 80
My Friend, Myself, and She who then received
The same admonishment, have called the place
By a memorial name, uncouth indeed
As e'er by Mariner was giv'n to Bay
Or Foreland on a new-discovered coast,
And, POINT RASH-JUDGMENT is the Name it bears.

Michael

A PASTORAL POEM

If from the public way you turn your steps
Up the tumultuous brook of Green-head Gill,
You will suppose that with an upright path
Your feet must struggle; in such bold ascent
The pastoral Mountains front you, face to face.
But, courage! for beside that boisterous Brook
The mountains have all opened out themselves,
And made a hidden valley of their own.
No habitation there is seen; but such
As journey thither find themselves alone   10
With a few sheep, with rocks and stones, and kites
That overhead are sailing in the sky.
It is in truth an utter solitude,
Nor should I have made mention of this Dell
But for one object which you might pass by,
Might see and notice not. Beside the brook
There is a straggling heap of unhewn stones!
And to that place a story appertains,
Which, though it be ungarnished with events,
Is not unfit, I deem, for the fire-side,   20
Or for the summer shade. It was the first,
The earliest of those tales that spake to me
Of Shepherds, dwellers in the vallies, men
Whom I already loved, not verily
For their own sakes, but for the fields and hills
Where was their occupation and abode.
And hence this Tale, while I was yet a boy
Careless of books, yet having felt the power
Of Nature, by the gentle agency
Of natural objects led me on to feel   30
For passions that were not my own, and think
At random and imperfectly indeed
On man; the heart of man and human life.
Therefore, although it be a history
Homely and rude, I will relate the same
For the delight of a few natural hearts,

And with yet fonder feeling, for the sake
Of youthful Poets, who among these Hills
Will be my second self when I am gone.

Upon the Forest-side in Grasmere Vale   40
There dwelt a Shepherd, Michael was his name,
An old man, stout of heart, and strong of limb.
His bodily frame had been from youth to age
Of an unusual strength: his mind was keen,
Intense and frugal, apt for all affairs,
And in his Shepherd's calling he was prompt
And watchful more than ordinary men.
Hence he had learned the meaning of all winds,
Of blasts of every tone, and often-times
When others heeded not, He heard the South   50
Make subterraneous music, like the noise
Of Bagpipers on distant Highland hills;
The Shepherd, at such warning, of his flock
Bethought him, and he to himself would say
The winds are now devising work for me!
And truly at all times the storm, that drives
The Traveller to a shelter, summoned him
Up to the mountains: he had been alone
Amid the heart of many thousand mists
That came to him and left him on the heights.   60
So lived he till his eightieth year was passed.

And grossly that man errs, who should suppose
That the green Valleys, and the Streams and Rocks
Were things indifferent to the Shepherd's thoughts.
Fields, where with chearful spirits he had breathed
The common air; the hills, which he so oft
Had climbed with vigorous steps; which had impressed
So many incidents upon his mind
Of hardship, skill or courage, joy or fear;
Which like a book preserved the memory   70
Of the dumb animals, whom he had saved,
Had fed or sheltered, linking to such acts,
So grateful in themselves, the certainty
Of honorable gains; these fields, these hills
Which were his living Being, even more

Than his own Blood—what could they less? had laid
Strong hold on his affections, were to him
A pleasurable feeling of blind love,
The pleasure which there is in life itself.

He had not passed his days in singleness.   80
He had a Wife, a comely Matron, old
Though younger than himself full twenty years.
She was a woman of a stirring life
Whose heart was in her house: two wheels she had
Of antique form, this large for spinning wool,
That small for flax, and if one wheel had rest,
It was because the other was at work.
The Pair had but one Inmate in their house,
An only Child, who had been born to them
When Michael telling o'er his years began   90
To deem that he was old, in Shepherd's phrase,
With one foot in the grave. This only son,
With two brave sheep dogs tried in many a storm,
The one of an inestimable worth,
Made all their Household. I may truly say,
That they were as a proverb in the vale
For endless industry. When day was gone,
And from their occupations out of doors
The Son and Father were come home, even then
Their labour did not cease, unless when all   100
Turned to their cleanly supper-board, and there
Each with a mess of pottage and skimmed milk,
Sate round their basket piled with oaten cakes,
And their plain home-made cheese. Yet when their meal
Was ended, Luke (for so the Son was named)
And his old Father, both betook themselves
To such convenient work, as might employ
Their hands by the fire-side; perhaps to card
Wool for the House-wife's spindle, or repair
Some injury done to sickle, flail, or scythe,   110
Or other implement of house or field.

Down from the ceiling by the chimney's edge,
Which in our ancient uncouth country style
Did with a huge projection overbrow

Large space beneath, as duly as the light
Of day grew dim, the House-wife hung a lamp;
An aged utensil, which had performed
Service beyond all others of its kind.
Early at evening did it burn and late,
Surviving Comrade of uncounted Hours   120
Which going by from year to year had found
And left the Couple neither gay perhaps
Nor chearful, yet with objects and with hopes
Living a life of eager industry.
And now, when Luke was in his eighteenth year,
There by the light of this old lamp they sate,
Father and Son, while late into the night
The House-wife plied her own peculiar work,
Making the cottage thro' the silent hours
Murmur as with the sound of summer flies.   130
Not with a waste of words, but for the sake
Of pleasure, which I know that I shall give
To many living now, I of this Lamp
Speak thus minutely: for there are no few
Whose memories will bear witness to my tale.
The Light was famous in its neighbourhood,
And was a public Symbol of the life,
The thrifty Pair had lived. For, as it chanced,
Their Cottage on a plot of rising ground
Stood single, with large prospect North and South,   140
High into Easedale, up to Dunmal-Raise,
And Westward to the village near the Lake.
And from this constant light so regular
And so far seen, the House itself by all
Who dwelt within the limits of the vale,
Both old and young, was named the Evening Star.

Thus living on through such a length of years,
The Shepherd, if he loved himself, must needs
Have loved his Help-mate; but to Michael's heart
This Son of his old age was yet more dear—   150
Effect which might perhaps have been produced
By that instinctive tenderness, the same
Blind Spirit, which is in the blood of all,
Or that a child, more than all other gifts,

Brings hope with it, and forward-looking thoughts,
And stirrings of inquietude, when they
By tendency of nature needs must fail.
From such, and other causes, to the thoughts
Of the old Man his only Son was now
The dearest object that he knew on earth.   160
Exceeding was the love he bare to him,
His Heart and his Heart's joy! For oftentimes
Old Michael, while he was a babe in arms,
Had done him female service, not alone
For dalliance and delight, as is the use
Of Fathers, but with patient mind enforced
To acts of tenderness; and he had rocked
His cradle with a woman's gentle hand.

And in a later time, ere yet the Boy
Had put on Boy's attire, did Michael love,   170
Albeit of a stern unbending mind,
To have the young one in his sight, when he
Had work by his own door, or when he sate
With sheep before him on his Shepherd's stool,
Beneath that large old Oak, which near their door
Stood, and from its enormous breadth of shade
Chosen for the Shearer's covert from the sun,
Thence in our rustic dialect was called
The CLIPPING TREE, a name which yet it bears.
There, while they two were sitting in the shade,   180
With others round them, earnest all and blithe,
Would Michael exercise his heart with looks
Of fond correction and reproof bestowed
Upon the child, if he disturbed the sheep
By catching at their legs, or with his shouts
Scared them, while they lay still beneath the shears.

And when by Heaven's good grace the Boy grew up
A healthy Lad, and carried in his cheek
Two steady roses that were five years old,
Then Michael from a winter coppice cut   190
With his own hand a sapling, which he hooped
With iron, making it throughout in all
Due requisites a perfect Shepherd's Staff,

And gave it to the Boy; wherewith equipped
He as a Watchman oftentimes was placed
At gate or gap, to stem or turn the flock,
And to his office prematurely called
There stood the urchin, as you will divine,
Something between a hindrance and a help,
And for this cause not always, I believe,   200
Receiving from his Father hire of praise.
Though nought was left undone, which staff or voice,
Or looks, or threatening gestures could perform.

    But soon as Luke, full ten years old, could stand
Against the mountain blasts, and to the heights,
Not fearing toil, nor length of weary ways,
He with his Father daily went, and they
Were as companions, why should I relate
That objects which the Shepherd loved before
Were dearer now? that from the Boy there came   210
Feelings and emanations, things which were
Light to the sun and music to the wind;
And that the Old Man's heart seemed born again.

    Thus in his Father's sight the Boy grew up:
And now when he had reached his eighteenth year,
He was his comfort and his daily hope.

While this good household thus were living on
From day to day, to Michael's ear there came
Distressful tidings. Long before the time
Of which I speak, the Shepherd had been bound   220
In surety for his Brother's Son, a man
Of an industrious life, and ample means,
But unforeseen misfortunes suddenly
Had pressed upon him, and old Michael now
Was summoned to discharge the forfeiture,
A grievous penalty, but little less
Than half his substance. This un-looked for claim
At the first hearing, for a moment took
More hope out of his life than he supposed
That any old man ever could have lost.   230
As soon as he had gathered so much strength
That he could look his trouble in the face,
It seemed that his sole refuge was to sell

A portion of his patrimonial fields.
Such was his first resolve; he thought again,
And his heart failed him. 'Isabel,' said he,
Two evenings after he had heard the news,
'I have been toiling more than seventy years,
And in the open sun-shine of God's love
Have we all lived, yet if these fields of ours   240
Should pass into a Stranger's hand, I think
That I could not lie quiet in my grave.
Our lot is a hard lot; the Sun itself
Has scarcely been more diligent than I,
And I have lived to be a fool at last
To my own family. An evil Man
That was, and made an evil choice, if he
Were false to us; and if he were not false,
There are ten thousand to whom loss like this
Had been no sorrow. I forgive him—but   250
'Twere better to be dumb than to talk thus.
When I began, my purpose was to speak
Of remedies and of a chearful hope.
Our Luke shall leave us, Isabel; the land
Shall not go from us, and it shall be free,
He shall possess it, free as is the wind
That passes over it. We have, thou knowest,
Another Kinsman, he will be our friend
In this distress. He is a prosperous man,
Thriving in trade, and Luke to him shall go,   260
And with his Kinsman's help and his own thrift,
He quickly will repair this loss, and then
May come again to us. If here he stay,
What can be done? Where every one is poor
What can be gained?' At this, the old man paused,
And Isabel sate silent, for her mind
Was busy, looking back into past times.
There's Richard Bateman, thought she to herself,
He was a parish-boy—at the church-door
They made a gathering for him, shillings, pence,   270
And halfpennies, wherewith the Neighbours bought
A Basket, which they filled with Pedlar's wares,
And with this Basket on his arm, the Lad
Went up to London, found a Master there,

Who out of many chose the trusty Boy
To go and overlook his merchandise
Beyond the seas, where he grew wond'rous rich,
And left estates and monies to the poor,
And at his birth-place built a Chapel, floored
With Marble, which he sent from foreign lands.   280
These thoughts, and many others of like sort,
Passed quickly thro' the mind of Isabel,
And her face brightened. The Old Man was glad,
And thus resumed. 'Well! Isabel, this scheme
These two days has been meat and drink to me.
Far more than we have lost is left us yet.
—We have enough—I wish indeed that I
Were younger, but this hope is a good hope.
—Make ready Luke's best garments, of the best
Buy for him more, and let us send him forth   290
To-morrow, or the next day, or to-night:
—If he could go, the Boy should go to-night.'
Here Michael ceased, and to the fields went forth
With a light heart. The House-wife for five days
Was restless morn and night, and all day long
Wrought on with her best fingers to prepare
Things needful for the journey of her Son.
But Isabel was glad when Sunday came
To stop her in her work; for, when she lay
By Michael's side, she for the two last nights   300
Heard him, how he was troubled in his sleep:
And when they rose at morning she could see
That all his hopes were gone. That day at noon
She said to Luke, while they two by themselves
Were sitting at the door, 'Thou must not go,
We have no other Child but thee to lose,
None to remember—do not go away,
For if thou leave thy Father he will die.'
The Lad made answer with a jocund voice,
And Isabel, when she had told her fears,   310
Recovered heart. That evening her best fare
Did she bring forth, and all together sate
Like happy people round a Christmas fire.

Next morning Isabel resumed her work,
And all the ensuing week the house appeared
As cheerful as a grove in Spring: at length
The expected letter from their Kinsman came,
With kind assurances that he would do
His utmost for the welfare of the Boy,
To which requests were added that forthwith   320
He might be sent to him. Ten times or more
The letter was read over; Isabel
Went forth to shew it to the neighbours round:
Nor was there at that time on English Land
A prouder heart than Luke's. When Isabel
Had to her house returned, the Old Man said
'He shall depart to-morrow.' To this word
The House-wife answered, talking much of things
Which, if at such short notice he should go,
Would surely be forgotten. But at length   330
She gave consent, and Michael was at ease.

Near the tumultuous brook of Green-head Gill,
In that deep Valley, Michael had designed
To build a Sheep-fold, and, before he heard
The tidings of his melancholy loss,
For this same purpose he had gathered up
A heap of stones, which close to the brook side
Lay thrown together, ready for the work.
With Luke that evening thitherward he walked;
And soon as they had reached the place he stopped   340
And thus the Old Man spake to him. 'My Son,
To-morrow thou wilt leave me; with full heart
I look upon thee, for thou art the same
That wert a promise to me ere thy birth,
And all thy life hast been my daily joy.
I will relate to thee some little part
Of our two histories; 'twill do thee good
When thou art from me, even if I should speak
Of things thou canst not know of.—After thou
First cam'st into the world, as it befalls   350
To new-born infants, thou didst sleep away
Two days, and blessings from thy Father's tongue
Then fell upon thee. Day by day passed on,

And still I loved thee with encreasing love.
Never to living ear came sweeter sounds
Than when I heard thee by our own fire-side
First uttering without words a natural tune,
When thou, a feeding babe, didst in thy joy
Sing at thy Mother's breast. Month followed month,
And in the open fields my life was passed   360
And in the mountains, else I think that thou
Hadst been brought up upon thy father's knees.
—But we were playmates, Luke; among these hills,
As well thou know'st, in us the old and young
Have played together, nor with me didst thou
Lack any pleasure which a boy can know.'
Luke had a manly heart; but at these words
He sobbed aloud; the Old Man grasped his hand,
And said, 'Nay do not take it so—I see
That these are things of which I need not speak.   370
—Even to the utmost I have been to thee
A kind and a good Father: and herein
I but repay a gift which I myself
Received at others' hands, for, though now old
Beyond the common life of man, I still
Remember them who loved me in my youth.
Both of them sleep together: here they lived
As all their Forefathers had done, and when
At length their time was come, they were not loth
To give their bodies to the family mold.   380
I wished that thou should'st live the life they lived.
But 'tis a long time to look back, my Son,
And see so little gain from sixty years.
These fields were burthened when they came to me;
'Till I was forty years of age, not more
Than half of my inheritance was mine.
I toiled and toiled; God blessed me in my work,
And 'till these three weeks past the land was free.
—It looks as if it never could endure
Another Master. Heaven forgive me, Luke,   390
If I judge ill for thee, but it seems good
That thou should'st go.' At this the Old Man paused,
Then, pointing to the Stones near which they stood,
Thus, after a short silence, he resumed:

'This was a work for us, and now, my Son,
It is a work for me. But, lay one Stone—
Here, lay it for me, Luke, with thine own hands.
I for the purpose brought thee to this place.
Nay, Boy, be of good hope:—we both may live
To see a better day. At eighty-four   400
I still am strong and stout;—do thou thy part,
I will do mine.—I will begin again
With many tasks that were resigned to thee;
Up to the heights, and in among the storms,
Will I without thee go again, and do
All works which I was wont to do alone,
Before I knew thy face.—Heaven bless thee, Boy!
Thy heart these two weeks has been beating fast
With many hopes—it should be so—yes—yes—
I knew that thou could'st never have a wish   410
To leave me, Luke, thou hast been bound to me
Only by links of love, when thou art gone
What will be left to us!—But, I forget
My purposes. Lay now the corner-stone,
As I requested, and hereafter, Luke,
When thou art gone away, should evil men
Be thy companions, let this Sheep-fold be
Thy anchor and thy shield; amid all fear
And all temptation, let it be to thee
An emblem of the life thy Fathers lived,   420
Who, being innocent, did for that cause
Bestir them in good deeds. Now, fare thee well—
When thou return'st, thou in this place wilt see
A work which is not here, a covenant
'Twill be between us—but whatever fate
Befall thee, I shall love thee to the last,
And bear thy memory with me to the grave.'

The Shepherd ended here; and Luke stooped down,
And as his Father had requested, laid
The first stone of the Sheep-fold; at the sight   430
The Old Man's grief broke from him, to his heart
He pressed his Son, he kissed him and wept;
And to the House together they returned.

Next morning, as had been resolved, the Boy
Began his journey, and when he had reached
The public Way, he put on a bold face;
And all the Neighbours as he passed their doors
Came forth, with wishes and with farewell prayers,
That followed him 'till he was out of sight.
A good report did from their Kinsman come,   440
Of Luke and his well-doing; and the Boy
Wrote loving letters, full of wond'rous news,
Which, as the House-wife phrased it, were throughout
The prettiest letters that were ever seen.
Both parents read them with rejoicing hearts.
So, many months passed on: and once again
The Shepherd went about his daily work
With confident and cheerful thoughts; and now
Sometimes when he could find a leisure hour
He to that valley took his way, and there   450
Wrought at the Sheep-fold. Meantime Luke began
To slacken in his duty, and at length
He in the dissolute city gave himself
To evil courses: ignominy and shame
Fell on him, so that he was driven at last
To seek a hiding-place beyond the seas.

There is a comfort in the strength of love;
'Twill make a thing endurable, which else
Would break the heart:—Old Michael found it so.
I have conversed with more than one who well   460
Remember the Old Man, and what he was
Years after he had heard this heavy news.
His bodily frame had been from youth to age
Of an unusual strength. Among the rocks
He went, and still looked up upon the sun,
And listened to the wind; and as before
Performed all kinds of labour for his Sheep,
And for the land his small inheritance.
And to that hollow Dell from time to time
Did he repair, to build the Fold of which   470
His flock had need. 'Tis not forgotten yet
The pity which was then in every heart
For the Old Man—and 'tis believed by all

That many and many a day he thither went,
And never lifted up a single stone.
There, by the Sheep-fold, sometimes was he seen
Sitting alone, with that his faithful Dog,
Then old, beside him, lying at his feet.
The length of full seven years from time to time
He at the building of this Sheep-fold wrought,   480
And left the work unfinished when he died.

Three years, or little more, did Isabel,
Survive her Husband: at her death the estate
Was sold, and went into a Stranger's hand.
The Cottage which was named The Evening Star
Is gone, the ploughshare has been through the ground
On which it stood; great changes have been wrought
In all the neighbourhood, yet the Oak is left
That grew beside their Door; and the remains
Of the unfinished Sheep-fold may be seen   490
Beside the boisterous brook of Green-head Gill.

'I travelled among unknown Men'

I travelled among unknown Men,
    In Lands beyond the Sea;
Nor England! did I know till then
    What love I bore to thee.

'Tis past, that melancholy dream!
    Nor will I quit thy shore
A second time; for still I seem
    To love thee more and more.

Among thy mountains did I feel
    The joy of my desire;   10
And She I cherished turned her wheel
    Beside an English fire.

Thy mornings shewed—thy nights concealed
    The bowers where Lucy played;
And thine is, too, the last green field
    Which Lucy's eyes surveyed!

To a Sky-Lark

Up with me! up with me into the clouds!
    For thy song, Lark, is strong;
Up with me, up with me into the clouds!
    Singing, singing,
With all the heav'ns about thee ringing,
    Lift me, guide me, till I find
That spot which seems so to thy mind!

I have walked through wildernesses dreary,
    And today my heart is weary;
    Had I now the soul of a Faery,   10
    Up to thee would I fly.
There is madness about thee, and joy divine
    In that song of thine;
Up with me, up with me, high and high,
To thy banqueting-place in the sky!
    Joyous as Morning,
    Thou art laughing and scorning;
Thou hast a nest, for thy love and thy rest:
And, though little troubled with sloth,
Drunken Lark! thou would'st be loth   20
To be such a Traveller as I.
    Happy, happy Liver!
With a soul as strong as a mountain River,
Pouring out praise to the Almighty Giver,
Joy and jollity be with us both!
Hearing thee, or else some other,
    As merry a Brother,
I on the earth will go plodding on,
By myself, chearfully, till the day is done.

Alice Fell

The Post-boy drove with fierce career,
For threat'ning clouds the moon had drowned;
When suddenly I seemed to hear
A moan, a lamentable sound.

As if the wind blew many ways
I heard the sound, and more and more:
It seemed to follow with the Chaise,
And still I heard it as before.

At length I to the Boy called out,
He stopped his horses at the word;   10
But neither cry, nor voice, nor shout,
Nor aught else like it could be heard.

The Boy then smacked his whip, and fast
The horses scampered through the rain;
And soon I heard upon the blast
The voice, and bade him halt again.

Said I, alighting on the ground,
'What can it be, this piteous moan?'
And there a little Girl I found,
Sitting behind the Chaise, alone.   20

'My Cloak!' the word was last and first,
And loud and bitterly she wept,
As if her very heart would burst;
And down from off the Chaise she leapt.

'What ails you, Child?' She sobbed, 'Look here!'
I saw it in the wheel entangled,
A weather beaten Rag as e'er
From any garden scare-crow dangled.

'Twas twisted betwixt nave and spoke;
Her help she lent, and with good heed   30
Together we released the Cloak;
A wretched, wretched rag indeed!

'And whither are you going, Child,
Tonight along these lonesome ways?'
'To Durham' answered she half wild—
'Then come with me into the chaise.'

She sate like one past all relief;
Sob after sob she forth did send
In wretchedness, as if her grief
Could never, never, have an end.   40

'My Child, in Durham do you dwell?'
She checked herself in her distress,
And said, 'My name is Alice Fell;
I'm fatherless and motherless.

And I to Durham, Sir, belong.'
And then, as if the thought would choke
Her very heart, her grief grew strong;
And all was for her tattered Cloak.

The chaise drove on; our journey's end
Was nigh; and, sitting by my side,   50
As if she'd lost her only friend
She wept, nor would be pacified.

Up to the Tavern-door we post;
Of Alice and her grief I told;
And I gave money to the Host,
To buy a new Cloak for the old.

'And let it be a duffil grey,
As warm a cloak as man can sell!'
Proud Creature was she the next day,
The little Orphan, Alice Fell!   60

Beggars

She had a tall Man's height, or more;
No bonnet screened her from the heat;
A long drab-coloured Cloak she wore,
A Mantle reaching to her feet:
What other dress she had I could not know;
Only she wore a Cap that was as white as snow.

In all my walks, through field or town,
Such Figure had I never seen:
Her face was of Egyptian brown:
Fit person was she for a Queen,   10
   To head those ancient Amazonian files:
Or ruling Bandit's Wife, among the Grecian Isles.

Before me begging did she stand,
Pouring out sorrows like a sea;
Grief after grief:—on English Land
Such woes I knew could never be;
   And yet a boon I gave her; for the Creature
Was beautiful to see; a Weed of glorious feature!

I left her, and pursued my way;
And soon before me did espy   20
A pair of little Boys at play,
Chasing a crimson butterfly;
   The Taller followed with his hat in hand,
Wreathed round with yellow flow'rs, the gayest of the land.

The Other wore a rimless crown,
With leaves of laurel stuck about:
And they both followed up and down,
Each whooping with a merry shout;
   Two Brothers seemed they, eight and ten years old;
And like that Woman's face as gold is like to gold. 30

They bolted on me thus, and lo!
Each ready with a plaintive whine;
Said I, 'Not half an hour ago
Your Mother has had alms of mine.'
   'That cannot be,' one answered, 'She is dead.'
'Nay but I gave her pence, and she will buy you bread.'

'She has been dead, Sir, many a day.'
'Sweet Boys, you're telling me a lie;
It was your Mother, as I say—'
And in the twinkling of an eye,   40
   'Come, come!' cried one; and, without more ado,
Off to some other play they both together flew.

To a Butterfly

Stay near me—do not take thy flight!
A little longer stay in sight!
Much converse do I find in Thee,
Historian of my Infancy!
Float near me; do not yet depart!
Dead times revive in thee:
Thou bring'st, gay Creature as thou art!
A solemn image to my heart,
My Father's Family!

Oh! pleasant, pleasant were the days,   10
The time, when in our childish plays
My sister Emmeline and I
Together chaced the Butterfly!
A very hunter did I rush
Upon the prey:—with leaps and springs
I followed on from brake to bush;
But She, God love her! feared to brush
The dust from off its wings.

To the Cuckoo

O blithe New-comer! I have heard,
I hear thee and rejoice:
O Cuckoo! shall I call thee Bird,
Or but a wandering Voice?

While I am lying on the grass,
I hear thy restless shout:
From hill to hill it seems to pass,
About, and all about!

To me, no Babbler with a tale
Of sunshine and of flowers,   10
Thou tellest, Cuckoo! in the vale
Of visionary hours.

Thrice welcome, Darling of the Spring!
Even yet thou art to me
No Bird; but an invisible Thing,
A voice, a mystery.

The same whom in my School-boy days
I listened to; that Cry
Which made me look a thousand ways;
In bush, and tree, and sky.   20

To seek thee did I often rove
Through woods and on the green;
And thou wert still a hope, a love;
Still longed for, never seen!

And I can listen to thee yet;
Can lie upon the plain
And listen, till I do beget
That golden time again.

O blessed Bird! the earth we pace
Again appears to be   30
An unsubstantial, faery place;
That is fit home for Thee!

'My heart leaps up when I behold'

My heart leaps up when I behold
    A Rainbow in the sky:
So was it when my life began;
So is it now I am a Man;
So be it when I shall grow old,
    Or let me die!
The Child is Father of the Man;
And I could wish my days to be
Bound each to each by natural piety.

To H.C., Six Years Old

O Thou! whose fancies from afar are brought;
Who of thy words dost make a mock apparel,
And fittest to unutterable thought
The breeze-like motion and the self-born carol;
Thou Faery Voyager! that dost float
In such clear water, that thy Boat
May rather seem
To brood on air than on an earthly stream;
Suspended in a stream as clear as sky,
Where earth and heaven do make one imagery;   10
O blessed Vision! happy Child!
That art so exquisitely wild,
I think of thee with many fears
For what may be thy lot in future years.

I thought of times when Pain might be thy guest,
Lord of thy house and hospitality;
And grief, uneasy Lover! never rest
But when she sate within the touch of thee.
Oh! too industrious folly!
Oh! vain and causeless melancholy!   20
Nature will either end thee quite;
Or, lengthening out thy season of delight,
Preserve for thee, by individual right,
A young Lamb's heart among the full-grown flocks.
What hast Thou to do with sorrow,
Or the injuries of tomorrow?
Thou art a Dew-drop, which the morn brings forth,
Not doomed to jostle with unkindly shocks;
Or to be trailed along the soiling earth;
A Gem that glitters while it lives,   30
And no forewarning gives;
But, at the touch of wrong, without a strife,
Slips in a moment out of life.

'Among all lovely things my Love had been'

Among all lovely things my Love had been;
Had noted well the stars, all flowers that grew
About her home; but she had never seen
A Glow-worm, never one, and this I knew.

While riding near her home one stormy night
A single Glow-worm did I chance to espy;
I gave a fervent welcome to the sight,
And from my Horse I leapt; great joy had I.

Upon a leaf the Glow-worm did I lay,
To bear it with me through the stormy night: 10
And, as before, it shone without dismay;
Albeit putting forth a fainter light.

When to the Dwelling of my Love I came,
I went into the Orchard quietly;
And left the Glow-worm, blessing it by name,
Laid safely by itself, beneath a Tree.

The whole next day, I hoped, and hoped with fear;
At night the Glow-worm shone beneath the Tree:
I led my Lucy to the spot, 'Look here!'
Oh! joy it was for her, and joy for me!   20

To a Butterfly

I've watched you now a full half hour,
Self-poised upon that yellow flower;
And, little Butterfly! indeed
I know not if you sleep, or feed.
How motionless! not frozen seas
More motionless! and then
What joy awaits you, when the breeze
Hath found you out among the trees,
And calls you forth again!

This plot of Orchard-ground is ours; 10
My trees they are, my Sister's flowers;
Stop here whenever you are weary,
And rest as in a sanctuary!
Come often to us, fear no wrong;
Sit near us on the bough!
We'll talk of sunshine and of song;
And summer days, when we were young,
Sweet childish days, that were as long
    As twenty days are now!

'These chairs they have no words to utter'

These chairs they have no words to utter,
No fire is in the grate to stir or flutter,
The ceiling and floor are mute as a stone,
My chamber is hushed and still,
    And I am alone,
    Happy and alone.

Oh! who would be afraid of life?
  The passion the sorrow and the strife,
    When he may lie
    Sheltered so easily? 10
May lie in peace on his bed,
Happy as they who are dead.

Half an hour afterwards

I have thoughts that are fed by the sun;
  The things which I see
  Are welcome to me,
  Welcome every one;
  I do not wish to lie
    Dead, dead,
Dead without any company
  Here alone on my bed, 20
With thoughts that are fed by the sun
And hopes that are welcome everyone,
    Happy am I.

O life there is about thee
A deep delicious peace;
I would not be without thee,
   Stay, oh stay!
Yet be thou ever as now,
Sweetness and breath with the quiet of death,
   Peace, peace, peace.

Resolution and Independence

There was a roaring in the wind all night;
The rain came heavily and fell in floods;
But now the sun is rising calm and bright;
The birds are singing in the distant woods;
Over his own sweet voice the Stock-dove broods;
The Jay makes answer as the Magpie chatters;
And all the air is filled with pleasant noise of waters.

All things that love the sun are out of doors;
The sky rejoices in the morning's birth;
The grass is bright with rain-drops; on the moors   10
The Hare is running races in her mirth;
And with her feet she from the plashy earth
Raises a mist; which, glittering in the sun,
Runs with her all the way, wherever she doth run.

I was a Traveller then upon the moor;
I saw the Hare that raced about with joy;
I heard the woods, and distant waters, roar;
Or heard them not, as happy as a Boy:
The pleasant season did my heart employ:
My old remembrances went from me wholly;   20
And all the ways of men, so vain and melancholy.

But, as it sometimes chanceth, from the might
Of joy in minds that can no farther go,
As high as we have mounted in delight
In our dejection do we sink as low,
To me that morning did it happen so;

And fears, and fancies, thick upon me came;
Dim sadness, and blind thoughts I knew not nor could name.

I heard the Sky-lark singing in the sky;
And I bethought me of the playful Hare: 30
Even such a happy Child of earth am I;
Even as these blissful Creatures do I fare;
Far from the world I walk, and from all care;
But there may come another day to me,
Solitude, pain of heart, distress, and poverty.

My whole life I have lived in pleasant thought,
As if life's business were a summer mood;
As if all needful things would come unsought
To genial faith, still rich in genial good;
But how can He expect that others should   40
Build for him, sow for him, and at his call
Love him, who for himself will take no heed at all?

I thought of Chatterton, the marvellous Boy,
The sleepless Soul that perished in its pride;
Of Him who walked in glory and in joy
Behind his plough, upon the mountain-side:
By our own spirits are we deified;
We Poets in our youth begin in gladness;
But thereof comes in the end despondency and madness.

Now, whether it were by peculiar grace,   50
A leading from above, a something given,
Yet it befel, that, in this lonely place,
When up and down my fancy thus was driven,
And I with these untoward thoughts had striven,
I saw a Man before me unawares:
The oldest Man he seemed that ever wore grey hairs.

My course I stopped as soon as I espied
The Old Man in that naked wilderness:
Close by a Pond, upon the further side,
He stood alone: a minute's space I guess   60
I watched him, he continuing motionless:
To the Pool's further margin then I drew;
He being all the while before me full in view.

As a huge Stone is sometimes seen to lie
Couched on the bald top of an eminence;
Wonder to all who do the same espy
By what means it could thither come, and whence;
So that it seems a thing endued with sense:
Like a Sea-beast crawled forth, which on a shelf
Of rock or sand reposeth, there to sun itself. 70

Such seemed this Man, not all alive nor dead,
Nor all asleep; in his extreme old age:
His body was bent double, feet and head
Coming together in their pilgrimage;
As if some dire constraint of pain, or rage
Of sickness felt by him in times long past,
A more than human weight upon his frame had cast.

Himself he propped, his body, limbs, and face,
Upon a long grey Staff of shaven wood:
And, still as I drew near with gentle pace, 80
Beside the little pond or moorish flood
Motionless as a Cloud the Old Man stood;
That heareth not the loud winds when they call;
And moveth altogether, if it move at all.

At length, himself unsettling, he the Pond
Stirred with his Staff, and fixedly did look
Upon the muddy water, which he conned,
As if he had been reading in a book:
And now such freedom as I could I took;
And, drawing to his side, to him did say, 90
'This morning gives us promise of a glorious day.'

A gentle answer did the Old Man make,
In courteous speech which forth he slowly drew:
And him with further words I thus bespake,
'What kind of work is that which you pursue?
This is a lonesome place for one like you.'
He answered me with pleasure and surprize;
And there was, while he spake, a fire about his eyes.

His words came feebly, from a feeble chest,
Yet each in solemn order followed each, 100
With something of a lofty utterance drest;
Choice word, and measured phrase; above the reach
Of ordinary men; a stately speech!
Such as grave Livers do in Scotland use,
Religious men, who give to God and Man their dues.

He told me that he to this pond had come
To gather Leeches, being old and poor:
Employment hazardous and wearisome!
And he had many hardships to endure:
From Pond to Pond he roamed, from moor to moor, 110
Housing, with God's good help, by choice or chance:
And in this way he gained an honest maintenance.

The Old Man still stood talking by my side;
But now his voice to me was like a stream
Scarce heard; nor word from word could I divide;
And the whole Body of the man did seem
Like one whom I had met with in a dream;
Or like a Man from some far region sent;
To give me human strength, and strong admonishment.

My former thoughts returned: the fear that kills; 120
The hope that is unwilling to be fed;
Cold, pain, and labour, and all fleshly ills;
And mighty Poets in their misery dead.
And now, not knowing what the Old Man had said,
My question eagerly did I renew,
'How is it that you live, and what is it you do?'

He with a smile did then his words repeat;
And said, that, gathering Leeches, far and wide
He travelled; stirring thus about his feet
The waters of the Ponds where they abide. 130
'Once I could meet with them on every side;
But they have dwindled long by slow decay;
Yet still I persevere, and find them where I may.'

While he was talking thus, the lonely place,
The Old Man's shape, and speech, all troubled me:
In my mind's eye I seemed to see him pace
About the weary moors continually,
Wandering about alone and silently.
While I these thoughts within myself pursued,
He, having made a pause, the same discourse renewed.   140

And soon with this he other matter blended,
Chearfully uttered, with demeanour kind,
But stately in the main; and, when he ended,
I could have laughed myself to scorn, to find
In that decrepit Man so firm a mind.
'God,' said I, 'be my help and stay secure;
I'll think of the Leech-gatherer on the lonely moor.'

Travelling

This is the spot:—how mildly does the sun
Shine in between these fading leaves! the air
In the habitual silence of this wood
Is more than silent: and this bed of heath,
Where shall we find so sweet a resting place?
Come!—let me see thee sink into a dream
Of quiet thoughts,—protracted till thine eye
Be calm as water, when the winds are gone
And no one can tell whither.—my sweet friend!
We two have had such happy hours together   10
That my heart melts in me to think of it.

'Within our happy Castle there dwelt one'

Within our happy Castle there dwelt one
Whom without blame I may not overlook:
For never sun on living creature shone
Who more devout enjoyment with us took.
Here on his hours he hung as on a book;

On his own time he here would float away;
As doth a fly upon a summer brook:
But, go tomorrow, or belike, today,
Seek for him, he is fled; and whither none could say.

Thus often would he leave our peaceful home,   10
And find elsewhere his business or delight.
Out of our Valley's limits did he roam:
Full many a time, upon a stormy night,
His voice came to us from the neighbouring height:
Oft did we see him driving full in view
At mid-day, when the sun was shining bright:
What ill was on him, what he had to do,
A mighty wonder bred among our quiet crew.

Ah! piteous sight it was to see this Man.
When he came back to us a withered flower;   20
Or like a sinful creature pale and wan:
Down would he lie, and without strength or power
Look at the common grass from hour to hour:
And oftentimes, how long I fear to say,
Where apple-trees in blossom made a bower,
Retired in that sunshiny shade he lay.
And, like a naked Indian, slept himself away.

Great wonder to our gentle tribe it was
Whenever from our Valley he withdrew;
For happier soul no living creature has   30
Than he had, being here the long day through.
Some thought he was a lover and did woo;
Some thought far worse of him, and did him wrong;
But Verse was what he had been wedded to:
And his own mind did, like a tempest strong,
Come to him thus; and drove the weary Man along.

With him there often walked in friendly wise,
Or lay upon the moss, by brook or tree,
A noticeable Man, with large dark eyes,
And a pale face, that seemed undoubtedly   40
As if a *blooming* face it *ought* to be:
Heavy his low-hung lip did oft appear,

A face divine of heaven-born ideotcy!
Profound his forehead was, though not severe;
Yet some did think that he had little business here.

Ah! God forefend! his was a lawful right.
Noisy he was, and gamesome as a boy:
His limbs would toss about him with delight,
Like branches when strong winds the trees annoy.
He lacked not implement, device, or toy,   50
To cheat away the hours that silent were:
He would have taught you how you might employ
Yourself; and many did to him repair,
And, certes, not in vain:—he had inventions rare.

Instruments had he, playthings for the ear,
Long blades of grass plucked round him as he lay;
These served to catch the wind as it came near;
Glasses he had with many colours gay;
Others that did all little things display;
The beetle with his radiance manifold,   60
A mailed angel on a battle day.
And leaves and flowers, and herbage green and gold,
And all the glorious sights which fairies do behold.

He would entice that other man to hear
His music, and to view his imagery:
And sooth, these two did love each other dear,
As far as love in such a place could be:
There did they lie from earthly labour free,
Most happy livers as were ever seen!
If but a bird, to keep them company,   70
Or butterfly sate down, they were, I ween,
As pleas'd as if the same had been a Maiden Queen.

'The world is too much with us'

The world is too much with us; late and soon,
Getting and spending, we lay waste our powers:
Little we see in nature that is ours;

We have given our hearts away, a sordid boon!
This Sea that bares her bosom to the moon;
The Winds that will be howling at all hours
And are up-gathered now like sleeping flowers;
For this, for every thing, we are out of tune;
It moves us not—Great God! I'd rather be
A Pagan suckled in a creed outworn;   10
So might I, standing on this pleasant lea,
Have glimpses that would make me less forlorn;
Have sight of Proteus coming from the sea;
Or hear old Triton blow his wreathed horn.

'With Ships the sea was sprinkled far and nigh'

With Ships the sea was sprinkled far and nigh,
Like stars in heaven, and joyously it showed;
Some lying fast at anchor in the road,
Some veering up and down, one knew not why.
A goodly Vessel did I then espy
Come like a Giant from a haven broad;
And lustily along the Bay she strode,
Her tackling rich, and of apparel high.
This Ship was nought to me, nor I to her,
Yet I pursued her with a Lover's look;   10
This Ship to all the rest did I prefer:
When will she turn, and whither? She will brook
No tarrying; where she comes the winds must stir:
On went She, and due north her journey took.

'Dear Native Brooks your ways have I pursued'

Dear Native Brooks your ways have I pursued
How fondly! whether you delight in screen
Of shady woods to rest yourselves unseen,
Or from your lofty dwellings scarcely viewed
But by the mountain eagle, your bold brood
Pure as the morning, angry, boisterous, keen,

Green as sea water, foaming white and green,
Comes roaring like a joyous multitude.
Nor have I been your follower in vain;
For not to speak of life and its first joys   10
Bound to your goings by a tender chain
Of flowers and delicate dreams that entertain
Loose minds when Men are growing into Boys,
My manly heart has owed to your rough noise
Triumph and thoughts no bondage could restrain.

'Great Men have been among us'

Great Men have been among us; hands that penned
And tongues that uttered wisdom, better none:
The later Sydney, Marvel, Harrington,
Young Vane, and others who called Milton Friend.
These Moralists could act and comprehend:
They knew how genuine glory was put on;
Taught us how rightfully a nation shone
In splendor: what strength was, that would not bend
But in magnanimous meekness. France, 'tis strange,
Hath brought forth no such souls as we had then.   10
Perpetual emptiness! unceasing change!
No single Volume paramount, no code,
No master spirit, no determined road;
But equally a want of Books and Men!

Composed by the Sea-Side, near Calais

AUGUST, 1802

Fair Star of Evening, Splendor of the West,
Star of my Country! on the horizon's brink
Thou hangest, stooping, as might seem, to sink
On England's bosom; yet well pleased to rest,
Meanwhile, and be to her a glorious crest
Conspicuous to the Nations. Thou, I think,
Should'st be my Country's emblem; and should'st wink,

Bright Star! with laughter on her banners, drest
In thy fresh beauty. There! that dusky spot
Beneath thee, it is England; there it lies.   10
Blessings be on you both! one hope, one lot,
One life, one glory! I, with many a fear
For my dear Country, many heartfelt sighs,
Among Men who do not love her linger here.

'It is a beauteous Evening, calm and free'

It is a beauteous Evening, calm and free;
The holy time is quiet as a Nun
Breathless with adoration; the broad sun
Is sinking down in its tranquillity;
The gentleness of heaven is on the Sea:
Listen! the mighty Being is awake
And doth with his eternal motion make
A sound like thunder—everlastingly.
Dear Child! dear Girl! that walkest with me here,
If thou appear'st untouched by solemn thought,   10
Thy nature is not therefore less divine:
Thou liest in Abraham's bosom all the year;
And worshipp'st at the Temple's inner shrine,
God being with thee when we know it not.

To Toussaint L'Ouverture

Toussaint, the most unhappy Man of Men!
Whether the rural Milk-maid by her Cow
Sing in thy hearing, or thou liest now
Alone in some deep dungeon's earless den,
O miserable Chieftain! where and when
Wilt thou find patience? Yet die not; do thou
Wear rather in thy bonds a chearful brow:
Though fallen Thyself, never to rise again,
Live, and take comfort. Thou hast left behind
Powers that will work for thee; air, earth, and skies;   10

There's not a breathing of the common wind
That will forget thee; thou hast great allies;
Thy friends are exultations, agonies,
And love, and Man's unconquerable mind.

Composed Upon Westminster Bridge

SEPT. 2, 1802

Earth has not any thing to shew more fair:
Dull would he be of soul who could pass by
A sight so touching in its majesty:
This City now doth like a garment wear
The beauty of the morning; silent, bare,
Ships, towers, domes, theatres, and temples lie
Open unto the fields, and to the sky;
All bright and glittering in the smokeless air.
Never did sun more beautifully steep
In his first splendor valley, rock, or hill;   10
Ne'er saw I, never felt, a calm so deep!
The river glideth at his own sweet will:
Dear God! the very houses seem asleep;
And all that mighty heart is lying still!

London

1802

Milton! thou should'st be living at this hour:
England hath need of thee: she is a fen
Of stagnant waters: altar, sword and pen,
Fireside, the heroic wealth of hall and bower,
Have forfeited their ancient English dower
Of inward happiness. We are selfish men;
Oh! raise us up, return to us again;
And give us manners, virtue, freedom, power.
Thy soul was like a Star and dwelt apart:
Thou hadst a voice whose sound was like the sea;   10

Pure as the naked heavens, majestic, free,
So didst thou travel on life's common way,
In chearful godliness; and yet thy heart
The lowliest duties on itself did lay.

'Nuns fret not at their Convent's narrow room'

Nuns fret not at their Convent's narrow room;
And Hermits are contented with their Cells;
And Students with their pensive Citadels:
Maids at the Wheel, the Weaver at his Loom,
Sit blithe and happy; Bees that soar for bloom,
High as the highest Peak of Furness Fells,
Will murmur by the hour in Foxglove bells:
In truth, the prison, unto which we doom
Ourselves, no prison is: and hence to me,
In sundry moods, 'twas pastime to be bound   10
Within the Sonnet's scanty plot of ground:
Pleased if some Souls (for such there needs must be)
Who have felt the weight of too much liberty,
Should find short solace there, as I have found.

'She was a Phantom of delight'

She was a Phantom of delight
When first she gleamed upon my sight;
A lovely Apparition, sent
To be a moment's ornament;
Her eyes as stars of Twilight fair;
Like Twilight's, too, her dusky hair;
But all things else about her drawn
From May-time and the chearful Dawn;
A dancing Shape, an Image gay,
To haunt, to startle, and way-lay.   10

I saw her upon nearer view,
A Spirit, yet a Woman too!

Her household motions light and free,
And steps of virgin liberty;
A countenance in which did meet
Sweet records, promises as sweet;
A Creature not too bright or good
For human nature's daily food;
For transient sorrows, simple wiles,
Praise, blame, love, kisses, tears, and smiles.   20

And now I see with eye serene
The very pulse of the machine;
A Being breathing thoughtful breath;
A Traveller betwixt life and death;
The reason firm, the temperate will,
Endurance, foresight, strength and skill;
A perfect Woman; nobly planned,
To warn, to comfort, and command;
And yet a Spirit still, and bright
With something of an angel light.   30

Ode to Duty

Stern Daughter of the Voice of God!
O Duty! if that name thou love
Who art a Light to guide, a Rod
To check the erring, and reprove;
Thou who art victory and law
When empty terrors overawe;
From vain temptations dost set free;
From strife and from despair; a glorious ministry.

There are who ask not if thine eye
Be on them; who, in love and truth,   10
Where no misgiving is, rely
Upon the genial sense of youth:
Glad Hearts! without reproach or blot;
Who do thy work, and know it not:
May joy be theirs while life shall last!
And Thou, if they should totter, teach them to stand fast!

Serene will be our days and bright,
And happy will our nature be,
When love is an unerring light,
And joy its own security.   20
And blessed are they who in the main
This faith, even now, do entertain:
Live in the spirit of this creed;
Yet find that other strength, according to their need.

I, loving freedom, and untried;
No sport of every random gust,
Yet being to myself a guide,
Too blindly have reposed my trust:
Resolved that nothing e'er should press
Upon my present happiness,   30
I shoved unwelcome tasks away;
But thee I now would serve more strictly, if I may.

Through no disturbance of my soul,
Or strong compunction in me wrought,
I supplicate for thy controul;
But in the quietness of thought:
Me this unchartered freedom tires;
I feel the weight of chance desires:
My hopes no more must change their name,
I long for a repose which ever is the same.   40

Yet not the less would I throughout
Still act according to the voice
Of my own wish; and feel past doubt
That my submissiveness was choice:
Not seeking in the school of pride
For 'precepts over dignified,'
Denial and restraint I prize
No farther than they breed a second Will more wise.

Stern Lawgiver! yet thou dost wear
The Godhead's most benignant grace;   50
Nor know we any thing so fair
As is the smile upon thy face;
Flowers laugh before thee on their beds;

And Fragrance in thy footing treads;
Thou dost preserve the Stars from wrong;
And the most ancient Heavens through Thee are fresh and strong.

To humbler functions, awful Power!
I call thee: I myself commend
Unto thy guidance from this hour;
Oh! let my weakness have an end!   60
Give unto me, made lowly wise,
The spirit of self-sacrifice;
The confidence of reason give;
And in the light of truth thy Bondman let me live!

Ode

Paulò majora canamus.

There was a time when meadow, grove, and stream,
The earth, and every common sight,
       To me did seem
     Apparelled in celestial light,
The glory and the freshness of a dream.
It is not now as it has been of yore;—
      Turn wheresoe'er I may,
        By night or day,
The things which I have seen I now can see no more.

     The Rainbow comes and goes,   10
     And lovely is the Rose,
     The Moon doth with delight
Look round her when the heavens are bare;
      Waters on a starry night
      Are beautiful and fair;
     The sunshine is a glorious birth;
     But yet I know, where'er I go,
That there hath passed away a glory from the earth.

Now, while the Birds thus sing a joyous song,
     And while the young Lambs bound   20

As to the tabor's sound,
To me alone there came a thought of grief:
A timely utterance gave that thought relief,
And I again am strong.
The Cataracts blow their trumpets from the steep,
No more shall grief of mine the season wrong;
I hear the Echoes through the mountains throng,
The Winds come to me from the fields of sleep,
And all the earth is gay,
Land and sea   30
Give themselves up to jollity,
And with the heart of May
Doth every Beast keep holiday,
Thou Child of Joy
Shout round me, let me hear thy shouts, thou happy
Shepherd Boy!

Ye blessed Creatures, I have heard the call
Ye to each other make; I see
The heavens laugh with you in your jubilee;
My heart is at your festival,
My head hath its coronal,   40
The fullness of your bliss, I feel—I feel it all.
Oh evil day! if I were sullen
While the Earth herself is adorning,
This sweet May-morning,
And the Children are pulling,
On every side,
In a thousand vallies far and wide,
Fresh flowers; while the sun shines warm,
And the Babe leaps up on his mother's arm:—
I hear, I hear, with joy I hear!   50
—But there's a Tree, of many one,
A single Field which I have looked upon,
Both of them speak of something that is gone:
The Pansy at my feet
Doth the same tale repeat:
Whither is fled the visionary gleam?
Where is it now, the glory and the dream?

Our birth is but a sleep and a forgetting:
The Soul that rises with us, our life's Star,
          Hath had elsewhere its setting,   60
              And cometh from afar:
          Not in entire forgetfulness,
          And not in utter nakedness,
But trailing clouds of glory do we come
              From God, who is our home:
Heaven lies about us in our infancy!
Shades of the prison-house begin to close
              Upon the growing Boy,
But He beholds the light, and whence it flows,
              He sees it in his joy;   70
The Youth, who daily farther from the East
          Must travel, still is Nature's Priest,
              And by the vision splendid
              Is on his way attended;
At length the Man perceives it die away,
And fade into the light of common day.

Earth fills her lap with pleasures of her own;
Yearnings she hath in her own natural kind,
And, even with something of a Mother's mind,
              And no unworthy aim,   80
          The homely Nurse doth all she can
To make her Foster-child, her Inmate Man,
          Forget the glories he hath known,
And that imperial palace whence he came.

Behold the Child among his new-born blisses,
A four year's Darling of a pigmy size!
See, where 'mid work of his own hand he lies,
Fretted by sallies of his Mother's kisses,
With light upon him from his Father's eyes!
See, at his feet, some little plan or chart,   90
Some fragment from his dream of human life,
Shaped by himself with newly-learned art;
              A wedding or a festival,
              A mourning or a funeral;
                  And this hath now his heart,
                  And unto this he frames his song:

Then will he fit his tongue
To dialogues of business, love, or strife;
But it will not be long
Ere this be thrown aside,   100
And with new joy and pride
The little Actor cons another part,
Filling from time to time his 'humorous stage'
With all the Persons, down to palsied Age,
That Life brings with her in her Equipage;
As if his whole vocation
Were endless imitation.

Thou, whose exterior semblance doth belie
Thy Soul's immensity;
Thou best Philosopher, who yet dost keep   110
Thy heritage, thou Eye among the blind,
That, deaf and silent, read'st the eternal deep,
Haunted for ever by the eternal mind,—
Mighty Prophet! Seer blest!
On whom those truths do rest,
Which we are toiling all our lives to find;
Thou, over whom thy Immortality
Broods like the Day, a Master o'er a Slave,
A Presence which is not to be put by;
To whom the grave   120
Is but a lonely bed without the sense or sight
Of day or the warm light,
A place of thought where we in waiting lie;
Thou little Child, yet glorious in the might
Of untamed pleasures, on thy Being's height,
Why with such earnest pains dost thou provoke
The Years to bring the inevitable yoke,
Thus blindly with thy blessedness at strife?
Full soon thy Soul shall have her earthly freight,
And custom lie upon thee with a weight,   130
Heavy as frost, and deep almost as life!

O joy! that in our embers
Is something that doth live,
That nature yet remembers
What was so fugitive!

The thought of our past years in me doth breed
Perpetual benedictions: not indeed
For that which is most worthy to be blest;
Delight and liberty, the simple creed
Of Childhood, whether fluttering or at rest,   140
With new-born hope for ever in his breast:—
          Not for these I raise
             The song of thanks and praise;
      But for those obstinate questionings
      Of sense and outward things,
      Fallings from us, vanishings;
      Blank misgivings of a Creature
Moving about in worlds not realized,
High instincts, before which our mortal Nature
Did tremble like a guilty Thing surprized: 150
      But for those first affections,
      Those shadowy recollections,
          Which, be they what they may,
Are yet the fountain light of all our day,
Are yet a master light of all our seeing;
          Uphold us, cherish us, and make
Our noisy years seem moments in the being
Of the eternal Silence: truths that wake,
          To perish never;
Which neither listlessness, nor mad endeavour,   160
          Nor Man nor Boy,
Nor all that is at enmity with joy,
Can utterly abolish or destroy!
      Hence, in a season of calm weather,
          Though inland far we be,
Our Souls have sight of that immortal sea
          Which brought us hither,
          Can in a moment travel thither,
And see the Children sport upon the shore,
And hear the mighty waters rolling evermore.   170

Then, sing ye Birds, sing, sing a joyous song!
          And let the young Lambs bound
          As to the tabor's sound!
We in thought will join your throng,
          Ye that pipe and ye that play,

Ye that through your hearts today
Feel the gladness of the May!
What though the radiance which was once so bright
Be now for ever taken from my sight,
Though nothing can bring back the hour 180
Of splendour in the grass, of glory in the flower;
We will grieve not, rather find
Strength in what remains behind,
In the primal sympathy
Which having been must ever be,
In the soothing thoughts that spring
Out of human suffering,
In the faith that looks through death,
In years that bring the philosophic mind.

And oh ye Fountains, Meadows, Hills, and Groves, 190
Think not of any severing of our loves!
Yet in my heart of hearts I feel your might;
I only have relinquished one delight
To live beneath your more habitual sway.
I love the Brooks which down their channels fret,
Even more than when I tripped lightly as they;
The innocent brightness of a new-born Day
Is lovely yet;
The Clouds that gather round the setting sun
Do take a sober colouring from an eye 200
That hath kept watch o'er man's mortality;
Another race hath been, and other palms are won.
Thanks to the human heart by which we live,
Thanks to its tenderness, its joys, and fears,
To me the meanest flower that blows can give
Thoughts that do often lie too deep for tears.

'I wandered lonely as a Cloud'

I wandered lonely as a Cloud
That floats on high o'er Vales and Hills,
When all at once I saw a crowd
A host of dancing Daffodils;

Along the Lake, beneath the trees,
Ten thousand dancing in the breeze.

The waves beside them danced, but they
Outdid the sparkling waves in glee:—
A Poet could not but be gay
In such a laughing company:
I gazed—and gazed—but little thought
What wealth the shew to me had brought:

For oft when on my couch I lie
In vacant or in pensive mood,
They flash upon that inward eye
Which is the bliss of solitude,
And then my heart with pleasure fills,
And dances with the Daffodils.

Stepping Westward

While my Fellow-traveller and I were walking by the side of Loch
Ketterine, one fine evening after sun-set, in our road to a Hut where in
the course of our Tour we had been hospitably entertained some weeks
before, we met, in one of the loneliest parts of that solitary region, two
well-dressed Women, one of whom said to us, by way of greeting, 'What
you are stepping westward?'

'What you are stepping westward?'—'Yea'
—'Twould be a wildish destiny,
If we, who thus together roam
In a strange Land, and far from home,
Were in this place the guests of Chance:
Yet who would stop, or fear to advance,
Though home or shelter he had none,
With such a Sky to lead him on?

The dewy ground was dark and cold;
Behind, all gloomy to behold;
And stepping westward seemed to be
A kind of *heavenly* destiny;
I liked the greeting, 'twas a sound

Of something without place or bound;
And seemed to give me spiritual right
To travel through that region bright.

The voice was soft, and she who spake
Was walking by her native Lake:
The salutation had to me
The very sound of courtesy: 20
Its power was felt; and while my eye
Was fixed upon the glowing sky,
The echo of the voice enwrought
A human sweetness with the thought
Of travelling through the world that lay
Before me in my endless way.

The Solitary Reaper

Behold her, single in the field,
Yon solitary Highland Lass!
Reaping and singing by herself;
Stop here, or gently pass!
Alone she cuts, and binds the grain,
And sings a melancholy strain;
O listen! for the Vale profound
Is overflowing with the sound.

No Nightingale did ever chaunt
So sweetly to reposing bands   10
Of Travellers in some shady haunt,
Among Arabian Sands:
No sweeter voice was ever heard
In spring-time from the Cuckoo-bird,
Breaking the silence of the seas
Among the farthest Hebrides.

Will no one tell me what she sings?
Perhaps the plaintive numbers flow
For old, unhappy, far-off things,
And battles long ago: 20

Or is it some more humble lay,
Familiar matter of today?
Some natural sorrow, loss, or pain,
That has been, and may be again!

Whate'er the theme, the Maiden sang
As if her song could have no ending;
I saw her singing at her work,
And o'er the sickle bending;
I listened till I had my fill:
And, as I mounted up the hill,   30
The music in my heart I bore,
Long after it was heard no more.

Elegiac Stanzas

SUGGESTED BY A PICTURE OF PEELE CASTLE, IN A
STORM, PAINTED BY SIR GEORGE BEAUMONT

I was thy Neighbour once, thou rugged Pile!
Four summer weeks I dwelt in sight of thee:
I saw thee every day; and all the while
Thy Form was sleeping on a glassy sea.

So pure the sky, so quiet was the air!
So like, so very like, was day to day!
Whene'er I looked, thy Image still was there;
It trembled, but it never passed away.

How perfect was the calm! it seemed no sleep;
No mood, which season takes away, or brings: 10
I could have fancied that the mighty Deep
Was even the gentlest of all gentle Things.

Ah! THEN, if mine had been the Painter's hand,
To express what then I saw; and add the gleam,
The light that never was, on sea or land,
The consecration, and the Poet's dream;

I would have planted thee, thou hoary Pile!
Amid a world how different from this!
Beside a sea that could not cease to smile;
On tranquil land, beneath a sky of bliss: 20

Thou shouldst have seemed a treasure-house, a mine
Of peaceful years; a chronicle of heaven:—
Of all the sunbeams that did ever shine
The very sweetest had to thee been given.

A Picture had it been of lasting ease,
Elysian quiet, without toil or strife;
No motion but the moving tide, a breeze,
Or merely silent Nature's breathing life.

Such, in the fond delusion of my heart,
Such Picture would I at that time have made: 30
And seen the soul of truth in every part;
A faith, a trust, that could not be betrayed.

So once it would have been,—'tis so no more;
I have submitted to a new controul:
A power is gone, which nothing can restore;
A deep distress hath humanized my Soul.

Not for a moment could I now behold
A smiling sea and be what I have been:
The feeling of my loss will ne'er be old;
This, which I know, I speak with mind serene.   40

Then, Beaumont, Friend! who would have been the Friend,
If he had lived, of Him whom I deplore,
This Work of thine I blame not, but commend;
This sea in anger, and the dismal shore.

Oh 'tis a passionate Work!—yet wise and well;
Well chosen is the spirit that is here;
That Hulk which labours in the deadly swell,
This rueful sky, this pageantry of fear!

And this huge Castle, standing here sublime,
I love to see the look with which it braves, 50
Cased in the unfeeling armour of old time,
The light'ning, the fierce wind, and trampling waves.

Farewell, farewell the Heart that lives alone,
Housed in a dream, at distance from the Kind!
Such happiness, wherever it be known,
Is to be pitied; for 'tis surely blind.

But welcome fortitude, and patient chear,
And frequent sights of what is to be borne!
Such sights, or worse, as are before me here.—
Not without hope we suffer and we mourn. 60

A Complaint

There is a change—and I am poor;
Your Love hath been, nor long ago,
A Fountain at my fond Heart's door,
Whose only business was to flow;
And flow it did; not taking heed
Of its own bounty, or my need.

What happy moments did I count!
Blessed was I then all bliss above!
Now, for this consecrated Fount
Of murmuring, sparkling, living love, 10
What have I? Shall I dare to tell?
A comfortless, and hidden WELL.

A Well of love—it may be deep—
I trust it is, and never dry:
What matter? if the Waters sleep
In silence and obscurity.
—Such change, and at the very door
Of my fond Heart, hath made me poor.

Gipsies

Yet are they here?—the same unbroken knot
Of human Beings, in the self-same spot!
    Men, Women, Children, yea the frame
    Of the whole Spectacle the same!
Only their fire seems bolder, yielding light:
Now deep and red, the colouring of night;
    That on their Gipsy-faces falls,
    Their bed of straw and blanket-walls.
—Twelve hours, twelve bounteous hours, are gone while I
Have been a Traveller under open sky,   10
    Much witnessing of change and chear,
    Yet as I left I find them here!

The weary Sun betook himself to rest.
—Then issued Vesper from the fulgent West,
    Outshining like a visible God
    The glorious path in which he trod.
And now, ascending, after one dark hour,
And one night's diminution of her power,
    Behold the mighty Moon! this way
    She looks as if at them—but they   20
Regard not her:—oh better wrong and strife
Better vain deeds or evil than such life!
    The silent Heavens have goings on;
    The stars have tasks—but these have none.

St Paul's

Pressed with conflicting thoughts of love and fear
I parted from thee, Friend! and took my way
Through the great City, pacing with an eye
Downcast, ear sleeping, and feet masterless
That were sufficient guide unto themselves,
And step by step went pensively. Now, mark!
Not how my trouble was entirely hushed,
(That might not be) but how by sudden gift,

Gift of Imagination's holy power,
My soul in her uneasiness received   10
An anchor of stability. It chanced
That while I thus was pacing I raised up
My heavy eyes and instantly beheld,
Saw at a glance in that familiar spot,
A visionary scene—a length of street
Laid open in its morning quietness,
Deep, hollow, unobstructed, vacant, smooth,
And white with winter's purest white, as fair,
As fresh and spotless as he ever sheds
On field or mountain. Moving Form was none   20
Save here and there a shadowy Passenger,
Slow, shadowy, silent, dusky, and beyond
And high above this winding length of street,
This noiseless and unpeopled avenue,
Pure, silent, solemn, beautiful, was seen
The huge majestic Temple of St Paul
In awful sequestration, through a veil,
Through its own sacred veil of falling snow.

'Surprized by joy—impatient as the Wind'

Surprized by joy—impatient as the Wind
I wished to share the transport—Oh! with whom
But Thee, long buried in the silent Tomb,
That spot which no vicissitude can find?
Love, faithful love recalled thee to my mind—
But how could I forget thee!—Through what power
Even for the least division of an hour,
Have I been so beguiled as to be blind
To my most grievous loss?—That thought's return
Was the worst pang that sorrow ever bore,   10
Save one, one only, when I stood forlorn,
Knowing my heart's best treasure was no more;
That neither present time, nor years unborn
Could to my sight that heavenly face restore.

Yew-Trees

There is a Yew-tree, pride of Lorton Vale,
Which to this day stands single, in the midst
Of its own darkness, as it stood of yore,
Not loth to furnish weapons for the Bands
Of Umfraville or Percy ere they marched
To Scotland's Heaths; or Those that crossed the Sea
And drew their sounding bows at Azincour,
Perhaps at earlier Crecy, or Poictiers.
Of vast circumference and gloom profound
This solitary Tree!—a living thing   10
Produced too slowly ever to decay;
Of form and aspect too magnificent
To be destroyed. But worthier still of note
Are those fraternal Four of Borrowdale,
Joined in one solemn and capacious grove;
Huge trunks!—and each particular trunk a growth
Of intertwisted fibres serpentine
Up-coiling, and inveterately convolved,—
Nor uninformed with Phantasy, and looks
That threaten the prophane;—a pillared shade,   20
Upon whose grassless floor of red-brown hue,
By sheddings from the pining umbrage tinged
Perennially—beneath whose sable roof
Of boughs, as if for festal purpose, decked
With unrejoicing berries, ghostly Shapes
May meet at noontide—Fear and trembling Hope,
Silence and Foresight—Death the Skeleton
And Time the Shadow,—there to celebrate,
As in a natural temple scattered o'er
With altars undisturbed of mossy stone,   30
United worship; or in mute repose
To lie, and listen to the mountain flood
Murmuring from Glaramara's inmost caves.

The River Duddon

CONCLUSION

I thought of Thee, my partner and my guide,
As being past away.—Vain sympathies!
For, *backward*, Duddon! as I cast my eyes,
I see what was, and is, and will abide;
Still glides the Stream, and shall for ever glide;
The Form remains, the Function never dies;
While *we*, the brave, the mighty, and the wise,
We Men, who in our morn of youth defied
The elements, must vanish;—be it so!
Enough, if something from our hands have power   10
To live, and act, and serve the future hour;
And if, as tow'rd the silent tomb we go,
Thro' love, thro' hope, and faith's transcendent dower,
We feel that we are greater than we know.

Airey-Force Valley

——Not a breath of air
Ruffles the bosom of this leafy glen.
From the brook's margin, wide around, the trees
Are stedfast as the rocks; the brook itself,
Old as the hills that feed it from afar,
Doth rather deepen that disturb the calm
Where all things else are still and motionless.
And yet, even now, a little breeze, perchance
Escaped from boisterous winds that rage without,
Has entered, by the sturdy oaks unfelt,   10
But to its gentle touch how sensitive
Is the light ash! that, pendent from the brow
Of yon dim cave, in seeming silence makes
A soft eye-music of slow-waving boughs,
Powerful almost as vocal harmony
To stay the wanderer's steps and soothe his thoughts.

Extempore Effusion Upon the Death of James Hogg

When first, descending from the moorlands,
I saw the Stream of Yarrow glide
Along a bare and open valley,
The Ettrick Shepherd was my guide.

When last along its banks I wandered,
Through groves that had begun to shed
Their golden leaves upon the pathways,
My steps the border minstrel led.

The mighty Minstrel breathes no longer,
'Mid mouldering ruins low he lies;   10
And death upon the braes of Yarrow,
Has closed the Shepherd-poet's eyes:

Nor has the rolling year twice measured,
From sign to sign, its stedfast course,
Since every mortal power of Coleridge
Was frozen at its marvellous source;

The rapt One, of the godlike forehead,
The heaven-eyed creature sleeps in earth:
And Lamb, the frolic and the gentle,
Has vanished from his lonely hearth.   20

Like clouds that rake the mountain-summits,
Or waves that own no curbing hand,
How fast has brother followed brother,
From sunshine to the sunless land!

Yet I, whose lids from infant slumbers
Were earlier raised, remain to hear
A timid voice, that asks in whispers,
'Who next will drop and disappear?'

Our haughty life is crowned with darkness,
Like London with its own black wreath,   30
On which with thee, O Crabbe! forth-looking,
I gazed from Hampstead's breezy heath.

As if but yesterday departed,
Thou too art gone before; but why,
O'er ripe fruit, seasonably gathered,
Should frail survivors heave a sigh?

Mourn rather for that holy Spirit,
Sweet as the spring, as ocean deep;
For Her who, ere her summer faded,
Has sunk into a breathless sleep.   40

No more of old romantic sorrows,
For slaughtered Youth or love-lorn Maid!
With sharper grief is Yarrow smitten,
And Ettrick mourns with her their Poet dead.

FROM THE PRELUDE

BOOK ONE

Introduction—Childhood and School-Time

Oh there is blessing in this gentle breeze
That blows from the green fields and from the clouds
And from the sky: it beats against my cheek,
And seems half-conscious of the joy it gives.
O welcome Messenger! O welcome Friend!
A captive greets thee, coming from a house
Of bondage, from yon City's walls set free,
A prison where he hath been long immured.
Now I am free, enfranchised and at large,
May fix my habitation where I will.   10
What dwelling shall receive me? In what Vale
Shall be my harbour? Underneath what grove
Shall I take up my home, and what sweet stream
Shall with its murmurs lull me to my rest?
The earth is all before me: with a heart
Joyous, nor scared at its own liberty,
I look about, and should the guide I chuse
Be nothing better than a wandering cloud,
I cannot miss my way. I breathe again;
Trances of thought and mountings of the mind   20
Come fast upon me: it is shaken off,
As by miraculous gift 'tis shaken off,
That burthen of my own unnatural self,
The heavy weight of many a weary day
Not mine, and such as were not made for me.
Long months of peace (if such bold word accord
With any promises of human life),
Long months of ease and undisturbed delight
Are mine in prospect; whither shall I turn
By road or pathway or through open field,   30
Or shall a twig or any floating thing
Upon the river, point me out my course?

Enough that I am free; for months to come
May dedicate myself to chosen tasks;
May quit the tiresome sea and dwell on shore,
If not a Settler on the soil, at least
To drink wild water, and to pluck green herbs,
And gather fruits fresh from their native bough.
Nay more, if I may trust myself, this hour
Hath brought a gift that consecrates my joy;   40
For I, methought, while the sweet breath of Heaven
Was blowing on my body, felt within
A corresponding mild creative breeze,
A vital breeze which travelled gently on
O'er things which it had made, and is become
A tempest, a redundant energy
Vexing its own creation. 'Tis a power
That does not come unrecognized, a storm,
Which, breaking up a long-continued frost
Brings with it vernal promises, the hope   50
Of active days, of dignity and thought,
Of prowess in an honorable field,
Pure passions, virtue, knowledge, and delight,
The holy life of music and of verse.

.   .   .   .   .   .

—Was it for this
That one, the fairest of all Rivers, loved
To blend his murmurs with my Nurse's song,
And from his alder shades and rocky falls,
And from his fords and shallows, sent a voice
That flowed along my dreams? For this, didst Thou,
O Derwent, travelling over the green Plains
Near my 'sweet Birthplace', didst thou, beauteous Stream,
Make ceaseless music through the night and day
Which with its steady cadence, tempering   280
Our human waywardness, composed my thoughts
To more than infant softness, giving me,
Among the fretful dwellings of mankind,
A knowledge, a dim earnest, of the calm
Which Nature breathes among the hills and groves.
When, having left his Mountains, to the Towers
Of Cockermouth that beauteous River came,
Behind my Father's House he passed, close by,

Along the margin of our Terrace Walk.
He was a Playmate whom we dearly loved.   290
Oh! many a time have I, a five years' Child,
A naked Boy, in one delightful Rill,
A little Mill-race severed from his stream,
Made one long bathing of a summer's day,
Basked in the sun, and plunged, and basked again
Alternate all a summer's day, or coursed
Over the sandy fields, leaping through groves
Of yellow grunsel, or when crag and hill,
The woods, and distant Skiddaw's lofty height,
Were bronzed with a deep radiance, stood alone   300
Beneath the sky, as if I had been born
On Indian Plains, and from my Mother's hut
Had run abroad in wantonness, to sport,
A naked Savage, in the thunder shower.

    Fair seed-time had my soul, and I grew up
Fostered alike by beauty and by fear;
Much favored in my birthplace, and no less
In that beloved Vale to which, erelong,
I was transplanted. Well I call to mind
('Twas at an early age, ere I had seen   310
Nine summers) when upon the mountain slope
The frost and breath of frosty wind had snapped
The last autumnal crocus, 'twas my joy
To wander half the night among the Cliffs
And the smooth Hollows, where the woodcocks ran
Along the open turf. In thought and wish
That time, my shoulder all with springes hung,
I was a fell destroyer. On the heights
Scudding away from snare to snare, I plied
My anxious visitation, hurrying on,   320
Still hurrying, hurrying onward; moon and stars
Were shining o'er my head; I was alone,
And seemed to be a trouble to the peace
That was among them. Sometimes it befel
In these night-wanderings, that a strong desire
O'erpowered my better reason, and the bird
Which was the captive of another's toils
Became my prey; and, when the deed was done

I heard among the solitary hills
Low breathings coming after me, and sounds   330
Of undistinguishable motion, steps
Almost as silent as the turf they trod.

Nor less in springtime when on southern banks
The shining sun had from his knot of leaves
Decoyed the primrose flower, and when the Vales
And woods were warm, was I a plunderer then
In the high places, on the lonesome peaks
Where'er, among the mountains and the winds,
The Mother Bird had built her lodge. Though mean
My object, and inglorious, yet the end   340
Was not ignoble. Oh! when I have hung
Above the raven's nest, by knots of grass
And half-inch fissures in the slippery rock
But ill sustained, and almost, as it seemed,
Suspended by the blast which blew amain,
Shouldering the naked crag; Oh! at that time,
While on the perilous ridge I hung alone,
With what strange utterance did the loud dry wind
Blow through my ears! the sky seemed not a sky
Of earth, and with what motion moved the clouds!   350

The mind of Man is framed even like the breath
And harmony of music. There is a dark
Invisible workmanship that reconciles
Discordant elements, and makes them move
In one society. Ah me! that all
The terrors, all the early miseries,
Regrets, vexations, lassitudes, that all
The thoughts and feelings which have been infused
Into my mind, should ever have made up
The calm existence that is mine when I   360
Am worthy of myself! Praise to the end!
Thanks likewise for the means! But I believe
That Nature, oftentimes, when she would frame
A favored Being, from his earliest dawn
Of infancy doth open out the clouds,
As at the touch of lightning, seeking him
With gentlest visitation; not the less,

Though haply aiming at the self-same end,
Does it delight her sometimes to employ
Severer interventions, ministry   370
More palpable, and so she dealt with me.

  One evening (surely I was led by her)
I went alone into a Shepherd's Boat,
A Skiff that to a Willow tree was tied
Within a rocky Cave, its usual home.
'Twas by the shores of Patterdale, a Vale
Wherein I was a Stranger, thither come
A School-boy Traveller, at the Holidays.
Forth rambled from the Village Inn alone,
No sooner had I sight of this small Skiff,   380
Discovered thus by unexpected chance,
Than I unloosed her tether and embarked.
The moon was up, the Lake was shining clear
Among the hoary mountains; from the Shore
I pushed, and struck the oars and struck again
In cadence, and my little Boat moved on
Even like a Man who walks with stately step
Though bent on speed. It was an act of stealth
And troubled pleasure; not without the voice
Of mountain-echoes did my Boat move on,   390
Leaving behind her still on either side
Small circles glittering idly in the moon,
Until they melted all into one track
Of sparkling light. A rocky Steep uprose
Above the Cavern of the Willow tree
And now, as suited one who proudly rowed
With his best skill, I fixed a steady view
Upon the top of that same craggy ridge,
The bound of the horizon, for behind
Was nothing but the stars and the grey sky.   400
She was an elfin Pinnace; lustily
I dipped my oars into the silent Lake,
And, as I rose upon the stroke, my Boat
Went heaving through the water, like a Swan;
When from behind that craggy Steep, till then
The bound of the horizon, a huge Cliff,
As if with voluntary power instinct,

Upreared its head. I struck, and struck again,
And, growing still in stature, the huge Cliff
Rose up between me and the stars, and still,   410
With measured motion, like a living thing,
Strode after me. With trembling hands I turned,
And through the silent water stole my way
Back to the Cavern of the Willow tree.
There, in her mooring-place, I left my Bark,
And, through the meadows homeward went, with grave
And serious thoughts; and after I had seen
That spectacle, for many days, my brain
Worked with a dim and undetermined sense
Of unknown modes of being; in my thoughts   420
There was a darkness, call it solitude,
Or blank desertion, no familiar shapes
Of hourly objects, images of trees,
Of sea or sky, no colours of green fields;
But huge and mighty Forms that do not live
Like living men moved slowly through my mind
By day and were the trouble of my dreams.

    Wisdom and Spirit of the universe!
Thou Soul that art the Eternity of Thought!
That giv'st to forms and images a breath   430
And everlasting motion! not in vain,
By day or star-light thus from my first dawn
Of Childhood didst Thou intertwine for me
The passions that build up our human Soul,
Not with the mean and vulgar works of Man,
But with high objects, with enduring things,
With life and nature, purifying thus
The elements of feeling and of thought,
And sanctifying, by such discipline,
Both pain and fear, until we recognize   440
A grandeur in the beatings of the heart.

    Nor was this fellowship vouchsafed to me
With stinted kindness. In November days,
When vapours rolling down the valleys made
A lonely scene more lonesome; among woods
At noon, and 'mid the calm of summer nights,

When, by the margin of the trembling Lake,
Beneath the gloomy hills I homeward went
In solitude, such intercourse was mine;
'Twas mine among the fields both day and night,   450
And by the waters all the summer long.

   And in the frosty season, when the sun
Was set, and visible for many a mile
The cottage windows through the twilight blazed,
I heeded not the summons:—happy time
It was, indeed, for all of us; to me
It was a time of rapture: clear and loud
The village clock tolled six; I wheeled about,
Proud and exulting, like an untired horse,
That cares not for its home.—All shod with steel,   460
We hissed along the polished ice in games
Confederate, imitative of the chace
And woodland pleasures, the resounding horn,
The Pack loud bellowing, and the hunted hare.
So through the darkness and the cold we flew,
And not a voice was idle; with the din,
Meanwhile, the precipices rang aloud;
The leafless trees, and every icy crag
Tinkled like iron; while the distant hills
Into the tumult sent an alien sound   470
Of melancholy, not unnoticed; while the stars,
Eastward, were sparkling clear, and in the west
The orange sky of evening died away.

   Not seldom from the uproar I retired
Into a silent bay, or sportively
Glanced sideway, leaving the tumultuous throng,
To cut across the image of a star
That gleamed upon the ice. And oftentimes
When we had given our bodies to the wind,
And all the shadowy banks, on either side,   480
Came sweeping through the darkness, spinning still
The rapid line of motion; then at once
Have I, reclining back upon my heels,
Stopped short, yet still the solitary Cliffs
Wheeled by me, even as if the earth had rolled

With visible motion her diurnal round.
Behind me did they stretch in solemn train
Feebler and feebler, and I stood and watched
Till all was tranquil as a dreamless sleep.

    Ye Presences of Nature, in the sky   490
Or on the earth! Ye Visions of the hills!
And Souls of lonely places! can I think
A vulgar hope was yours when Ye employed
Such ministry, when Ye through many a year
Haunting me thus among my boyish sports,
On caves and trees, upon the woods and hills,
Impressed upon all forms the characters
Of danger or desire, and thus did make
The surface of the universal earth
With triumph, and delight, and hope, and fear,   500
Work like a sea?

               Not uselessly employed,
I might pursue this theme through every change
Of exercise and play, to which the year
Did summon us in its delightful round.
We were a noisy crew, the sun in heaven
Beheld not vales more beautiful than ours,
Nor saw a race in happiness and joy
More worthy of the fields where they were sown.
I would record with no reluctant voice
The woods of autumn and their hazel bowers   510
With milk-white clusters hung; the rod and line,
True symbol of the foolishness of hope,
Which with its strong enchantment led us on
By rocks and pools, shut out from every star
All the green summer, to forlorn cascades
Among the windings of the mountain brooks.
—Unfading recollections! at this hour
The heart is almost mine with which I felt
From some hill-top, on sunny afternoons
The Kite high up among the fleecy clouds   520
Pull at its rein, like an impatient Courser,
Or, from the meadows sent on gusty days,
Beheld her breast the wind, then suddenly
Dashed headlong; and rejected by the storm.

   Ye lowly Cottages in which we dwelt,
A ministration of your own was yours,
A sanctity, a safeguard, and a love!
Can I forget you, being as ye were
So beautiful among the pleasant fields
In which ye stood? Or can I here forget   530
The plain and seemly countenance with which
Ye dealt out your plain comforts? Yet had ye
Delights and exultations of your own.
Eager and never weary we pursued
Our home amusements by the warm peat-fire
At evening, when with pencil and with slate,
In square divisions parcelled out, and all
With crosses and with cyphers scribbled o'er,
We schemed and puzzled, head opposed to head
In strife too humble to be named in Verse.   540
Or round the naked table, snow-white deal,
Cherry or maple, sate in close array,
And to the combat, Lu or Whist, led on
A thick-ribbed Army; not as in the world
Neglected and ungratefully thrown by
Even for the very service they had wrought,
But husbanded through many a long campaign.
Uncouth assemblage was it, where no few
Had changed their functions, some, plebeian cards,
Which Fate beyond the promise of their birth   550
Had glorified, and called to represent
The persons of departed Potentates.
Oh! with what echoes on the Board they fell!
Ironic Diamonds, Clubs, Hearts, Diamonds, Spades,
A congregation piteously akin.
Cheap matter did they give to boyish wit,
Those sooty knaves, precipitated down
With scoffs and taunts, like Vulcan out of Heaven;
The paramount Ace, a moon in her eclipse;
Queens, gleaming through their splendour's last decay;   560
And Monarchs, surly at the wrongs sustained
By royal visages. Meanwhile, abroad
The heavy rain was falling, or the frost
Raged bitterly, with keen and silent tooth,
And, interrupting oft the impassioned game,

From Esthwaite's neighbouring Lake the splitting ice,
While it sank down towards the water, sent,
Among the meadows and the hills, its long
And dismal yellings, like the noise of wolves
When they are howling round the Bothnic Main.   570

   Nor, sedulous as I have been to trace
How Nature by extrinsic passion first
Peopled my mind with beauteous forms or grand
And made me love them, may I well forget
How other pleasures have been mine, and joys
Of subtler origin; how I have felt,
Not seldom, even in that tempestuous time,
Those hallowed and pure motions of the sense
Which seem, in their simplicity, to own
An intellectual charm, that calm delight   580
Which, if I err not, surely must belong
To those first-born affinities that fit
Our new existence to existing things,
And, in our dawn of being, constitute
The bond of union betwixt life and joy.

Yes, I remember, when the changeful earth,
And twice five seasons on my mind had stamped
The faces of the moving year, even then,
A Child, I held unconscious intercourse
With the eternal Beauty, drinking in   590
A pure organic pleasure from the lines
Of curling mist, or from the level plain
Of waters coloured by the steady clouds.
The Sands of Westmoreland, the Creeks and Bays
Of Cumbria's rocky limits, they can tell
How when the Sea threw off his evening shade
And to the Shepherd's huts beneath the crags
Did send sweet notice of the rising moon,
How I have stood, to fancies such as these,
Engrafted in the tenderness of thought,   600
A stranger, linking with the spectacle
No conscious memory of a kindred sight,
And bringing with me no peculiar sense
Of quietness or peace, yet I have stood,

Even while mine eye has moved o'er three long leagues
Of shining water, gathering, as it seemed,
Through every hair-breadth of that field of light,
New pleasure, like a bee among the flowers.

Thus, often in those fits of vulgar joy
Which, through all seasons, on a child's pursuits   610
Are prompt attendants, 'mid that giddy bliss
Which, like a tempest, works along the blood
And is forgotten; even then I felt
Gleams like the flashing of a shield. The earth
And common face of Nature spake to me
Rememberable things; sometimes, 'tis true,
By chance collisions and quaint accidents
Like those ill-sorted unions, work supposed
Of evil-minded fairies, yet not vain,
Nor profitless, if haply they impressed   620
Collateral objects and appearances,
Albeit lifeless then, and doomed to sleep
Until maturer seasons called them forth
To impregnate and to elevate the mind.
—And if the vulgar joy by its own weight
Wearied itself out of the memory,
The scenes which were a witness of that joy
Remained, in their substantial lineaments
Depicted on the brain, and to the eye
Were visible, a daily sight. And thus   630
By the impressive discipline of fear,
By pleasure and repeated happiness,
So frequently repeated, and by force
Of obscure feelings representative
Of joys that were forgotten, these same scenes,
So beauteous and majestic in themselves,
Though yet the day was distant, did at length
Become habitually dear, and all
Their hues and forms were by invisible links
Allied to the affections.   640

I began
My story early, feeling, as I fear,
The weakness of a human love, for days

Disowned by memory, ere the birth of spring
Planting my snowdrops among winter snows.
Nor will it seem to thee, my Friend! so prompt
In sympathy, that I have lengthened out,
With fond and feeble tongue, a tedious tale.
Meanwhile, my hope has been that I might fetch
Invigorating thoughts from former years,
Might fix the wavering balance of my mind,   650
And haply meet reproaches, too, whose power
May spur me on, in manhood now mature,
To honorable toil. Yet should these hopes
Be vain, and thus should neither I be taught
To understand myself, nor thou to know
With better knowledge how the heart was framed
Of him thou lovest, need I dread from thee
Harsh judgments, if I am so loth to quit
Those recollected hours that have the charm
Of visionary things, and lovely forms   660
And sweet sensations, that throw back our life
And almost make our Infancy itself
A visible scene, on which the sun is shining?
.   .   .   .

BOOK TWO

School-Time (continued)

Thus far, O Friend! have we, though leaving much
Unvisited, endeavoured to retrace
My life through its first years, and measured back
The way I travelled when I first began
To love the woods and fields. The passion yet
Was in its birth, sustained, as might befal,
By nourishment that came unsought; for still,
From week to week, from month to month, we lived
A round of tumult. Duly were our games
Prolonged in summer till the day-light failed;   10
No chair remained before the doors, the bench
And threshold steps were empty; fast asleep

The Labourer, and the Old Man who had sate,
A later lingerer, yet the revelry
Continued, and the loud uproar: at last,
When all the ground was dark, and the huge clouds
Were edged with twinkling stars, to bed we went,
With weary joints, and with a beating mind.
Ah! is there one who ever has been young,
And needs a monitory voice to tame   20
The pride of virtue, and of intellect?
And is there one, the wisest and the best
Of all mankind, who does not sometimes wish
For things which cannot be, who would not give,
If so he might, to duty and to truth
The eagerness of infantine desire?
A tranquillizing spirit presses now
On my corporeal frame: so wide appears
The vacancy between me and those days,
Which yet have such self-presence in my mind   30
That, sometimes, when I think of them, I seem
Two consciousnesses, conscious of myself
And of some other Being. A grey Stone
Of native rock, left midway in the Square
Of our small market Village, was the home
And centre of these joys, and when returned
After long absence, thither I repaired,
I found that it was split, and gone to build
A smart Assembly-room that perked and flared
With wash and rough-cast, elbowing the ground   40
Which had been ours. But let the fiddle scream,
And be ye happy! yet, my Friends! I know
That more than one of you will think with me
Of those soft starry nights, and that old Dame
From whom the stone was named, who there had sate
And watched her Table with its huxter's wares,
Assiduous thro' the length of sixty years.

We ran a boisterous race; the year span round
With giddy motion. But the time approached
That brought with it a regular desire   50
For calmer pleasures, when the beauteous forms
Of Nature were collaterally attached

To every scheme of holiday delight,
And every boyish sport, less grateful else,
And languidly pursued.
                        When summer came
It was the pastime of our afternoons
To beat along the plain of Windermere
With rival oars, and the selected bourne
Was now an Island musical with birds
That sang for ever; now a Sister Isle   60
Beneath the oaks' umbrageous covert, sown
With lillies of the valley like a field;
And now a third small Island where remained
An old stone Table, and a mouldered Cave,
A Hermit's history. In such a race,
So ended, disappointment could be none,
Uneasiness, or pain, or jealousy:
We rested in the shade, all pleased alike,
Conquered and Conqueror. Thus the pride of strength,
And the vain-glory of superior skill   70
Were interfused with objects which subdued
And tempered them, and gradually produced
A quiet independence of the heart.
And to my Friend, who knows me, I may add,
Unapprehensive of reproof, that hence
Ensued a diffidence and modesty,
And I was taught to feel, perhaps too much,
The self-sufficing power of solitude.

   No delicate viands sapped our bodily strength;
More than we wished we knew the blessing then   80
Of vigorous hunger, for our daily meals
Were frugal, Sabine fare! and then, exclude
A little weekly stipend, and we lived
Through three divisions of the quartered year
In pennyless poverty. But now, to School
Returned, from the half-yearly holidays,
We came with purses more profusely filled,
Allowance which abundantly sufficed
To gratify the palate with repasts
More costly than the Dame of whom I spake,   90
That ancient Woman, and her board supplied.

Hence inroads into distant Vales, and long
Excursions far away among the hills,
Hence rustic dinners on the cool green ground,
Or in the woods, or near a river side,
Or by some shady fountain, while soft airs
Among the leaves were stirring, and the sun
Unfelt, shone sweetly round us in our joy.

Nor is my aim neglected, if I tell
How twice in the long length of those half-years   100
We from our funds, perhaps, with bolder hand
Drew largely, anxious for one day, at least,
To feel the motion of the galloping Steed;
And with the good old Inn-keeper, in truth,
On such occasion sometimes we employed
Sly subterfuge; for the intended bound
Of the day's journey was too distant far
For any cautious man, a Structure famed
Beyond its neighbourhood, the antique Walls
Of that large Abbey which within the Vale   110
Of Nightshade, to St. Mary's honour built,
Stands yet, a mouldering Pile, with fractured Arch,
Belfry, and Images, and living Trees,
A holy Scene! Along the smooth green turf
Our Horses grazed: to more than inland peace
Left by the sea wind passing overhead
(Though wind of roughest temper) trees and towers
May in that Valley oftentimes be seen,
Both silent and both motionless alike;
Such is the shelter that is there, and such   120
The safeguard for repose and quietness.

Our steeds remounted, and the summons given,
With whip and spur we by the Chauntry flew
In uncouth race, and left the cross-legged Knight,
And the stone-Abbot, and that single Wren
Which one day sang so sweetly in the Nave
Of the old Church, that, though from recent showers
The earth was comfortless, and, touched by faint
Internal breezes, sobbings of the place,
And respirations, from the roofless walls   130

The shuddering ivy dripped large drops, yet still,
So sweetly 'mid the gloom the invisible Bird
Sang to itself, that there I could have made
My dwelling-place, and lived for ever there
To hear such music. Through the Walls we flew
And down the valley, and a circuit made
In wantonness of heart, through rough and smooth
We scampered homeward. Oh! ye Rocks and Streams,
And that still Spirit of the evening air!
Even in this joyous time I sometimes felt   140
Your presence, when with slackened step we breathed
Along the sides of the steep hills, or when,
Lighted by gleams of moonlight from the sea,
We beat with thundering hoofs the level sand.

  Upon the Eastern Shore of Windermere,
Above the crescent of a pleasant Bay,
There stood an Inn, no homely-featured Shed,
Brother of the surrounding Cottages,
But 'twas a splendid place, the door beset
With Chaises, Grooms, and Liveries, and within   150
Decanters, Glasses, and the blood-red Wine.
In ancient times, or ere the Hall was built
On the large Island, had this Dwelling been
More worthy of a Poet's love, a Hut,
Proud of its one bright fire, and sycamore shade.
But though the rhymes were gone which once inscribed
The threshold, and large golden characters
On the blue-frosted Signboard had usurped
The place of the old Lion, in contempt
And mockery of the rustic painter's hand,   160
Yet to this hour the spot to me is dear
With all its foolish pomp. The garden lay
Upon a slope surmounted by the plain
Of a small Bowling-green; beneath us stood
A grove, with gleams of water through the trees
And over the tree-tops; nor did we want
Refreshment, strawberries and mellow cream.
And there, through half an afternoon, we played
On the smooth platform, and the shouts we sent
Made all the mountains ring. But ere the fall   170

Of night, when in our pinnace we returned
Over the dusky Lake, and to the beach
Of some small Island steered our course with one,
The Minstrel of our troop, and left him there,
And rowed off gently, while he blew his flute
Alone upon the rock, Oh! then the calm
And dead still water lay upon my mind
Even with a weight of pleasure, and the sky
Never before so beautiful, sank down
Into my heart, and held me like a dream.   180

Thus daily were my sympathies enlarged,
And thus the common range of visible things
Grew dear to me: already I began
To love the sun, a Boy I loved the sun,
Not as I since have loved him, as a pledge
And surety of our earthly life, a light
Which while we view we feel we are alive,
But, for this cause, that I had seen him lay
His beauty on the morning hills, had seen
The western mountain touch his setting orb   190
In many a thoughtless hour, when, from excess
Of happiness, my blood appeared to flow
With its own pleasure, and I breathed with joy.
And from like feelings, humble though intense,
To patriotic and domestic love
Analogous, the moon to me was dear;
For I would dream away my purposes,
Standing to look upon her while she hung
Midway between the hills, as if she knew
No other region but belonged to thee,   200
Yea, appertained by a peculiar right
To thee and thy grey huts, my darling Vale!

Those incidental charms which first attached
My heart to rural objects, day by day
Grew weaker, and I hasten on to tell
How Nature, intervenient till this time,
And secondary, now at length was sought
For her own sake. But who shall parcel out
His intellect, by geometric rules,

Split, like a province, into round and square?   210
Who knows the individual hour in which
His habits were first sown, even as a seed,
Who that shall point, as with a wand, and say,
'This portion of the river of my mind
Came from yon fountain?' Thou, my Friend! art one
More deeply read in thy own thoughts; to thee
Science appears but, what in truth she is,
Not as our glory and our absolute boast,
But as a succedaneum, and a prop
To our infirmity. Thou art no slave   220
Of that false secondary power, by which
In weakness we create distinctions, then
Deem that our puny boundaries are things
Which we perceive, and not which we have made.
To thee, unblinded by these outward shows,
The unity of all has been revealed,
And thou wilt doubt with me, less aptly skilled
Than many are to class the cabinet
Of their sensations, and, in voluble phrase,
Run through the history and birth of each   230
As of a single independent thing.
Hard task to analyse a soul, in which,
Not only general habits and desires,
But each most obvious and particular thought,
Not in a mystical and idle sense,
But in the words of reason deeply weighed,
Hath no beginning.
                    Blessed the infant Babe,
(For with my best conjectures I would trace
The progress of our being) blest the Babe,
Nursed in his Mother's arms, the Babe who sleeps   240
Upon his Mother's breast, who, when his soul
Claims manifest kindred with an earthly soul,
Doth gather passion from his Mother's eye!
Such feelings pass into his torpid life
Like an awakening breeze, and hence his mind,
Even in the first trial of its powers,
Is prompt and watchful, eager to combine
In one appearance, all the elements
And parts of the same object, else detached

And loth to coalesce. Thus, day by day,   250
Subjected to the discipline of love,
His organs and recipient faculties
Are quickened, are more vigorous, his mind spreads,
Tenacious of the forms which it receives.
In one beloved presence, nay and more,
In that most apprehensive habitude
And those sensations which have been derived
From this beloved Presence, there exists
A virtue which irradiates and exalts
All objects through all intercourse of sense.   260
No outcast he, bewildered and depressed;
Along his infant veins are interfused
The gravitation and the filial bond
Of nature, that connect him with the world.
Emphatically such a Being lives,
An inmate of this *active* universe;
From nature largely he receives; nor so
Is satisfied, but largely gives again,
For feeling has to him imparted strength,
And powerful in all sentiments of grief,   270
Of exultation, fear, and joy, his mind,
Even as an agent of the one great mind,
Creates, creator and receiver both,
Working but in alliance with the works
Which it beholds.—Such, verily, is the first
Poetic spirit of our human life;
By uniform controul of after years
In most abated or suppressed, in some,
Through every change of growth or of decay,
Pre-eminent till death.   280
                    From early days,
Beginning not long after that first time
In which, a Babe, by intercourse of touch
I held mute dialogues with my Mother's heart,
I have endeavoured to display the means
Whereby the infant sensibility,
Great birthright of our Being, was in me
Augmented and sustained. Yet is a path
More difficult before me, and I fear
That in its broken windings we shall need

The chamois' sinews, and the eagle's wing: 290
For now a trouble came into my mind
From unknown causes. I was left alone,
Seeking the visible world, nor knowing why.
The props of my affections were removed,
And yet the building stood, as if sustained
By its own spirit! All that I beheld
Was dear to me, and from this cause it came,
That now to Nature's finer influxes
My mind lay open, to that more exact
And intimate communion which our hearts   300
Maintain with the minuter properties
Of objects which already are beloved,
And of those only. Many are the joys
Of youth; but oh! what happiness to live
When every hour brings palpable access
Of knowledge, when all knowledge is delight,
And sorrow is not there. The seasons came,
And every season to my notice brought
A store of transitory qualities
Which, but for this most watchful power of love   310
Had been neglected, left a register
Of permanent relations, else unknown.
Hence life, and change, and beauty, solitude
More active, even, than 'best society',
Society made sweet as solitude
By silent inobtrusive sympathies,
And gentle agitations of the mind
From manifold distinctions, difference
Perceived in things, where to the common eye,
No difference is; and hence, from the same source 320
Sublimer joy. For I would walk alone,
In storm and tempest, or in starlight nights
Beneath the quiet Heavens; and, at that time,
Have felt whate'er there is of power in sound
To breathe an elevated mood, by form
Or image unprofaned; and I would stand,
Beneath some rock, listening to sounds that are
The ghostly language of the ancient earth,
Or make their dim abode in distant winds.
Thence did I drink the visionary power.   330

I deem not profitless those fleeting moods
Of shadowy exultation: not for this,
That they are kindred to our purer mind
And intellectual life; but that the soul,
Remembering how she felt, but what she felt
Remembering not, retains an obscure sense
Of possible sublimity, to which,
With growing faculties she doth aspire,
With faculties still growing, feeling still
That whatsoever point they gain, they still   340
Have something to pursue.
                                    And not alone
In grandeur and in tumult, but no less
In tranquil scenes, that universal power
And fitness in the latent qualities
And essences of things, by which the mind
Is moved by feelings of delight, to me
Came strengthened with a superadded soul,
A virtue not its own. My morning walks
Were early; oft, before the hours of School
I travelled round our little Lake, five miles   350
Of pleasant wandering, happy time! more dear
For this, that one was by my side, a Friend
Then passionately loved; with heart how full
Will he peruse these lines, this page, perhaps
A blank to other men! for many years
Have since flowed in between us; and our minds,
Both silent to each other, at this time
We live as if those hours had never been.
Nor seldom did I lift our cottage latch
Far earlier, and before the vernal thrush   360
Was audible, among the hills I sate
Alone, upon some jutting eminence
At the first hour of morning, when the Vale
Lay quiet in an utter solitude.
How shall I trace the history, where seek
The origin of what I then have felt?
Oft in those moments such a holy calm
Did overspread my soul, that I forgot
That I had bodily eyes, and what I saw
Appeared like something in myself, a dream,   370

A prospect in my mind.
               'Twere long to tell
What spring and autumn, what the winter snows,
And what the summer shade, what day and night,
The evening and the morning, what my dreams
And what my waking thoughts supplied, to nurse
That spirit of religious love in which
I walked with Nature. But let this at least
Be not forgotten, that I still retained
My first creative sensibility,
That by the regular action of the world   380
My soul was unsubdued. A plastic power
Abode with me, a forming hand, at times
Rebellious, acting in a devious mood,
A local spirit of its own, at war
With general tendency, but for the most
Subservient strictly to the external things
With which it communed. An auxiliar light
Came from my mind which on the setting sun
Bestowed new splendor; the melodious birds,
The gentle breezes, fountains that ran on,   390
Murmuring so sweetly in themselves, obeyed
A like dominion; and the midnight storm
Grew darker in the presence of my eye.
Hence my obeisance, my devotion hence,
And hence my transport.
                 Nor should this, perchance,
Pass unrecorded, that I still had loved
The exercise and produce of a toil
Than analytic industry to me
More pleasing, and whose character I deem
Is more poetic, as resembling more   400
Creative agency. I mean to speak
Of that interminable building reared
By observation of affinities
In objects where no brotherhood exists
To common minds. My seventeenth year was come,
And, whether from this habit rooted now
So deeply in my mind, or from excess
Of the great social principle of life,
Coercing all things into sympathy,

To unorganic natures I transferred   410
My own enjoyments, or, the power of truth
Coming in revelation, I conversed
With things that really are, I at this time
Saw blessings spread around me like a sea.
Thus did my days pass on, and now at length
From Nature and her overflowing soul
I had received so much that all my thoughts
Were steeped in feeling. I was only then
Contented when with bliss ineffable
I felt the sentiment of Being spread   420
O'er all that moves, and all that seemeth still,
O'er all, that, lost beyond the reach of thought
And human knowledge, to the human eye
Invisible, yet liveth to the heart,
O'er all that leaps, and runs, and shouts, and sings,
Or beats the gladsome air, o'er all that glides
Beneath the wave, yea, in the wave itself
And mighty depth of waters. Wonder not
If such my transports were, for in all things
I saw one life, and felt that it was joy.   430
One song they sang, and it was audible,
Most audible then when the fleshly ear,
O'ercome by grosser prelude of that strain,
Forgot its functions, and slept undisturbed.

    If this be error, and another faith
Find easier access to the pious mind,
Yet were I grossly destitute of all
Those human sentiments which make this earth
So dear, if I should fail, with grateful voice
To speak of you, Ye Mountains and Ye Lakes,   440
And sounding Cataracts! Ye Mists and Winds
That dwell among the hills where I was born.
If, in my youth, I have been pure in heart,
If, mingling with the world, I am content
With my own modest pleasures, and have lived,
With God and Nature communing, removed
From little enmities and low desires,
The gift is yours; if in these times of fear,
This melancholy waste of hopes o'erthrown,

If, 'mid indifference and apathy   450
And wicked exultation, when good men,
On every side fall off we know not how,
To selfishness, disguised in gentle names
Of peace, and quiet, and domestic love,
Yet mingled, not unwillingly, with sneers
On visionary minds; if in this time
Of dereliction and dismay, I yet
Despair not of our nature; but retain
A more than Roman confidence, a faith
That fails not, in all sorrow my support,   460
The blessing of my life, the gift is yours,
Ye mountains! thine, O Nature! Thou hast fed
My lofty speculations; and in thee
For this uneasy heart of ours I find
A never-failing principle of joy,
And purest passion.
                        Thou, my Friend! wert reared
In the great City, 'mid far other scenes;
But we, by different roads at length have gained
The self-same bourne. And for this cause to Thee
I speak, unapprehensive of contempt,   470
The insinuated scoff of coward tongues,
And all that silent language which so oft
In conversation betwixt man and man
Blots from the human countenance all trace
Of beauty and of love. For Thou hast sought
The truth in solitude, and Thou art one,
The most intense of Nature's worshippers
In many things my Brother, chiefly here
In this my deep devotion.
                        Fare Thee well!
Health, and the quiet of a healthful mind
Attend thee! seeking oft the haunts of men,   480
And yet more often living with Thyself,
And for Thyself, so haply shall thy days
Be many, and a blessing to mankind.

BOOK THREE

Residence at Cambridge

. . . .

  A track pursuing not untrod before,
From deep analogies by thought supplied,
Or consciousnesses not to be subdued,
To every natural form, rock, fruit or flower,
Even the loose stones that cover the high-way,
I gave a moral life, I saw them feel,
Or linked them to some feeling: the great mass
Lay bedded in a quickening soul, and all
That I beheld respired with inward meaning.
Thus much for the one Presence, and the Life 130
Of the great whole; suffice it here to add
That whatsoe'er of Terror or of Love,
Or Beauty, Nature's daily face put on
From transitory passion, unto this
I was as wakeful, even, as waters are
To the sky's motion; in a kindred sense
Of passion was obedient as a lute
That waits upon the touches of the wind.
So was it with me in my solitude;
So often among multitudes of men. 140
Unknown, unthought of, yet I was most rich,
I had a world about me; 'twas my own,
I made it; for it only lived to me,
And to the God who looked into my mind.
Such sympathies would sometimes shew themselves
By outward gestures and by visible looks.
Some called it madness: such, indeed, it was,
If child-like fruitfulness in passing joy,
If steady moods of thoughtfulness, matured
To inspiration, sort with such a name; 150
If prophesy be madness; if things viewed
By Poets in old time, and higher up
By the first men, earth's first inhabitants,
May in these tutored days no more be seen
With undisordered sight: but leaving this

It was no madness: for I had an eye
Which in my strongest workings, evermore
Was looking for the shades of difference
As they lie hid in all exterior forms,
Near or remote, minute or vast, an eye   160
Which from a stone, a tree, or withered leaf,
To the broad ocean and the azure heavens,
Spangled with kindred multitudes of stars,
Could find no surface where its powerful might sleep,
Which spake perpetual logic to my soul,
And by an unrelenting agency
Did bind my feelings, even as in a chain.
    .   .   .   .   .   .

Beside the pleasant Mills of Trompington
I laughed with Chaucer; in the hawthorn shade
Heard him (while birds were warbling) tell his tales
Of amorous passion. And that gentle Bard,
Chosen by the Muses for their Page of State,   280
Sweet Spenser, moving through his clouded heaven
With the moon's beauty and the moon's soft pace,
I called him Brother, Englishman, and Friend.
Yea, our blind Poet, who, in his later day,
Stood almost single, uttering odious truth,
Darkness before, and danger's voice behind;
Soul awful! if the earth has ever lodged
An awful Soul, I seemed to see him here
Familiarly, and in his Scholar's dress
Bounding before me, yet a stripling Youth,   290
A Boy, no better, with his rosy cheeks
Angelical, keen eye, courageous look,
And conscious step of purity and pride.

Among the Band of my Compeers was one,
My class-fellow at School, whose chance it was
To lodge in the Apartments which had been,
Time out of mind, honored by Milton's name;
The very shell reputed of the abode
Which he had tenanted. O temperate Bard!
One afternoon, the first time I set foot   300
In this thy innocent Nest and Oratory,
Seated with others in a festive ring

Of common-place convention, I to thee
Poured out libations, to thy memory drank,
Within my private thoughts, till my brain reeled,
Never so clouded by the fumes of wine
Before that hour, or since. Thence forth I ran
From that assembly, through a length of streets,
Ran, Ostrich-like, to reach our Chapel Door
In not a desperate or opprobrious time,   310
Albeit long after the importunate Bell
Had stopped, with wearisome Cassandra voice
No longer haunting the dark winter night.
Call back, O Friend! a moment to thy mind,
The place itself and fashion of the rites.
Upshouldering in a dislocated lump,
With shallow ostentatious carelessness,
My Surplice, gloried in, and yet despised,
I clove in pride through the inferior throng
Of the plain Burghers, who in audience stood   320
On the last skirts of their permitted ground,
Beneath the pealing Organ. Empty thoughts!
I am ashamed of them; and that great Bard,
And thou, O Friend! who in thy ample mind
Hast stationed me for reverence and love,
Ye will forgive the weakness of that hour
In some of its unworthy vanities,
Brother of many more.

  .   .   .   .

BOOK FOUR

Summer Vacation

As one who hangs down-bending from the side
Of a slow-moving Boat, upon the breast
Of a still water, solacing himself
With such discoveries as his eye can make,   250
Beneath him, in the bottom of the deeps,
Sees many beauteous sights, weeds, fishes, flowers,
Grots, pebbles, roots of trees, and fancies more,

Yet often is perplexed, and cannot part
The shadow from the substance, rocks and sky,
Mountains and clouds, from that which is indeed
The region, and the things which there abide
In their true dwelling; now is crossed by gleam
Of his own image, by a sunbeam now,
And motions that are sent he knows not whence,   260
Impediments that make his task more sweet;
—Such pleasant office have we long pursued
Incumbent o'er the surface of past time
With like success; nor have we often looked
On more alluring shows (to me, at least,)
More soft, or less ambiguously descried,
Than those which now we have been passing by,
And where we still are lingering.

.   .   .   .

BOOK FIVE

Books

.   .   .   .

A thought is with me sometimes, and I say,
'Should earth by inward throes be wrenched throughout,
Or fire be sent from far to wither all   30
Her pleasant habitations, and dry up
Old Ocean in his bed left singed and bare,
Yet would the living Presence still subsist
Victorious; and composure would ensue,
And kindlings like the morning; presage sure,
Though slow, perhaps, of a returning day.'
But all the meditations of mankind,
Yea, all the adamantine holds of truth,
By reason built, or passion, which itself
Is highest reason in a soul sublime;   40
The consecrated works of Bard and Sage,
Sensuous or intellectual, wrought by men,
Twin labourers and heirs of the same hopes,
Where would they be? Oh! why hath not the mind

Some element to stamp her image on
In nature somewhat nearer to her own?
Why, gifted with such powers to send abroad
Her spirit, must it lodge in shrines so frail?

    One day, when in the hearing of a Friend,
I had given utterance to thoughts like these,   50
He answered with a smile that, in plain truth,
'Twas going far to seek disquietude;
But on the front of his reproof, confessed
That he, at sundry seasons, had himself
Yielded to kindred hauntings. And forthwith
Added, that once upon a summer's noon,
While he was sitting in a rocky cave
By the sea-side, perusing, as it chanced,
The famous History of the Errant Knight
Recorded by Cervantes, these same thoughts   60
Came to him; and to height unusual rose
While listlessly he sate, and having closed
The Book, had turned his eyes towards the Sea.
On Poetry and geometric Truth,
The knowledge that endures, upon these two,
And their high privilege of lasting life,
Exempt from all internal injury,
He mused: upon these chiefly: and at length,
His senses yielding to the sultry air,
Sleep seized him, and he passed into a dream.   70
He saw before him an Arabian Waste,
A Desart, and he fancied that himself
Was sitting there in the wide wilderness,
Alone, upon the sands. Distress of mind
Was growing in him when, behold! at once
To his great joy a Man was at his side,
Upon a dromedary mounted high.
He seemed an Arab of the Bedouin Tribes;
A Lance he bore, and underneath one arm
A Stone, and, in the opposite hand, a Shell   80
Of a surpassing brightness. Much rejoiced
The dreaming Man that he should have a Guide
To lead him through the Desart; and he thought,
While questioning himself what this strange freight

Which the Newcomer carried through the Waste
Could mean, the Arab told him that the Stone,
To give it in the language of the Dream,
Was Euclid's Elements; 'and this,' said he,
'This other,' pointing to the Shell, 'this Book
Is something of more worth.' 'And, at the word,   90
The Stranger', said my Friend continuing,
'Stretched forth the Shell towards me, with command
That I should hold it to my ear. I did so,
And heard that instant in an unknown Tongue,
Which yet I understood, articulate sounds,
A loud prophetic blast of harmony,
An Ode, in passion uttered, which foretold
Destruction to the Children of the Earth
By deluge now at hand. No sooner ceased
The Song, but with calm look, the Arab said   100
That all was true; that it was even so
As had been spoken; and that he himself
Was going then to bury those two Books:
The one that held acquaintance with the stars,
And wedded man to man by purest bond
Of nature, undisturbed by space or time;
The other that was a God, yea many Gods,
Had voices more than all the winds, and was
A joy, a consolation, and a hope.'
My friend continued, 'Strange as it may seem,   110
I wondered not, although I plainly saw
The one to be a Stone, the other a Shell,
Nor doubted once but that they both were Books,
Having a perfect faith in all that passed.
A wish was now ingendered in my fear
To cleave unto this Man, and I begged leave
To share his errand with him. On he passed
Not heeding me; I followed, and took note
That he looked often backward with wild look,
Grasping his twofold treasure to his side.   120
Upon a Dromedary, Lance in rest,
He rode, I keeping pace with him, and now
I fancied that he was the very Knight
Whose Tale Cervantes tells, yet not the Knight,
But was an Arab of the Desert too;

Of these was neither, and was both at once.
His countenance, meanwhile, grew more disturbed,
And, looking backwards when he looked, I saw
A glittering light, and asked him whence it came.
"It is," said he, "the waters of the deep   130
Gathering upon us," quickening then his pace
He left me: I called after him aloud;
He heeded not; but with his twofold charge
Beneath his arm, before me full in view
I saw him riding o'er the Desert Sands,
With the fleet waters of the drowning world
In chace of him; whereat I waked in terror,
And saw the Sea before me, and the Book,
In which I had been reading at my side.'

    Full often, taking from the world of sleep   140
This Arab Phantom, which my Friend beheld,
This Semi-Quixote, I to him have given
A substance, fancied him a living man,
A gentle Dweller in the Desert, crazed
By love and feeling and internal thought,
Protracted among endless solitudes;
Have shaped him, in the oppression of his brain,
Wandering upon this quest, and thus equipped.
And I have scarcely pitied him; have felt
A reverence for a Being thus employed,   150
And thought that in the blind and awful lair
Of such a madness, reason did lie couched.
Enow there are on earth to take in charge
Their Wives, their Children, and their virgin Loves,
Or whatsoever else the heart holds dear;
Enow to think of these; yea, will I say,
In sober contemplation of the approach
Of such great overthrow, made manifest
By certain evidence, that I, methinks,
Could share that Maniac's anxiousness, could go   160
Upon like errand. Oftentimes, at least,
Me hath such deep entrancement half-possessed,
When I have held a volume in my hand
Poor earthly casket of immortal Verse!
Shakespeare, or Milton, Labourers divine!

.   .   .   .

                    My drift hath scarcely,   290
I fear, been obvious; for I have recoiled
From showing as it is the monster birth
Engendered by these too industrious times.
Let few words paint it: 'tis a Child, no Child,
But a dwarf Man; in knowledge, virtue, skill;
In what he is not, and in what he is,
The noontide shadow of a man complete;
A worshipper of worldly seemliness,
Not quarrelsome; for that were far beneath
His dignity; with gifts he bubbles o'er   300
As generous as a fountain; selfishness
May not come near him, gluttony or pride;
The wandering Beggars propagate his name,
Dumb creatures find him tender as a nun.
Yet deem him not for this a naked dish
Of goodness merely; he is garnished out.
Arch are his notices, and nice his sense
Of the ridiculous; deceit and guile,
Meanness and falsehood, he detects, can treat
With apt and graceful laughter; nor is blind   310
To the broad follies of the licensed world;
Though shrewd, yet innocent himself withal
And can read lectures upon innocence.
He is fenced round, nay armed, for aught we know
In panoply complete; and fear itself,
Natural or supernatural alike,
Unless it leap upon him in a dream,
Touches him not. Briefly, the moral part
Is perfect, and in learning and in books
He is a prodigy. His discourse moves slow,   320
Massy and ponderous as a prison door,
Tremendously embossed with terms of art;
Rank growth of propositions overruns
The Stripling's brain; the path in which he treads
Is choked with grammars; cushion of Divine
Was never such a type of thought profound
As is the pillow where he rests his head.
The Ensigns of the Empire which he holds,
The globe and sceptre of his royalties,

Are telescopes, and crucibles, and maps.   330
Ships he can guide across the pathless sea,
And tell you all their cunning; he can read
The inside of the earth, and spell the stars;
He knows the policies of foreign Lands;
Can string you names of districts, cities, towns,
The whole world over, tight as beads of dew
Upon a gossamer thread; he sifts, he weighs;
Takes nothing upon trust: his Teachers stare,
The Country People pray for God's good grace,
And tremble at his deep experiments.   340
All things are put to question; he must live
Knowing that he grows wiser every day,
Or else not live at all; and seeing, too,
Each little drop of wisdom as it falls
Into the dimpling cistern of his heart.
Meanwhile old Grandame Earth is grieved to find
The playthings, which her love designed for him,
Unthought of: in their woodland beds the flowers
Weep, and the river sides are all forlorn.

    Now this is hollow, 'tis a life of lies   350
From the beginning, and in lies must end.
Forth bring him to the air of common sense,
And, fresh and shewy as it is, the Corps
Slips from us into powder. Vanity
That is his soul, there lives he, and there moves;
It is the soul of every thing he seeks;
That gone, nothing is left which he can love.
Nay, if a thought of purer birth should rise
To carry him towards a better clime,
Some busy helper still is on the watch   360
To drive him back and pound him like a Stray
Within the pinfold of his own conceit,
Which is his home, his natural dwelling place.
Oh! give us once again the Wishing-Cap
Of Fortunatus, and the invisible Coat
Of Jack the Giant-killer, Robin Hood,
And Sabra in the forest with St. George!
The child, whose love is here, at least, doth reap
One precious gain, that he forgets himself.

These mighty workmen of our late age   370
Who with a broad highway have overbridged
The froward chaos of futurity,
Tamed to their bidding; they who have the art
To manage books, and things, and make them work
Gently on infant minds, as does the sun
Upon a flower; the Tutors of our Youth
The Guides, the Wardens of our faculties,
And Stewards of our labour, watchful men
And skilful in the usury of time,
Sages, who in their prescience would controul   380
All accidents, and to the very road
Which they have fashioned would confine us down,
Like engines, when will they be taught
That in the unreasoning progress of the world
A wiser Spirit is at work for us,
A better eye than theirs, most prodigal
Of blessings, and most studious of our good,
Even in what seem our most unfruitful hours?

There was a Boy, ye knew him well, ye Cliffs
And Islands of Winander! many a time   390
At evening, when the stars had just begun
To move along the edges of the hills,
Rising or setting, would he stand alone
Beneath the trees, or by the glimmering Lake,
And there, with fingers interwoven, both hands
Pressed closely, palm to palm, and to his mouth
Uplifted, he, as through an instrument,
Blew mimic hootings to the silent owls
That they might answer him.—And they would shout
Across the wat'ry Vale, and shout again,   400
Responsive to his call, with quivering peals,
And long halloos, and screams, and echoes loud
Redoubled and redoubled; concourse wild
Of mirth and jocund din! And when it chanced
That pauses of deep silence mocked his skill,
Then sometimes, in that silence, while he hung
Listening, a gentle shock of mild surprize
Has carried far into his heart the voice
Of mountain torrents; or the visible scene

Would enter unawares into his mind   410
With all its solemn imagery, its rocks,
Its woods, and that uncertain Heaven, received
Into the bosom of the steady Lake.

   This Boy was taken from his Mates, and died
In childhood, ere he was full ten years old.
—Fair are the woods, and beauteous is the spot,
The Vale where he was born; the Churchyard hangs
Upon a Slope above the Village School,
And there, along that bank, when I have passed
At evening, I believe that oftentimes   420
A full half-hour together I have stood
Mute—looking at the Grave in which he lies.
Even now, methinks, before my sight I have
That self-same Village Church; I see her sit,
The throned Lady spoken of erewhile,
On her green hill; forgetful of this Boy
Who slumbers at her feet; forgetful, too,
Of all her silent neighbourhood of graves,
And listening only to the gladsome sounds
That, from the rural School ascending, play   430
Beneath her and about her. May she long
Behold a race of young Ones like to those
With whom I herded! (easily, indeed,
We might have fed upon a fatter soil
Of Arts and Letters, but be that forgiven)
A race of real children, not too wise,
Too learned, or too good; but wanton, fresh,
And bandied up and down by love and hate;
Fierce, moody, patient, venturous, modest, shy;
Mad at their sports like withered leaves in winds;   440
Though doing wrong, and suffering, and full oft
Bending beneath our life's mysterious weight
Of pain and fear; yet still in happiness
Not yielding to the happiest upon earth.
Simplicity in habit, truth in speech,
Be these the daily strengtheners of their minds!
May books and nature be their early joy!
And knowledge, rightly honored with that name,
Knowledge not purchased with the loss of power!

Well do I call to mind the very week   450
When I was first entrusted to the care
Of that sweet Valley; when its paths, its shores,
And brooks, were like a dream of novelty
To my half-infant thoughts; that very week
While I was roving up and down alone,
Seeking I knew not what, I chanced to cross
One of those open fields, which, shaped like ears,
Make green peninsulas on Esthwaite's Lake:
Twilight was coming on; yet through the gloom,
I saw distinctly on the opposite Shore   460
A heap of garments, left, as I supposed,
By one who there was bathing; long I watched,
But no one owned them; meanwhile the calm Lake
Grew dark, with all the shadows on its breast,
And, now and then, a fish up-leaping, snapped
The breathless stillness. The succeeding day,
(Those unclaimed garments telling a plain Tale)
Went there a Company, and, in their Boat
Sounded with grappling irons, and long poles.
At length, the dead Man, 'mid that beauteous scene   470
Of trees, and hills and water, bolt upright
Rose with his ghastly face; a spectre shape
Of terror even! and yet no vulgar fear,
Young as I was, a Child not nine years old,
Possessed me, for my inner eye had seen
Such sights before, among the shining streams
Of Fairy Land, the Forests of Romance:
Thence came a spirit hallowing what I saw
With decoration and ideal grace;
A dignity, a smoothness, like the works   480
Of Grecian Art, and purest Poesy.
. . . .

Here must I pause: this only will I add,
From heart-experience, and in the humblest sense
Of modesty, that he, who, in his youth   610
A wanderer among the woods and fields,
With living Nature hath been intimate,
Not only in that raw unpractised time
Is stirred to ecstasy, as others are,
By glittering verse; but, he doth furthermore,

In measure only dealt out to himself,
Receive enduring touches of deep joy
From the great Nature that exists in works
Of mighty Poets. Visionary Power
Attends upon the motions of the winds   620
Embodied in the mystery of words;
There darkness makes abode, and all the host
Of shadowy things do work their changes there,
As in a mansion like their proper home;
Even forms and substances are circumfused
By that transparent veil with light divine;
And through the turnings intricate of Verse,
Present themselves as objects recognised,
In flashes, and with a glory scarce their own.

.   .   .   .

BOOK SIX

Cambridge and the Alps

.   .   .   .   .   .

When the third Summer brought its liberty
A Fellow Student and myself, he too
A Mountaineer, together sallied forth   340
And, Staff in hand, on foot pursued our way
Towards the distant Alps. An open slight
Of College cares and study was the scheme,
Nor entertained without concern for those
To whom my worldly interests were dear:
But Nature then was sovereign in my heart,
And mighty forms seizing a youthful Fancy
Had given a charter to irregular hopes.
In any age, without an impulse sent
From work of Nations, and their goings-on,   350
I should have been possessed by like desire:
But 'twas a time when Europe was rejoiced,
France standing on the top of golden hours,
And human nature seeming born again.
Bound, as I said, to the Alps, it was our lot
To land at Calais on the very eve

Of that great federal Day; and there we saw,
In a mean City, and among a few,
How bright a face is worn when joy of one
Is joy of tens of millions. Southward thence   360
We took our way direct through Hamlets, Towns,
Gaudy with reliques of that Festival,
Flowers left to wither on triumphal Arcs,
And window-Garlands. On the public roads,
And once three days successively through paths
By which our toilsome journey was abridged,
Among sequestered villages we walked,
And found benevolence and blessedness
Spread like a fragrance everywhere, like Spring
That leaves no corner of the Land untouched.   370

 . . . .

Sweet coverts did we cross of pastoral life,
Enticing Vallies, greeted them, and left
Too soon, while yet the very flash and gleam
Of salutation were not passed away.   440
Oh! sorrow for the Youth who could have seen
Unchastened, unsubdued, unawed, unraised
To patriarchal dignity of mind
And pure simplicity of wish and will,
Those sanctified abodes of peaceful Man.
My heart leaped up when first I did look down
On that which was first seen of these deep haunts,
A green recess, an aboriginal vale
Quiet, and lorded over and possessed
By naked huts, wood-built, and sown like tents   450
Or Indian cabins over the fresh lawns,
And by the river side. That day we first
Beheld the summit of Mont Blanc, and grieved
To have a soulless image on the eye
Which had usurped upon a living thought
That never more could be: the wondrous Vale
Of Chamouny did, on the following dawn,
With its dumb cataracts and streams of ice,
A motionless array of mighty waves,
Five rivers broad and vast, make rich amends,   460
And reconciled us to realities.
There small birds warble from the leafy trees,

The Eagle soareth in the element;
There doth the Reaper bind the yellow sheaf,
The Maiden spread the haycock in the sun,
While Winter like a tamed Lion walks
Descending from the mountain to make sport
Among the cottages by beds of flowers.

.   .   .   .

　　Yet still in me, mingling with these delights
Was something of stern mood, an under-thirst
Of vigour, never utterly asleep.   490
Far different dejection once was mine,
A deep and genuine sadness then I felt;
The circumstances I will here relate
Even as they were. Upturning with a Band
Of Travellers, from the Valais we had clomb
Along the road that leads to Italy;
A length of hours, making of these our Guides,
Did we advance, and having reached an Inn
Among the mountains, we together ate
Our noon's repast, from which the Travellers rose,   500
Leaving us at the Board. Ere long we followed,
Descending by the beaten road that led
Right to a rivulet's edge, and there broke off.
The only track now visible was one
Upon the further side, right opposite,
And up a lofty Mountain. This we took
After a little scruple, and short pause,
And climbed with eagerness, though not, at length,
Without surprise and some anxiety
On finding that we did not overtake   510
Our Comrades gone before. By fortunate chance,
While every moment now encreased our doubts,
A Peasant met us, and from him we learned
That to the place which had perplexed us first
We must descend, and there should find the road
Which in the stony channel of the Stream
Lay a few steps, and then along its Banks;
And further, that thenceforward all our course
Was downwards, with the current of that Stream.
Hard of belief, we questioned him again,   520
And all the answers which the Man returned

To our inquiries, in their sense and substance,
Translated by the feelings which we had,
Ended in this; that we had crossed the Alps.

   Imagination! lifting up itself
Before the eye and progress of my Song
Like an unfathered vapour; here that Power,
In all the might of its endowments, came
Athwart me; I was lost as in a cloud,
Halted, without a struggle to break through.   530
And now recovering, to my Soul I say
'I recognise thy glory'. In such strength
Of usurpation, in such visitings
Of awful promise, when the light of sense
Goes out in flashes that have shewn to us
The invisible world, doth Greatness make abode,
There harbours whether we be young or old.
Our destiny, our nature, and our home,
Is with infinitude, and only there;
With hope it is, hope that can never die,   540
Effort, and expectation, and desire,
And something evermore about to be.
The mind beneath such banners militant
Thinks not of spoils or trophies, nor of aught
That may attest its prowess, blest in thoughts
That are their own perfection and reward,
Strong in itself, and in the access of joy
Which hides it like the overflowing Nile.

   The dull and heavy slackening that ensued
Upon those tidings by the Peasant given   550
Was soon dislodged; downwards we hurried fast,
And entered with the road which we had missed
Into a narrow chasm. The brook and road
Were fellow-travellers in this gloomy Pass,
And with them did we journey several hours
At a slow step. The immeasurable height
Of woods decaying, never to be decayed,
The stationary blasts of water-falls,
And every where along the hollow rent
Winds thwarting winds, bewildered and forlorn,   560

The torrents shooting from the clear blue sky,
The rocks that muttered close upon our ears,
Black drizzling crags that spake by the way-side
As if a voice were in them, the sick sight
And giddy prospect of the raving stream,
The unfettered clouds and region of the heavens,
Tumult and peace, the darkness and the light
Were all like workings of one mind, the features
Of the same face, blossoms upon one tree,
Characters of the great Apocalypse,   570
The types and symbols of Eternity,
Of first and last, and midst, and without end.

.   .   .   .

BOOK SEVEN
Residence in London

.   .   .   .

These last words uttered, to my argument
I was returning, when, with sundry Forms
Mingled, that in the way which I must tread
Before me stand, thy image rose again,   350
Mary of Buttermere! She lives in peace
Upon the spot where she was born and reared;
Without contamination does she live
In quietness, without anxiety:
Beside the mountain-Chapel sleeps in earth
Her new-born Infant, fearless as a lamb
That thither comes, from some unsheltered place,
To rest beneath the little rock-like Pile
When storms are blowing. Happy are they both
Mother and Child! These feelings, in themselves   360
Trite, do yet scarcely seem so when I think
Of those ingenuous moments of our youth,
Ere yet by use we have learned to slight the crimes
And sorrows of the world. Those days are now
My theme; and, 'mid the numerous scenes which they
Have left behind them, foremost I am crossed
Here by remembrance of two figures: One

A rosy Babe, who, for a twelvemonth's space
Perhaps, had been of age to deal about
Articulate prattle, Child as beautiful   370
As ever sate upon a Mother's knee;
The other was the Parent of that Babe;
But on the Mother's cheek the tints were false,
A painted bloom. 'Twas at a Theatre
That I beheld this Pair; the Boy had been
The pride and pleasure of all lookers-on
In whatsoever place, but seemed in this
A sort of Alien scattered from the clouds.
Of lusty vigour, more than infantine,
He was in limbs, in face a Cottage rose   380
Just three parts blown; a Cottage Child, but ne'er
Saw I, by Cottage or elsewhere, a Babe
By Nature's gifts so honored. Upon a Board
Whence an attendant of the Theatre
Served out refreshments, had this Child been placed,
And there he sate, environed with a Ring
Of chance Spectators, chiefly dissolute men
And shameless women; treated and caressed,
Ate, drank, and with the fruit and glasses played,
While oaths, indecent speech, and ribaldry   390
Were rife about him as are songs of birds
In spring-time after showers. The Mother, too,
Was present! but of her I know no more
Than hath been said, and scarcely at this time
Do I remember her. But I behold
The lovely Boy as I beheld him then,
Among the wretched and the falsely gay,
Like one of those who walked with hair unsinged
Amid the fiery furnace. He hath since
Appeared to me oft times as if embalmed   400
By Nature; through some special privilege,
Stopped at the growth he had; destined to live,
To be, to have been, come and go, a Child
And nothing more, no partner in the years
That bear us forward to distress and guilt,
Pain and abasement, beauty in such excess
Adorned him in that miserable place.
So have I thought of him a thousand times,

And seldom otherwise. But he perhaps
Mary! may now have lived till he could look   410
With envy on thy nameless Babe that sleeps
Beside the mountain Chapel, undisturbed!

.   .   .   .

O Friend! one feeling was there which belonged
To this great City, by exclusive right;
How often in the overflowing Streets,
Have I gone forward with the Crowd, and said
Unto myself, the face of every one
That passes by me is a mystery.
Thus have I looked, nor ceased to look, oppressed
By thoughts of what, and whither, when and how,   600
Until the shapes before my eyes became
A second-sight procession, such as glides
Over still mountains, or appears in dreams;
And all the ballast of familiar life,
The present, and the past; hope, fear; all stays,
All laws of acting, thinking, speaking man
Went from me, neither knowing me, nor known.
And once, far-travelled in such mood, beyond
The reach of common indications, lost
Amid the moving pageant, 'twas my chance   610
Abruptly to be smitten with the view
Of a blind Beggar, who, with upright face,
Stood propped against a Wall, upon his Chest
Wearing a written paper, to explain
The story of the Man, and who he was.
My mind did at this spectacle turn round
As with the might of waters, and it seemed
To me that in this Label was a type,
Or emblem, of the utmost that we know,
Both of ourselves and of the universe;   620
And, on the shape of the unmoving man,
His fixèd face and sightless eyes, I looked
As if admonished from another world.

Though reared upon the base of outward things,
These, chiefly, are such structures as the mind
Builds for itself. Scenes different there are,
Full-formed, which take, with small internal help,

Possession of the faculties; the peace
Of night, for instance, the solemnity
Of nature's intermediate hours of rest,   630
When the great tide of human life stands still,
The business of the day to come unborn,
Of that gone by, locked up as in the grave;
The calmness, beauty, of the spectacle,
Sky, stillness, moonshine, empty streets, and sounds
Unfrequent as in desarts; at late hours
Of winter evenings when unwholesome rains
Are falling hard, with people yet astir,
The feeble salutation from the voice
Of some unhappy Woman, now and then   640
Heard as we pass; when no one looks about,
Nothing is listened to. But these, I fear,
Are falsely catalogued, things that are, are not,
Even as we give them welcome, or assist,
Are prompt, or are remiss. What say you then,
To times, when half the City shall break out
Full of one passion, vengeance, rage, or fear,
To executions, to a Street on fire,
Mobs, riots, or rejoicings? From these sights
Take one, an annual Festival, the Fair   650
Holden where Martyrs suffered in past time,
And named of Saint Bartholomew; there see
A work that's finished to our hands, that lays,
If any spectacle on earth can do,
The whole creative powers of man asleep!
For once the Muse's help will we implore,
And she shall lodge us, wafted on her wings,
Above the press and danger of the Crowd,
Upon some Showman's platform: what a hell
For eyes and ears! what anarchy and din   660
Barbarian and infernal! 'tis a dream,
Monstrous in colour, motion, shape, sight, sound.
Below, the open space, through every nook
Of the wide area, twinkles, is alive
With heads; the midway region and above
Is thronged with staring pictures, and huge scrolls,
Dumb proclamations of the prodigies;
And chattering monkeys dangling from their poles,

And children whirling in their roundabouts;
With those that stretch the neck, and strain the eyes,   670
And crack the voice in rivalship, the crowd
Inviting; with buffoons against buffoons
Grimacing, writhing, screaming; him who grinds
The hurdy-gurdy, at the fiddle weaves;
Rattles the salt-box, thumps the kettle-drum,
And him who at the trumpet puffs his cheeks,
The silver-collared Negro with his timbrel,
Equestrians, Tumblers, Women, Girls, and Boys,
Blue-breeched, pink-vested, and with towering plumes.
—All moveables of wonder from all parts,   680
Are here, Albinos, painted Indians, Dwarfs,
The Horse of Knowledge, and the learned Pig,
The Stone-eater, the Man that swallows fire,
Giants, Ventriloquists, the Invisible Girl,
The Bust that speaks, and moves its goggling eyes,
The Wax-work, Clock-work, all the marvellous craft
Of modern Merlins, wild Beasts, Puppet-shows,
All out-o'-th'-way, far-fetched, perverted things,
All freaks of Nature, all Promethean thoughts
Of man; his dulness, madness, and their feats,   690
All jumbled up together to make up
This Parliament of Monsters. Tents and Booths
Meanwhile, as if the whole were one vast Mill,
Are vomiting, receiving, on all sides,
Men, Women, three-years' Children, Babes in arms.

      Oh, blank confusion! and a type not false
Of what the mighty City is itself
To all except a Straggler here and there,
To the whole swarm of its inhabitants;
An undistinguishable world to men,   700
The slaves unrespited of low pursuits,
Living amid the same perpetual flow
Of trivial objects, melted and reduced
To one identity, by differences
That have no law, no meaning, and no end;
Oppression under which even highest minds
Must labour, whence the strongest are not free.
But though the picture weary out the eye,

By nature an unmanageable sight,
It is not wholly so to him who looks   710
In steadiness, who hath among least things
An under-sense of greatest; sees the parts
As parts, but with a feeling of the whole.
This, of all acquisitions first, awaits
On sundry and most widely different modes
Of education; nor with least delight
On that through which I passed. Attention comes,
And comprehensiveness and memory,
From early converse with the works of God
Among all regions; chiefly where appear   720
Most obviously simplicity and power.
By influence habitual to the mind
The mountain's outline and its steady form
Gives a pure grandeur, and its presence shapes
The measure and the prospect of the soul
To majesty; such virtue have the forms
Perennial of the ancient hills; nor less
The changeful language of their countenances
Gives movement to the thoughts, and multitude,
With order and relation. This, if still,   730
As hitherto, with freedom I may speak,
And the same perfect openness of mind,
Not violating any just restraint,
As I would hope, of real modesty,
This did I feel in that vast receptacle.
The Spirit of Nature was upon me here;
The Soul of Beauty and enduring life
Was present as a habit, and diffused,
Through meagre lines and colours, and the press
Of self-destroying, transitory things,   740
Composure and ennobling harmony.
    .   .   .   .

BOOK EIGHT

Retrospect.—Love of Nature Leading to Love of Mankind

. . . .

With deep devotion, Nature, did I feel
In that great City what I owed to thee,
High thoughts of God and Man, and love of Man,
Triumphant over all those loathsome sights
Of wretchedness and vice; a watchful eye,
Which with the outside of our human life
Not satisfied, must read the inner mind.
For I already had been taught to love
My Fellow-beings, to such habits trained   70
Among the woods and mountains, where I found
In thee a gracious Guide, to lead me forth
Beyond the bosom of my Family,
My Friends and youthful Playmates. 'Twas thy power
That raised the first complacency in me,
And noticeable kindliness of heart,
Love human to the Creature in himself
As he appeared, a Stranger in my path,
Before my eyes a Brother of this world;
Thou first didst with those motions of delight   80
Inspire me.—I remember, far from home
Once having strayed, while yet a very Child,
I saw a sight, and with what joy and love!
It was a day of exhalations, spread
Upon the mountains, mists and steam-like fogs
Redounding everywhere, not vehement,
But calm and mild, gentle and beautiful,
With gleams of sunshine on the eyelet spots
And loop-holes of the hills, wherever seen,
Hidden by quiet process, and as soon   90
Unfolded, to be huddled up again:
Along a narrow Valley and profound
I journeyed, when, aloft above my head,
Emerging from the silvery vapours, lo!
A Shepherd and his Dog! in open day:
Girt round with mists they stood and looked about

From that enclosure small, inhabitants
Of an aerial Island floating on,
As seemed, with that Abode in which they were,
A little pendant area of grey rocks,   100
By the soft wind breathed forward. With delight
As bland almost, one Evening I beheld,
And at as early age (the spectacle
Is common, but by me was then first seen)
A Shepherd in the bottom of a Vale
Towards the centre standing, who with voice,
And hand waved to and fro as need required
Gave signal to his Dog, thus teaching him
To chace along the mazes of steep crags
The Flock he could not see: and so the Brute   110
Dear Creature! with a Man's intelligence
Advancing, or retreating on his steps,
Through every pervious strait, to right or left,
Thridded a way unbaffled; while the Flock
Fled upwards from the terror of his Bark
Through rocks and seams of turf with liquid gold
Irradiate, that deep farewell light by which
The setting sun proclaims the love he bears
To mountain regions.

.   .   .   .

                              A rambling school-boy, thus   390
Have I beheld him; without knowing why,
Have felt his presence in his own domain
As of a Lord and Master; or a Power
Or Genius, under Nature, under God,
Presiding; and severest solitude
Seemed more commanding oft when he was there.
Seeking the Raven's Nest, and suddenly
Surprized with vapours, or on rainy days
When I have angled up the lonely brooks
Mine eyes have glanced upon him, few steps off,   400
In size a Giant, stalking through the fog,
His Sheep like Greenland Bears. At other times
When round some shady promontory turning,
His Form hath flashed upon me, glorified
By the deep radiance of the setting sun:
Or him have I descried in distant sky,

A solitary object and sublime,
Above all height! like an aerial Cross,
As it is stationed on some spiry Rock
Of the Chartreuse, for worship. Thus was Man   410
Ennobled outwardly before mine eyes,
And thus my heart at first was introduced
To an unconscious love and reverence
Of human nature; hence the human form
To me was like an index of delight,
Of grace and honour, power and worthiness.
Meanwhile, this Creature, spiritual almost
As those of Books; but more exalted far,
Far more of an imaginative form,
Was not a Corin of the groves, who lives   420
For his own fancies, or to dance by the hour
In coronal, with Phillis in the midst,
But, for the purposes of kind, a Man
With the most common; Husband, Father; learned,
Could teach, admonish, suffered with the rest
From vice and folly, wretchedness and fear;
Of this I little saw, cared less for it,
But something must have felt.

  .   .   .   .

                   There was a Copse
An upright bank of wood and woody rock   560
That opposite our rural Dwelling stood,
In which a sparkling patch of diamond light
Was in bright weather duly to be seen
On summer afternoons, within the wood
At the same place. 'Twas doubtless nothing more
Than a black rock, which, wet with constant springs,
Glistered far seen from out its lurking-place
As soon as ever the declining sun
Had smitten it. Beside our cottage hearth,
Sitting with open door, a hundred times   570
Upon this lustre have I gazed, that seemed
To have some meaning which I could not find:
And now it was a burnished shield, I fancied,
Suspended over a Knight's Tomb, who lay
Inglorious, buried in the dusky wood;
An entrance now into some magic cave

Or Palace for a Fairy of the rock;
Nor would I, though not certain whence the cause
Of the effulgence, thither have repaired
Without a precious bribe, and day by day   580
And month by month I saw the spectacle,
Nor ever once have visited the spot
Unto this hour. Thus sometimes were the shapes
Of wilful fancy grafted upon feelings
Of the imagination, and they rose
In worth accordingly.
. . . .

Preceptress stern, that didst instruct me next,
London! to thee I willingly return.
Erewhile my Verse played only with the flowers   680
Enwrought upon thy mantle, satisfied
With this amusement, and a simple look
Of child-like inquisition, now and then
Cast upwards on thine eye to puzzle out
Some inner meanings, which might harbour there.
Yet did I not give way to this light mood
Wholly beguiled, as one incapable
Of higher things, and ignorant that high things
Were round me. Never shall I forget the hour
The moment rather say when having thridded   690
The labyrinth of suburban Villages,
At length I did unto myself first seem
To enter the great City. On the Roof
Of an itinerant Vehicle I sate,
With vulgar men about me, vulgar forms
Of houses, pavement, streets, of men and things,
Mean shapes on every side: but, at the time,
When to myself it fairly might be said,
The very moment that I seemed to know
The threshold now is overpassed, Great God!   700
That aught *external* to the living mind
Should have such mighty sway! yet so it was
A weight of Ages did at once descend
Upon my heart; no thought embodied, no
Distinct remembrances; but weight and power,
Power growing with the weight: alas! I feel
That I am trifling: 'twas a moment's pause.

All that took place within me, came and went
As in a moment, and I only now
Remember that it was a thing divine.   710

   As when a traveller hath from open day
With torches passed into some Vault of Earth,
The Grotto of Antiparos, or the Den
Of Yordas among Craven's mountain tracts;
He looks and sees the Cavern spread and grow,
Widening itself on all sides, sees, or thinks
He sees, erelong, the roof above his head,
Which instantly unsettles and recedes
Substance and shadow, light and darkness, all
Commingled, making up a Canopy   720
Of Shapes and Forms and Tendencies to Shape,
That shift and vanish, change and interchange
Like Spectres, ferment quiet and sublime,
Which, after a short space, works less and less,
Till every effort, every motion gone,
The scene before him lies in perfect view,
Exposed and lifeless, as a written book.
But let him pause awhile, and look again
And a new quickening shall succeed, at first
Beginning timidly, then creeping fast   730
Through all which he beholds; the senseless mass,
In its projections, wrinkles, cavities,
Through all its surface, with all colours streaming,
Like a magician's airy pageant, parts
Unites, embodying everywhere some pressure
Or image, recognised or new, some type
Or picture of the world; forests and lakes,
Ships, rivers, towers, the Warrior clad in Mail,
The prancing Steed, the Pilgrim with his Staff,
The mitred Bishop and the throned King,   740
A Spectacle to which there is no end.
.   .   .   .

BOOK NINE

Residence in France

.　　.　　.　　.　　.　　.　　.　　.

   Where silent zephyrs sported with the dust
Of the Bastille I sate in the open sun,
And from the rubbish gathered up a stone
And pocketed the relick in the guise
Of an Enthusiast, yet, in honest truth
Though not without some strong incumbences,
And glad, (could living man be otherwise?)
I looked for something that I could not find,   70
Affecting more emotion than I felt,
For 'tis most certain that the utmost force
Of all these various objects which may shew
The temper of my mind as then it was
Seemed less to recompense the Traveller's pains,
Less moved me, gave me less delight, than did
A single picture merely, hunted out
Among other sights, the Magdalene of le Brun,
A Beauty exquisitely wrought, fair face
And rueful, with its ever-flowing tears.   80

.　　.　　.　　.　　.　　.　　.

   A knot of military Officers,
That to a Regiment appertained which then
Was stationed in the City, were the chief
Of my associates: some of these wore Swords   130
Which had been seasoned in the Wars, and all
Were men well-born, at least laid claim to such
Distinction, as the Chivalry of France.

.　　.　　.　　.　　.　　.　　.

   Among that band of Officers was one,
Already hinted at, of other mold,
A Patriot, thence rejected by the rest
And with an oriental loathing spurned,
As of a different Cast. A meeker Man
Than this lived never, or a more benign,
Meek, though enthusiastic to the height   300
Of highest expectation. Injuries

Made him more gracious, and his nature then
Did breathe its sweetness out most sensibly
As aromatic flowers on alpine turf
When foot hath crushed them. He through events
Of that great change wandered in perfect faith,
As through a Book, an old Romance or Tale
Of Fairy, or some dream of actions wrought
Behind the summer clouds. By birth he ranked
With the most noble, but unto the poor   310
Among mankind he was in service bound
As by some tie invisible, oaths professed
To a religious Order. Man he loved
As Man, and to the mean and the obscure,
And all the homely in their homely works,
Transferred a courtesy which had no air
Of condescension, but did rather seem
A passion and a gallantry, like that
Which he, a Soldier, in his idler day
Had payed to Woman. Somewhat vain he was,   320
Or seemed so, yet it was not vanity
But fondness, and a kind of radiant joy
That covered him about when he was bent
On works of love or freedom, or revolved
Complacently the progress of a cause
Whereof he was a part; yet this was meek
And placid, and took nothing from the Man
That was delightful. Oft in solitude
With him did I discourse about the end
Of civil government, and its wisest forms,   330
Of ancient prejudice, and chartered rights,
Allegiance, faith, and laws by time matured,
Custom and habit, novelty and change,
Of self-respect, and virtue in the Few
For patrimonial honour set apart,
And ignorance in the labouring Multitude.
.   .   .   .

                        And when we chanced
One day to meet a hunger-bitten Girl,
Who crept along, fitting her languid self
Unto a Heifer's motion, by a cord
Tied to her arm, and picking thus from the lane

Its sustenance, while the Girl with her two hands
Was busy knitting, in a heartless mood
Of solitude, and at the sight my Friend
In agitation said, "Tis against *that*
Which we are fighting,' I with him believed   520
Devoutly that a spirit was abroad
Which could not be withstood, that poverty
At least like this, would in a little time
Be found no more, that we should see the earth
Unthwarted in her wish to recompense
The industrious, and the lowly Child of Toil,
All institutes for ever blotted out
That legalised exclusion, empty pomp
Abolished, sensual state and cruel power
Whether by edict of the one or few,   530
And finally, as sum and crown of all,
Should see the People having a strong hand
In making their own Laws, whence better days
To all mankind.

  .   .   .   .

BOOK TEN

Residence in France and French Revolution

  .   .   .   .   .   .

This was the time in which enflamed with hope,
To Paris I returned. Again I ranged,
More eagerly than I had done before,   40
Through the wide City, and in progress passed
The Prison where the unhappy Monarch lay,
Associate with his Children and his Wife
In bondage, and the Palace lately stormed
With roar of cannon, and a numerous Host.
I crossed (a blank and empty area then)
The Square of the Carousel, few weeks back
Heaped up with dead and dying, upon these
And other sights looking as doth a man
Upon a volume whose contents he knows   50
Are memorable, but from him locked up,

Being written in a tongue he cannot read,
So that he questions the mute leaves with pain
And half upbraids their silence. But that night
When on my bed I lay, I was most moved
And felt most deeply in what world I was;
My room was high and lonely, near the roof
Of a large Mansion or Hotel, a spot
That would have pleased me in more quiet times,
Nor was it wholly without pleasure then.   60
With unextinguished taper I kept watch,
Reading at intervals. The fear gone by
Pressed on me almost like a fear to come.
I thought of those September Massacres,
Divided from me by a little month,
And felt and touched them, a substantial dread;
The rest was conjured up from tragic fictions,
And mournful Calendars of true history,
Remembrances and dim admonishments.
'The horse is taught his manage, and the wind   70
Of heaven wheels round and treads in his own steps,
Year follows year, the tide returns again,
Day follows day, all things have second birth;
The earthquake is not satisfied at once.'
And in such way I wrought upon myself,
Until I seemed to hear a voice that cried,
To the whole City, 'Sleep no more.' To this
Add comments of a calmer mind, from which
I could not gather full security,
But at the best it seemed a place of fear,   80
Unfit for the repose of night,
Defenceless as a wood where tigers roam.
        .   .   .   .   .   .

O Friend! few happier moments have been mine
Through my whole life than that when first I heard
That this foul Tribe of Moloch was o'erthrown,
And their chief Regent levelled with the dust.
The day was one which haply may deserve   470
A separate chronicle. Having gone abroad
From a small Village where I tarried then,
To the same far-secluded privacy
I was returning. Over the smooth Sands

Of Leven's ample Æstuary lay
My journey, and beneath a genial sun;
With distant prospect among gleams of sky
And clouds, and intermingled mountain tops,
In one inseparable glory clad,
Creatures of one ethereal substance, met   480
In Consistory, like a diadem
Or crown of burning Seraphs, as they sit
In the Empyrean. Underneath this show
Lay, as I knew, the nest of pastoral vales
Among whose happy fields I had grown up
From childhood. On the fulgent spectacle
Which neither changed, nor stirred, nor passed away,
I gazed, and with a fancy more alive
On this account, that I had chanced to find
That morning, ranging through the churchyard graves   490
Of Cartmell's rural Town, the place in which
An honored Teacher of my youth was laid.
While we were Schoolboys he had died among us,
And was born hither, as I knew, to rest
With his own Family. A plain Stone, inscribed
With name, date, office, pointed out the spot,
To which a slip of verses was subjoined,
(By his desire, as afterwards I learned)
A fragment from the Elegy of Gray.
A week, or little less, before his death   500
He had said to me, 'my head will soon lie low;'
And when I saw the turf that covered him,
After the lapse of full eight years, those words,
With sound of voice, and countenance of the Man,
Came back upon me, so that some few tears
Fell from me in my own despite. And now,
Thus travelling smoothly o'er the level Sands,
I thought with pleasure of the Verses graven
Upon his Tombstone, saying to myself
He loved the Poets, and if now alive,   510
Would have loved me, as one not destitute
Of promise, nor belying the kind hope
Which he had formed, when I at his command,
Began to spin, at first, my toilsome Songs.

Without me and within, as I advanced,
All that I saw, or felt, or communed with
Was gentleness and peace. Upon a small
And rocky Island near, a fragment stood
(Itself like a sea rock) of what had been
A Romish Chapel, where in ancient times   520
Masses were said at the hour which suited those
Who crossed the Sands with ebb of morning tide.
Not far from this still Ruin all the Plain
Was spotted with a variegated crowd
Of Coaches, Wains, and Travellers, horse and foot,
Wading, beneath the conduct of their Guide
In loose procession through the shallow Stream
Of inland water; the great Sea meanwhile
Was at safe distance, far retired. I paused,
Unwilling to proceed, the scene appeared   530
So gay and chearful; when a Traveller
Chancing to pass, I carelessly inquired
If any news were stirring; he replied
In the familiar language of the day
That, *Robespierre was dead*. Nor was a doubt,
On further question, left within my mind
But that the tidings were substantial truth;
That he and his supporters all were fallen.

Great was my glee of spirit, great my joy
In vengeance, and eternal justice, thus   540
Made manifest. 'Come now ye golden times,'
Said I, forth-breathing on those open Sands
A Hymn of triumph, 'as the morning comes
Out of the bosom of the night, come Ye:
Thus far our trust is verified; behold!
They who with clumsy desperation brought
Rivers of Blood, and preached that nothing else
Could cleanse the Augean Stable, by the might
Of their own helper have been swept away;
Their madness is declared and visible,   550
Elsewhere will safety now be sought, and Earth
March firmly towards righteousness and peace.'
Then schemes I framed more calmly, when and how
The madding Factions might be tranquillised,

And, though through hardships manifold and long,
The mighty renovation would proceed;
Thus, interrupted by uneasy bursts
Of exultation, I pursued my way
Along that very Shore which I had skimmed
In former times, when, spurring from the Vale   560
Of Nightshade, and St. Mary's mouldering Fane,
And the Stone Abbot, after circuit made
In wantonness of heart, a joyous Crew
Of School-boys, hastening to their distant home,
Along the margin of the moonlight Sea,
We beat with thundering hoofs the level Sand.
.   .   .   .

   This was the time when, all things tending fast
To depravation, the Philosophy
That promised to abstract the hopes of man
Out of his feelings, to be fixed thenceforth
For ever in a purer element
Found ready welcome. Tempting region that   810
For Zeal to enter and refresh herself,
Where passions had the privilege to work,
And never hear the sound of their own names;
But, speaking more in charity, the dream
Was flattering to the young ingenuous mind
Pleased with extremes, and not the least with that
Which makes the human Reason's naked self
The object of its fervour. What delight!
How glorious! in self-knowledge and self-rule,
To look through all the frailties of the world,   820
And, with a resolute mastery shaking off
The accidents of nature, time, and place,
That make up the weak being of the past,
Build social freedom on its only basis:
The freedom of the individual mind,
Which, to the blind restraint of general laws
Superior, magisterially adopts
One guide, the light of circumstances, flashed
Upon an independent intellect.
.   .   .   .

                              Time may come
When some dramatic Story may afford

Shapes livelier to convey to thee, my Friend,   880
What then I learned, or think I learned, of truth,
And the errors into which I was betrayed
By present objects, and by reasonings false
From the beginning, inasmuch as drawn
Out of a heart which had been turned aside
From Nature by external accidents,
And which was thus confounded more and more,
Misguiding and misguided. Thus I fared,
Dragging all passions, notions, shapes of faith,
Like culprits to the bar, suspiciously   890
Calling the mind to establish in plain day
Her titles and her honours, now believing,
Now disbelieving, endlessly perplexed
With impulse, motive, right and wrong, the ground
Of moral obligation, what the rule
And what the sanction, till, demanding *proof*,
And seeking it in everything, I lost
All feeling of conviction, and, in fine,
Sick, wearied out with contrarieties,
Yielded up moral questions in despair,   900
And for my future studies, as the sole
Employment of the enquiring faculty,
Turned towards mathematics, and their clear
And solid evidence—Ah! then it was
That Thou, most precious Friend! about this time
First known to me, didst lend a living help
To regulate my Soul, and then it was
That the belovèd Woman in whose sight
Those days were passed, now speaking in a voice
Of sudden admonition, like a brook   910
That does but cross a lonely road, and now
Seen, heard and felt, and caught at every turn,
Companion never lost through many a league,
Maintained for me a saving intercourse
With my true self; for, though impaired and changed
Much, as it seemed, I was no further changed
Than as a clouded, not a waning moon:
She, in the midst of all, preserved me still
A Poet, made me seek beneath that name
My office upon earth, and nowhere else;   920

And lastly, Nature's self, by human love
Assisted, through the weary labyrinth
Conducted me again to open day,
Revived the feelings of my earlier life,
Gave me that strength and knowledge full of peace,
Enlarged, and never more to be disturbed,
Which through the steps of our degeneracy,
All degradation of this age, hath still
Upheld me, and upholds me at this day
In the catastrophe (for so they dream,   930
And nothing less), when, finally, to close
And rivet up the gains of France, a Pope
Is summoned in to crown an Emperor;
This last opprobrium, when we see the dog
Returning to his vomit, when the sun
That rose in splendour, was alive, and moved
In exultation among living clouds,
Hath put his function and his glory off,
And, turned into gewgaw, a machine,
Sets like an opera phantom.   940

.   .   .   .

BOOK ELEVEN

Imagination, How Impaired and Restored

.   .   .   .   .   .

There are in our existence spots of time,
Which with distinct pre-eminence retain
A renovating Virtue, whence, depressed   260
By false opinion and contentious thought,
Or aught of heavier and more deadly weight
In trivial occupations, and the round
Of ordinary intercourse, our minds
Are nourished and invisibly repaired;
A virtue by which pleasure is enhanced,
That penetrates, enables us to mount
When high, more high, and lifts us up when fallen.
This efficacious spirit chiefly lurks
Among those passages of life in which   270

We have had deepest feeling that the mind
Is lord and master, and that outward sense
Is but the obedient servant of her will.
Such moments worthy of all gratitude,
Are scattered everywhere, taking their date
From our first childhood: in our childhood even
Perhaps are most conspicuous. Life with me,
As far as memory can look back, is full
Of this beneficent influence.
                              At a time
When scarcely (I was then not six years old)   280
My hand could hold a bridle, with proud hopes
I mounted, and we rode towards the hills:
We were a pair of Horsemen; honest James
Was with me, my encourager and guide.
We had not travelled long ere some mischance
Disjoined me from my Comrade, and, through fear
Dismounting, down the rough and stony Moor
I led my Horse, and stumbling on, at length
Came to a bottom, where in former times
A Murderer had been hung in iron chains.   290
The Gibbet-mast was mouldered down, the bones
And iron case were gone, but on the turf,
Hard by, soon after that fell deed was wrought,
Some unknown hand had carved the Murderer's name.
The monumental writing was engraven
In times long past, and still from year to year
By superstition of the neighbourhood
The grass is cleared away; and to this hour
The letters are all fresh and visible.
Faltering, and ignorant where I was, at length   300
I chanced to espy those characters inscribed
On the green sod: forthwith I left the spot
And, reascending the bare Common, saw
A naked Pool that lay beneath the hills,
The Beacon on the summit, and more near,
A Girl who bore a Pitcher on her head
And seemed with difficult steps to force her way
Against the blowing wind. It was, in truth,
An ordinary sight; but I should need
Colours and words that are unknown to man   310

To paint the visionary dreariness
Which, while I looked all round for my lost guide,
Did at that time invest the naked Pool,
The Beacon on the lonely Eminence,
The Woman, and her garments vexed and tossed
By the strong wind. When, in a blessed season
With those two dear Ones, to my heart so dear,
When in the blessed time of early love,
Long afterwards, I roamed about
In daily presence of this very scene,   320
Upon the naked pool and dreary crags,
And on the melancholy Beacon, fell
The spirit of pleasure and youth's golden gleam;
And think ye not with radiance more divine
From these remembrances, and from the power
They left behind? So feeling comes in aid
Of feeling, and diversity of strength
Attends us, if but once we have been strong.
Oh! mystery of Man, from what a depth
Proceed thy honours! I am lost, but see   330
In simple childhood something of the base
On which thy greatness stands; but this I feel,
That from thyself it is that thou must give,
Else never canst receive. The days gone by
Come back upon me from the dawn almost
Of life: the hiding-places of my power
Seem open; I approach, and then they close;
I see by glimpses now; when age comes on,
May scarcely see at all, and I would give,
While yet we may, as far as words can give,   340
A substance and a life to what I feel:
I would enshrine the spirit of the past
For future restoration. Yet another
Of these to me affecting incidents
With which we will conclude.

                                    One Christmas-time,
The day before the Holidays began,
Feverish, and tired, and restless, I went forth
Into the fields, impatient for the sight
Of those two Horses which should bear us home,
My Brothers and myself. There was a crag,   350

An Eminence, which from the meeting-point
Of two highways ascending, overlooked
At least a long half-mile of those two roads,
By each of which the expected Steeds might come,
The choice uncertain. Thither I repaired
Up to the highest summit. 'Twas a day
Stormy, and rough, and wild, and on the grass
I sate, half-sheltered by a naked wall;
Upon my right hand was a single sheep,
A whistling hawthorn on my left, and there,   360
With those companions at my side, I watched,
Straining my eyes intensely, as the mist
Gave intermitting prospect of the wood
And plain beneath. Ere I to School returned
That dreary time, ere I had been ten days
A dweller in my Father's House, he died,
And I and my two Brothers, Orphans then,
Followed his Body to the Grave. The event
With all the sorrow which it brought appeared
A chastisement; and when I called to mind   370
That day so lately passed, when from the crag
I looked in such anxiety of hope,
With trite reflections of morality,
Yet in the deepest passion, I bowed low
To God, who thus corrected my desires;
And afterwards, the wind and sleety rain,
And all the business of the elements,
The single sheep, and the one blasted tree,
And the bleak music of that old stone wall,
The noise of wood and water, and the mist   380
Which on the line of each of those two Roads
Advanced in such indisputable shapes,
All these were spectacles and sounds to which
I often would repair and thence would drink,
As at a fountain; and I do not doubt
That in this later time, when storm and rain
Beat on my roof at midnight, or by day
When I am in the woods, unknown to me
The workings of my spirit thence are brought.
. . . .

BOOK TWELVE
Same Subject (continued)

.   .   .   .

Be mine to follow with no timid step
Where knowledge leads me; it shall be my pride   250
That I have dared to tread this holy ground,
Speaking no dream but things oracular,
Matter not lightly to be heard by those
Who to the letter of the outward promise
Do read the invisible soul, by men adroit
In speech and for communion with the world
Accomplished, minds whose faculties are then
Most active when they are most eloquent,
And elevated most when most admired.
Men may be found of other mold than these,   260
Who are their own upholders, to themselves
Encouragement, and energy and will,
Expressing liveliest thoughts in lively words
As native passion dictates. Others, too,
There are among the walks of homely life
Still higher, men for contemplation framed,
Shy, and unpractised in the strife of phrase,
Meek men, whose very souls perhaps would sink
Beneath them, summoned to such intercourse:
Theirs is the language of the heavens, the power,   270
The thought, the image, and the silent joy;
Words are but under-agents in their souls;
When they are grasping with their greatest strength
They do not breathe among them: this I speak
In gratitude to God, who feeds our hearts
For his own service, knoweth, loveth us
When we are unregarded by the world.

.   .   .   .

BOOK THIRTEEN

Conclusion

In one of these excursions, travelling then
Through Wales on foot, and with a youthful Friend,
I left Bethkelet's huts at couching-time,
And westward took my way to see the sun
Rise from the top of Snowdon. Having reached
The Cottage at the Mountain's foot, we there
Rouzed up the Shepherd, who by ancient right
Of office is the Stranger's usual Guide,
And after short refreshment sallied forth.

It was a Summer's night, a close warm night,   10
Wan, dull and glaring, with a dripping mist
Low-hung and thick that covered all the sky,
Half threatening storm and rain; but on we went
Unchecked, being full of heart and having faith
In our tried Pilot. Little could we see,
Hemmed round on every side with fog and damp,
And, after ordinary travellers' chat
With our Conductor, silently we sank
Each into commerce with his private thoughts.
Thus did we breast the ascent, and by myself   20
Was nothing either seen or heard the while
Which took me from my musings, save that once
The Shepherd's Cur did to his own great joy
Unearth a hedgehog in the mountain crags
Round which he made a barking turbulent.
This small adventure, for even such it seemed
In that wild place and at the dead of night,
Being over and forgotten, on we wound
In silence as before. With forehead bent
Earthward, as if in opposition set   30
Against an enemy, I panted up
With eager pace, and no less eager thoughts.
Thus might we wear perhaps an hour away,
Ascending at loose distance each from each,
And I, as chanced, the foremost of the Band;

When at my feet the ground appeared to brighten,
And with a step or two seemed brighter still;
Nor had I time to ask the cause of this,
For instantly a Light upon the turf
Fell like a flash: I looked about, and lo!   40
The Moon stood naked in the Heavens, at height
Immense above my head, and on the shore
I found myself of a huge sea of mist,
Which, meek and silent, rested at my feet.
A hundred hills their dusky backs upheaved
All over this still Ocean, and beyond,
Far, far beyond, the vapours shot themselves,
In headlands, tongues, and promontory shapes,
Into the Sea, the real Sea, that seemed
To dwindle and give up its majesty,   50
Usurped upon as far as sight could reach.
Meanwhile, the Moon looked down upon this shew
In single glory, and we stood, the mist
Touching our very feet; and from the shore
At distance not the third part of a mile
Was a blue chasm; a fracture in the vapour,
A deep and gloomy breathing-place, through which
Mounted the roar of waters, torrents, streams
Innumerable, roaring with one voice.
The universal spectacle throughout   60
Was shaped for admiration and delight,
Grand in itself alone, but in that breach
Through which the homeless voice of waters rose,
That dark deep thoroughfare, had Nature lodged
The Soul, the Imagination of the whole.

   A meditation rose in me that night
Upon the lonely Mountain when the scene
Had passed away, and it appeared to me
The perfect image of a mighty Mind,
Of one that feeds upon infinity,   70
That is exalted by an underpresence,
The sense of God, or whatso'er is dim
Or vast in its own being; above all
One function of such mind had Nature there
Exhibited by putting forth, and that

With circumstance most awful and sublime,
That domination which she oftentimes
Exerts upon the outward face of things,
So moulds them, and endues, abstracts, combines,   80
Or by abrupt and unhabitual influence
Doth make one object so impress itself
Upon all others, and pervade them so,
That even the grossest minds must see and hear
And cannot chuse but feel. The Power which these
Acknowledge when thus moved, which Nature thus
Thrusts forth upon the senses, is the express
Resemblance, in the fulness of its strength
Made visible, a genuine Counterpart
And Brother of the glorious faculty
Which higher minds bear with them as their own.   90
This is the very spirit in which they deal
With all the objects of the universe;
They from their native selves can send abroad
Like transformations, for themselves create
A like existence, and, whene'er it is
Created for them, catch it by an instinct;
Them the enduring and the transient both
Serve to exalt; they build up greatest things
From least suggestions, ever on the watch,
Willing to work and to be wrought upon.   100
They need not extraordinary calls
To rouze them, in a world of life they live,
By sensible impressions not enthralled,
But quickened, rouzed, and made thereby more fit
To hold communion with the invisible world.
Such minds are truly from the Deity,
For they are Powers; and hence the highest bliss
That can be known is theirs, the consciousness
Of whom they are, habitually infused
Through every image, and through every thought,   110
And all impressions; hence religion, faith,
And endless occupation for the soul
Whether discursive or intuitive;
Hence sovereignty within and peace at will,
Emotion which best foresight need not fear,
Most worthy then of trust when most intense;

Hence chearfulness in every act of life;
Hence truth in moral judgements and delight
That fails not, in the external universe.

. . . .

   Oh! yet a few short years of useful life,
And all will be complete, thy race be run,
Thy monument of glory will be raised.   430
Then, though, too weak to tread the ways of truth,
This Age fall back to old idolatry,
Though men return to servitude as fast
As the tide ebbs, to ignominy and shame
By Nations sink together, we shall still
Find solace in the knowledge which we have,
Blessed with true happiness if we may be
United helpers forward of a day
Of firmer trust, joint-labourers in the work
(Should Providence such grace to us vouchsafe)   440
Of their redemption, surely yet to come.
Prophets of Nature, we to them will speak
A lasting inspiration, sanctified
By reason and by truth; what we have loved
Others will love; and we may teach them how;
Instruct them how the mind of man becomes
A thousand times more beautiful than the earth
On which he dwells, above this Frame of things
(Which, 'mid all revolutions in the hopes
And fears of men, doth still remain unchanged)   450
In beauty exalted, as it is itself
Of substance and of fabric more divine.

Notes

ABBREVIATIONS

C	Samuel Taylor Coleridge
DW	Dorothy Wordsworth
IF note	Notes by W, compiled in 1843 by Isabella Fenwick
Journal	*Journals of Dorothy Wordsworth*, ed. Mary Moorman (1971)
Moorman	Mary Moorman, *William Wordsworth: A Biography. The Early Years* (Oxford, 1957); *The Later Years* (Oxford, 1965)
MW	Mary Wordsworth
Notebooks	*The Notebooks of Samuel Taylor Coleridge*, ed. Kathleen Coburn (1957–)
Prose	*The Prose Works of William Wordsworth*, ed. W. J. B. Owen and Jane Worthington Smyser (Oxford, 1974)
PW	*The Poetical Works of William Wordsworth*, ed. E. de Selincourt and Helen Darbishire (Oxford, 1940–9)
W	William Wordsworth
Wordsworth's Hawkshead	T. W. Thompson, *Wordsworth's Hawkshead*, ed. Robert Woof (1970)

Letters of W, DW, and C are identified in the introduction and notes by date only. Texts can be found in: *Letters of William and Dorothy Wordsworth*, ed. E. de Selincourt; *The Early Years, 1787–1805*, revised Chester L. Shaver (Oxford, 1967); *The Middle Years, 1806–11*, revised Mary Moorman (Oxford, 1969); *1812–20*, revised Mary Moorman and Alan G. Hill (Oxford, 1970); *The Later Years, 1821–50*, revised Alan G. Hill (Oxford, 1978–88); *Collected Letters of Samuel Taylor Coleridge*, ed. Earl Leslie Griggs, 6 vols. (Oxford, 1956–71).

1 *Old Man Travelling*. Composed Apr.–June 1797. Published 1798.

  The Ruined Cottage. Composed Apr. 1797–Mar. 1798. Revised and developed 1802 and 1804. Published with further revision as Book One of *The Excursion* (1814).

2 l. 45. In the IF note W compared Southey's passions for *books* with his

own for *wandering* and said 'had I been born in a class which would have deprived me of what is called a liberal education, it is not unlikely that, being strong in body, I should have taken to a way of life such as that in which my Pedlar passed the greater part of his days. At all events, ... the character I have represented in his person is chiefly an idea of what I fancied my own character might have become in his circumstances ...'.

4 l. 99. 'All that relates to Margaret and the ruined cottage etc., was taken from observations made in the South-West of England' (IF note). Early on in their life in the south-west DW reported that 'The peasants are miserably poor ...' (30 Nov. 1795).

8 l. 264. purse ...

9 l. 295. W's quotation marks draw attention to a borrowing from Burns's *To W.S. ----n Ochiltree*, xv. 3.

ll. 330–6. See DW's Alfoxden *Journal*, 4 Feb. 1798: 'The moss rubbed from the pailings by the sheep that leave locks of wool, and the red marks with which they are spotted, upon the wood.'

13 ll. 460–2. James Butler points out that Bridport, near the W's home at Racedown, was a centre for the manufacture of twine for fishing nets. He explains how the spinner walked to and from the spinning wheel with the flex tied round her waist; James Butler (ed.), *The Ruined Cottage and the Pedlar* (Ithaca, NY, 1979), 70.

15 [*A Night-Piece*]. Composed Jan.–Mar. 1798. Published 1815. Wordsworth noted: 'Composed on the road between Nether Stowey and Alfoxden, extempore' (IF note). DW's *Journal*, 25 Jan. 1798 records the occasion: 'The sky spread over with one continuous cloud, whitened by the light of the moon, which, though her dim shape was seen, did not throw forth so strong a light as to chequer the earth with shadows. At once the clouds seemed to cleave asunder, and left her in the centre of a black-blue vault. She sailed along, followed by multitudes of stars, small, and bright, and sharp. Their brightness seemed concentrated, (half-moon).'

[*The Discharged Soldier*]. Composed Jan.–Mar. 1798. Not published by W, but incorporated into *Prelude*, iv. 364–504. For the place of the meeting above the Windermere Ferry see *Wordsworth's Hawkshead*, 139–41 and 375. DW's *Journal*, 27 and 31 Jan. 1798, records impressions used in the poem ll. 7–9 and 135–6. W's account of the soldier, 'Neglected and ungratefully thrown by | Even for the very service he [had] wrought' (*Prelude*, ii. 545–6) is further evidence to add to that in 'The Ruined Cottage' of his awareness of the impact of Britain's military operations on common people.

25 *Lines Written at a Small Distance from my House*. Composed 1–10 Mar. 1798. Published 1798. W noted: 'Composed in front of Alfoxden House. My little boy messenger on this occasion was the son of Basil

Montagu' (IF note). He was also called Basil in fact, not Edward, and appears again in 'Anecdote for Fathers'. This poem, no less than the more complex 'Tintern Abbey' published in the same volume of *Lyrical Ballads*, expresses some of the fundamental convictions on which the whole of W's poetry is based.

26 *Goody Blake and Harry Gill*. Composed 7–13 Mar. 1798. Published 1798. For the incident W drew on Erasmus Darwin's *Zoönomia; or, the Laws of Organic Life* (1794–6), which he had borrowed from Cottle, his publisher friend, in March 1798. W was aware, of course, at first hand of the distress of the peasantry. See DW's letter of 30 Nov. 1795: 'The peasants are miserably poor; their cottages are shapeless structures (I may almost say) of wood and clay—indeed they are not at all beyond what might be expected in savage life.'

30 *The Thorn*. Composed *c.* 19 Mar. 1798. Published 1798. W noted that the poem 'Arose out of my observing, on the ridge of Quantock Hill, on a stormy day, a thorn which I had often passed in calm and bright weather without noticing it. I said to myself, "Cannot I by some invention do as much to make this Thorn an impressive object as the storm has made it to my eyes at this moment." I began the poem accordingly and composed it with great rapidity' (IF note).

In the *Advertisement* to *Lyrical Ballads* 1798 W pointed out that 'The Thorn' 'is not supposed to be spoken in the author's own person: the character of the loquacious narrator will sufficiently shew itself in the course of the story'.

36 *The Idiot Boy*. Composed late Mar. 1798. Published 1798. In his important defence of the *Lyrical Ballads* in the letter to John Wilson of 7 June 1802, W discusses the poem and declares: 'I wrote the poem with exceeding delight and pleasure . . .'.

50 *Lines written in Early Spring*. Composed *c.* 12 Apr. 1798. Published 1798. W's note, composed more than forty years after the poem, indicates his astonishing power of recall for such moments as are the basis of this poem: 'Actually composed while I was sitting by the side of the brook that runs down from the *Comb*, in which stands the village of Alford, through the grounds of Alfoxden. It was a chosen resort of mine.' (IF note).

Anecdote for Fathers. Composed Apr.–May 1798. Published 1798. For the fuller context of the poem see note to 'The Tables Turned', p. 228. On 7 Mar. 1796 W reported amusingly of little Basil Montagu, the child of the poem: 'Basil is quite well quant au physique mais pour le moral il-y-a bien à craindre. Among other things he lies like a little devil.'

52 *We Are Seven*. Composed Apr.–May 1798. Published 1798. W noted 'The little Girl who is the heroine I met within the area of Goodrich

Castle in the year 1793. Having left the Isle of Wight and crost Salisbury Plain ... I proceeded by Bristol up the Wye, and so on to N. Wales to the Vale of Clwydd ... I composed it while walking in the grove of Alfoxden. My friends will not deem it too trifling to relate that while walking to and fro I composed the last stanza first, having begun with the last line. When it was all but finished, I came in and recited it to Mr Coleridge and my Sister, and said, "A prefatory stanza must be added, and I should sit down to our little tea-meal with greater pleasure if my task was finished." I mentioned in substance what I wished to be expressed, and Coleridge immediately threw off the stanza thus:

> A little child, dear brother Jem,—

I objected to the rhyme, dear brother Jem, as being ludicrous, but we all enjoyed the joke of hitching in our friend James Tobin's name, who was familiarly called Jem' (IF note).

55 *Expostulation and Reply.* Composed *c.* 23 May 1798. Published 1798. In the *Advertisement* to *Lyrical Ballads* (1798) W says that this and the following poem 'arose out of conversation with a friend who was somewhat unreasonably attached to modern books of moral philosophy'. This is usually taken to refer to William Hazlitt (1778–1830), who records in his splendid essay *My First Acquaintance with Poets* that, while visiting Alfoxden in May–June 1798, he 'got into a metaphysical argument with Wordsworth ... in which we neither of us succeeded in making ourselves perfectly clear and intelligible'.

ll. 13–15. The scene is in the Lake District and not Somerset.

56 *The Tables Turned.* Composed *c.* 23 May 1798. Published 1798. See note to previous poem. This poem is so central that reference from it could be made to almost all of W's mature work. In 1797–8 the Wordsworths and Coleridge were concerned not only with questions of perception, which is obvious from C's 'conversation poems', from 'Tintern Abbey' and the description of the Pedlar in 'The Ruined Cottage', but especially with the question of how best to educate a young mind. The Wordsworths were looking after Basil Montagu and were bringing him up, as DW explained in a letter of 19 Mar. 1797, in a system 'so simple that in this age of systems you will hardly be likely to follow it. We teach him nothing at present but what he learns from the evidence of his senses. He has an insatiable curiosity which we are always careful to satisfy to the best of our ability. It is directed to everything he sees, the sky, the fields, trees, shrubs, corn, the making of tools, carts, etc. ...' In 1797 it was suggested that W should oversee Thomas Wedgwood's scheme for educating a genius through strict control of sensory experience. See also W's attack on infant prodigies in *The Prelude*, v. 290–449.

57 *Lines written a few miles above Tintern Abbey*. Composed 11–13 July 1798. Published 1798. W noted: 'No poem of mine was composed under circumstances more pleasant for me to remember than this. I began it upon leaving Tintern, after crossing the Wye, and concluded it just as I was entering Bristol in the evening, after a ramble of 4 or 5 days, with my sister. Not a line of it was altered, and not any part of written down till I reached Bristol' (IF note).

l. l. W visited Tintern in Aug. 1793 and returned 10–13 July 1798.

l. 18. Moorman, i. 402, points out that William Gilpin, *Observations on the River Wye ... Relative Chiefly to Picturesque Beauty* (1782), observes: 'Many of the furnaces, on the banks of the river consume charcoal, which is manufactured on the spot; and the smoke, which is frequently seen issuing from the sides of the hills; and spreading its thin veil over a part of them, beautifully breaks their lines, and unites them with the sky' (p. 12).

59 ll. 74–5. See *The Prelude*, i–ii, for description of these pleasures.

60 l. 107. W notes the borrowing from Edward Young's *Night Thoughts* (1742–5), vi. 426: 'And half create the wondrous World they see'.

l. 129. In a poem of such joyous confidence the reference in 'evil tongues' to the Milton of *Paradise Lost*, vii. 25–6 may seem odd. But see the description of the poet amidst 'this time of dereliction and dismay' which closes *The Prelude*, ii. 435–66.

61 *The Fountain*. Composed Oct. 1798–Feb. 1797. Published 1800.

63 *The Two April Mornings*. Composed Oct. 1798–Feb. 1799. Published 1800.

64 l. 30. River Derwent flows through Cockermouth, W's birthplace in the north of the Lake District.

65 '*A slumber did my spirit seal*'. This and the two following poems were composed late 1798–early 1799 and published 1800. Much useless speculation has focused on these 'Lucy' poems in attempts to identify the original girl and to unravel W's psyche.In fairness it has to be said, however, that C started it, in a letter of 6 Apr. 1799: 'Some months ago Wordsworth transmitted to me a most sublime Epitaph ["A slumber . . ."] whether it had any reality, I cannot say.—Most probably in some gloomier moment he had fancied the moment in which his Sister might die.'

67 *Lucy Gray*. W noted: '. . . founded on a circumstance told me by my sister of a little girl who, not far from Halifax in Yorkshire, was bewildered in a snowstorm. Her footsteps were traced by her parents to the middle of the lock of a canal.'

69 *Nutting*. Composed Oct.–Dec. 1798. Published 1800. W recalled that the poem was 'intended as part of a poem on my own life, but struck

out as not being wanted there' (IF note). DW sent a text to C in a letter of 14 or 21 Dec. 1798 in which she also sent *The Prelude* descriptions of skating and stealing the boat.

l. 9. *my frugal Dame* was Ann Tyson, with whom W lodged whilst at Hawkshead School.

70 *'Three years she grew in sun and shower'*. Composed Feb. 1799. Published 1800. See note to 'A slumber did my spirit seal', above.

72 *The Brothers*. Composed 1800. Published 1800. As with so many of W's poems, this originates in a story told to W in an encounter while wandering. In Nov.–Dec. W, C and, until 5 Nov., John Wordsworth, toured the Lake District. On 12 Nov. in Ennerdale they heard the story of James Bowman who 'broke his neck ... by falling off a Crag—supposed to have layed down and slept—but walked in his sleep, and so came to this crag, and fell off—This was at Proud Knot on the mountain called Pillar up Ennerdale—his Pike staff stuck midway and stayed till it rotted away' (*Notebooks* entry 541).

l. 1. 'This Poem was intended to be the concluding poem of a series of pastorals, the scene of which was laid among the mountains of Cumberland and Westmoreland. I mention this to apologise for the abruptness with which the poem begins'—W.

75 ll. 137–43. 'The impressive circumstance here described actually took place some years ago in this country, upon an eminence called Kidstow Pike, one of the highest of the mountains that surround Haweswater. The summit of the pike was stricken by lightning; and every trace of one of the fountains disappeared, while the other continued to flow as before'—W.

76 ll. 180–1. 'There is not anything more worthy of remark in the manners of the inhabitants of these mountains than the tranquillity, I might say indifference, with which they think and talk upon the subject of death. Some of the country churchyards, as here described, do not contain a single tombstone, and most of them have a very small number'—W.

80 ll. 305–7. 'The Great Gavel—so called, I imagine, from its resemblance to the gable end of a house—is one of the highest of the Cumberland mountains. It stands at the head of the several vales of Ennerdale, Wastdale and Borrowdale. The Leeza is a river which flows into the Lake of Ennerdale; on issuing from the lake it changes its name and is called the End, Eyne, or Enna. It falls into the sea a little below Egremont'—W.

84 *Hart-Leap Well*. Composed early 1800. Published 1800. W noted: 'The first eight stanzas were composed extempore one winter evening in the cottage; when, after having tired myself with labouring at an awkward

passage in "The Brothers", I started with a sudden impulse to this to get rid of the other, and finished it in a day or two. My sister and I had past the place a few weeks before in our wild winter journey from Sockburn on the banks of the Tees to Grasmere. A peasant whom we met near the spot told us the story so far as concerned the name of the well, and the hart, and pointed out the stones' (IF note). W and DW saw the spot 17 Dec. 1799.

87 l. 97. See *Othello*, I. iii. 135. For W's exploitation of narrative *not* garnished with event see e.g. 'Michael', ll. 16–39 and 'The Idiot Boy'.

90 *Home at Grasmere*. Composed 1800. Not published by W. In 1798, at the height of the intimacy of the two poets, C suggested that W was uniquely fitted to write a philosophical poem. The project for *The Recluse* was eagerly embraced by W (see letters of 6 and 11 Mar. 1798) and verse such as 'The Ruined Cottage' was probably thought to fall within the scope of the plan. Preparatory self-examination produced the two-part *Prelude* of 1799 and composition after W had made his home in Grasmere from the end of 1799 became *Home at Grasmere*. The grand design of *The Recluse*, however, was not to be fulfilled. Only *The Excursion* (1814) was published, bearing the subtitle 'Being a Portion of *The Recluse*', and a Preface in which W revealed his ambitions for the whole.

l. 1. The Wordsworths arrived at Dove Cottage, Grasmere, on 20 Dec. 1799. 'Emma' in the poem is DW.

99 *Poems on the Naming of Places*. In 1800 the following *Advertisement* introduced the sequence: 'By Persons resident in the country and attached to rural objects, many places will be found unnamed or of unknown names, where little Incidents will have occurred, or feelings been experienced, which will have given to such places a private and peculiar interest. From a wish to give some sort of record to such Incidents or renew the gratification of such Feelings, Names have been given to Places by the Author and some of his Friends, and the following Poems written in consequence.'

To Joanna. Joanna Hutchinson (1780–1843), sister of Mary, whom W was to marry 4 Oct. 1802. The fact that Joanna did not live her early life 'Amid the smoke of cities' emphasizes that these poems are exercises of the imagination and not merely recitals of fact. In the 1800 *Lyrical Ballads* W appended the following note: 'In Cumberland and Westmoreland are several Inscriptions upon the native rock which from the wasting of Time and the rudeness of the Workmanship had been mistaken for Runic. They are without doubt Roman.

The Rotha, mentioned in this poem, is the River which flowing through the Lakes of Grasmere and Rydale falls into Windermere. On Helm-Crag, that impressive single Mountain at the head of the Vale of Grasmere, is a Rock which from most points of view bears a striking resemblance to an Old Woman cowering. Close by this rock is one of those fissures or Caverns, which in the language of the Country are called Dungeons. The other Mountains either immediately surround the Vale of Grasmere, or belong to the same Cluster.'

101 '*A narrow girdle of rough stones and crags*'. W's IF note establishes that the incident took place with DW and C on the eastern shore of Grasmere.

102 l. 16. *wreck*. Northern form of 'wrack'.

l. 36. *Osmunda named*. royal moonwort, *Osmunda regalis*.

l. 38. *Naiad*. Naiad, goddess of river or spring.

104 *Michael*. Composed Oct.–Dec. 1800. Published 1800. W noted: 'The Sheepfold, on which so much of the poem turns, remains, or rather the ruins of it. The character and circumstances of Luke were taken from a family to whom had belonged, many years before, the house we lived in at Town-End, along with some fields and woodlands on the eastern shore of Grasmere. The name of the Evening Star was not in fact given to this house but to another on the same side of the valley more to the north' (IF note).

The poem was very important to W. He sent a copy of *Lyrical Ballads* (1800) to Charles James Fox, the statesman, and in a long letter of 14 Jan. 1801 singled out 'The Brothers' and 'Michael' for special mention: 'You have felt that the most sacred of all property is the property of the Poor. The two poems I have mentioned were written with a view to shew that men who do not wear fine cloaths can feel deeply.' W's letter to his old friend Thomas Poole of 9 Apr. 1801 also describes his intentions in the poem: 'I have attempted to give a picture of a man, of strong mind and lively sensibility, agitated by two of the most powerful affections of the human heart; the parental affection, and the love of property, *landed* property, including the feelings of inheritance, home, and personal and family independence.'

l. 2. *Green-head Gill* is a mountain stream to the north-east of Grasmere. It runs through the area still known as Forest-side, l. 40. Dunmal-Raise, l. 141, is the pass north towards Keswick and Easedale, l. 141, runs westwards out of Grasmere.

108 l. 179. W's note 1800: 'Clipping is the word used in the North of England for shearing.'

110 l. 268. 'The story alluded to here is well known in the country. The chapel is called Ings Chapel; and is on the right hand side of the road leading from Kendal to Ambleside'—W's note 1800. Robert (not Richard) Bateman, a successful merchant, provided the money for the rebuilding of the Chapel of his birthplace.

112 l. 334. W's 1800 note: 'It may be proper to inform some readers, that a sheep-fold in these mountains is an unroofed building of stone walls,

with different divisions. It is generally placed by the side of a brook, for the convenience of washing the sheep; but it is also useful as a shelter for them, and as a place to drive them into, to enable the shepherds conveniently to single out one or more for any particular purpose.'

116   '*I travelled among unknown Men*'. Composed early 1801. Published 1807. W sent a copy to Mary Hutchinson 29 Apr. 1801, saying that it was to be read after 'She dwelt among th'untrodden ways'.

117   *To a Sky-Lark*. Composed Mar.–July 1802. Published 1807. It seems likely that this poem was amongst a number which C commented on to Southey, 29 July 1802, as being 'very excellent Compositions, but here and there a daring Humbleness of Language and Versification, and a strict adherence to matter of fact, even to prolixity . . .'. In a letter of 24 Oct. 1828 W told Barron Field that 'Coleridge used severely to condemn, and to treat contemptuously' this poem.

Alice Fell. Composed 12–13 Mar. 1802. Published 1807. DW's *Journal* 16 Feb. 1802 records the origin of the poem: 'Mr. Graham [Robert Grahame, solicitor of Glasgow] said he wished Wm had been with him the other day—he was riding in a post chaise and he heard a strange cry that he could not understand, the sound continued and he called to the chaise driver to stop. It was a little girl that was crying as if her heart would burst. She had got up behind the chaise and her cloak had been caught by the wheel and was jammed in and it hung there. She was crying after it. Poor thing. Mr. Graham took her into the chaise and the cloak was released from the wheel but the child's misery did not cease for her cloak was torn to rags; it had been a miserable cloak before, but she had no other and it was the greatest sorrow that could befal her. Her name was Alice Fell. She had no parents, and belonged to the next Town. At the next Town Mr. G. left money with some respectable people in the town to buy her a new cloak.'

119   *Beggars*. Composed 13–14 Mar. 1802. Published 1807.

121   *To a Butterfly* ('*Stay near me*'). Composed 14 Mar. 1802. Published 1807. W completed 'Beggars' on 14 Mar. and the memory of Spenser's poem *The Fate of the Butterflie* must have prompted the conversation and composition. DW records: W 'wrote the Poem to a Butterfly! He ate not a morsel, nor put on his stockings but sate with his shirt neck unbuttoned, and his waistcoat open while he did it. The thought first came upon him as we were talking about the pleasure we both always feel at the sight of a Butterfly. I told him that I used to chase them a little but that I was afraid of brushing the dust off their wings, and did not catch them—He told me how they used to kill all the white ones when he went to school because they were frenchmen.'

To the Cuckoo. Composed Mar.–June 1802. Published 1807.

122 '*My heart leaps up when I behold*'. Composed 26 Mar. 1802. Published 1807. In 1815 W printed ll. 7–9 as an epigraph to Ode ('There was a time'), the very lines C had emphasized when he printed the poem in *The Friend*, Essay v, as an expression of the truth that 'Men are ungrateful to others only when they have ceased to look back on their former selves with joy and tenderness. They exist in fragments' (see *The Friend*, ed. Barbara E. Rooke, 2 vols. (Princeton and London,1969), i. 40).

123 *To H. C., Six Years Old.* Composed Mar.–June 1802. Published 1807. C describes his son on 14 Oct. 1803 and quotes l. 12: 'Hartley is what he always was—a strange strange Boy—"*exquisitely wild*"! An utter Visionary! like the Moon among thin Clouds, he moves in a circle of Light of his own making—he alone, in a Light of his own. Of all human Beings I never yet saw one so utterly naked of *Self*—he has no Vanity, no Pride, no Resentment, and tho' *very passionate*, I have never yet saw him *angry with* any body.'

124 '*Among all lovely things my Love had been*'. Composed 12 Apr. 1802. Published 1807. DW's account of the writing, *Journal* 20 Apr. 1802, confirmed by W's letter of 16 Apr. 1802, gives a fascinating glimpse of W's absorption in composition: '. . . when William came to a well or a Trough which there is in Lord Darlington's Park he began to write that poem of the glow-worm. Not being able to write upon the long Trot. Interrupted in going through the Town of Staindrop. Finished it about 2 miles and a half beyond Staindrop. He did not feel the jogging of the horse while he was writing but when he had done he felt the effect of it and his fingers were cold with his gloves.' The poem, which W said recorded an incident in 1795, was ridiculed on its appearance in 1807 and not reprinted by W.

To a Butterfly ('*I've watched you*'). Composed 20 Apr. 1802. Published 1807.

125 '*These chairs they have no words to utter*'. Composed *c.* 22 Apr. 1802. Not published by W. DW's *Journal* 22 Apr. 1802: 'A fine mild morning. We walked into Easedale . . . [I] sate upon the grass till they [W and C] came from the Waterfall. I saw them there and heard Wm flinging stones into the River whose roaring was loud even where I was. When they returned William was repeating the poem "I have thoughts that are fed by the Sun". It had been called to his mind by the dying away of the stunning of the waterfall when he came behind a stone.'

l. 19. Cf. Chaucer, *The Knight's Tale*, l. 2779.

126 *Resolution and Independence.* Composed May–July 1802. Published 1807. W noted: 'This old man I met a few hundred yards from my

cottage at Town-End, Grasmere; and the account of him is taken from his own mouth. I was in the state of feeling described in the beginning of the poem, while crossing over Barton Fell from Mr Clarkson's, at the foot of Ullswater, towards Askam. The image of the hare I then observed on the ridge of the Fell' (IF note). DW's *Journal*, 3 Oct. 1800, describes the meeting. W crossed Barton Fell on 7 Apr. 1802.

127 l. 43. Thomas Chatterton (1752–70), author of purportedly fifteenth-century poems of Thomas Rowley. Killed himself in despair at poverty and lack of recognition. Became a symbol of the poet whose creative gifts are at once a blessing and a destructive power. This poem follows the metre of Chatterton's 'An Excelent Balade of Charitie'.

ll. 45–6. Robert Burns (1759–96), still a farmer when he wrote some of his finest work. Burns was thought to have hastened his early death through dissipation. The fact that he left at his death wife and children without support is also in W's mind at this time when his own marriage was approaching.

130 *Travelling*. Composed *c*. 4 May 1802. Published *PW*, iv. 423. This text from MS. See DW's *Journal* 4 May 1802.

'*Within our happy Castle there dwelt one*'. Composed May 1802. Published 1815 as 'Stanzas written in my Pocket-Copy of Thomson's "Castle of Indolence"'. James Thomson's poem (1748) was important in fostering the Spenserian stanza in the eighteenth century and was to C 'that most lovely Poem' (10 Mar. 1795).

In the IF note W said: 'Composed in the Orchard, Grasmere, Town-End. Coleridge was living with us much at the time; his son Hartley has said, that his father's character and habits are here preserved in a livelier way than anything that has been written about him.'

Despite some confusion caused by Arnold, it has been generally agreed that the first portrait is of W and the second of C. Both are highly literary in origin, however, drawing not just on Thomson but on Beattie's *The Minstrel* (1771–4) and even *Troilus and Criseyde*, passages of which W had translated in Dec. 1801, and, as Lucy Newlyn has pointed out in a penetrating discussion of the poem, they do not distinguish the poets but on the contrary merge and blur their separate identities.

132 '*The world is too much with us*'. Composed May 1802–Mar. 1804. Published 1807.

133 '*With Ships the sea was sprinkled far and nigh*'. Composed and published as above.

'*Dear Native Brooks your ways have I pursued*'. Composed May–Dec. 1802. W recalls the beloved river of his childhood, the Derwent, and appropriately alludes to C's 'Sonnet to the River Otter', which begins: 'Dear native Brook!'

134 '*Great Men have been among us*'. Composed May–Dec. 1802. Published 1807. In this roll-call of English Republicans W refers to Algernon Sidney (1622–83), author of *Discourse concerning Civil Government*; Andrew Marvell (1621–78); James Harrington (1611–77), author of *Commonwealth of Oceana*; Sir Henry Vane the younger (1613–62).

Composed by the Sea-Side, near Calais. Composed Aug. 1802. Published 1807. DW's *Journal* entry for the month includes: 'We had delightful walks after the heat of the day was passed away—seeing far off in the west the Coast of England like a cloud crested with Dover Castle, which was but like the summit of the cloud. The Evening star and the glory of the sky.'

135 '*It is a beauteous Evening, calm and free*'. Composed Aug. 1802. Published 1807. The 'Dear Child' is Caroline, daughter of W and Annette Vallon, although it could be construed as an address to DW. 'Abraham's bosom', see Luke 16:22, the repose of the happy after death, suggests that W is thinking of the child's transition from 'God, who is our home' to this world in the terms developed in Ode ('There was a time').

To Toussaint L'Ouverture. Composed Aug. 1802. Published *Morning Post* 2 Feb. 1803 and 1807. François Dominique Toussaint, surnamed L'Ouverture, was the son of a Negro slave. He was imprisoned in Paris in June 1802 because he resisted, as Governor of Haiti, Napoleon's edict re-establishing slavery. He died in imprisonment in Apr. 1803.

136 *Composed Upon Westminster Bridge*. Composed 31 July 1802–3 Sept. 1802. Published 1807. W noted that the poem was 'Composed on the roof of a coach on my way to France Sept. 1802' (IF note), but W and DW left on 31 July and returned to London 1 Sept. (The confusion is increased by the fact that all editions to 1836 date the poem 'Sept. 3 1803'.) It seems likely that W drafted the poem on the outward journey and completed it on 3 Sept. DW's *Journal*, 31 July, records: 'We mounted the Dover Coach at Charing Cross. It was a beautiful morning. The City, St. Paul's, with the River and a multitude of little Boats, made a most beautiful sight as we crossed Westminster Bridge. The houses were not overhung by their cloud of smoke and they were spread out endlessly, yet the sun shone so brightly with such a pure light that there was even something like the purity of one of nature's own grand spectacles.' For another poem which celebrates the transfigured city see 'St Paul's', pp. 151–2.

London, 1802. Composed Sept. 1802. Published 1807. Milton was, of course, the supreme example to W: a poet of austere and principled life and art.

137 'Nuns fret not at their Convent's narrow room'. Composed c. late 1802. Published 1807. Furness, l. 6, is the south-western part of the Lake District.

'She was a Phantom of delight'. Composed Oct. 1803–Mar. 1804. Published 1807. Christopher Wordsworth, Memoirs of William Wordsworth, 2 vols. (1851), ii. 306, cites Mr Justice Coleridge's record that W said the poem 'was written on "his dear wife", of whom he spoke in the sweetest manner; a manner full of the warmest love and admiration, yet with delicacy and reserve'.

138 Ode to Duty. Composed 1804–early 1807. Published 1807.

l. 1. See Paradise Lost, ix. 652–4. Eve explains:

> God so commanded, and left that command
> Sole daughter of his voice; the rest, we live
> Law to our selves, our reason is our law.

140 ll. 57–64. Glossed by W in 'Reply to "Mathetes"' (1809–10): 'in his character of Philosophical Poet, having thought of Morality as implying in its essence voluntary obedience, and producing the effect of order, he transfers, in the transport of imagination, the law of Moral to physical Natures, and, having contemplated, through the medium of that order, all modes of existence as subservient to one spirit, concludes his address to the power of Duty in the following words [this stanza]' (Prose, ii. 24–5).

Ode. ('There was a time'). Composed Mar. 1802–Mar. 1804. Published 1807. History of composition uncertain, but seems probable that stanzas i–iv belong to 1802 and the rest to 1804.

In his long IF note W describes the poem's origins in his childhood's 'sense of the indomitableness of the spirit within me'. C's 'Dejection: An Ode' (1802) engages in dialogue with stanzas i–iv and is, in turn, answered by the development of W's poem.

142 ll. 58 et seq. In the IF note W explains his poetic use of this fiction: '. . . a pre-existent state has entered into the popular creeds of many nations; and, among all persons acquainted with classic literature, is known as an ingredient in Platonic philosophy . . . I took hold of the notion of pre-existence as having sufficient foundation in humanity for authorizing me to make for my purpose the best use of it I could as a Poet.'

143 l. 103. W's quotation marks acknowledge a borrowing from Daniel's Musophilus in the sonnet to Fulke Greville, l. 1.

ll. 117–23. On our early 'intimation or assurance within us, that some part of our nature is imperishable' see Essays upon Epitaphs (1810), i. Prose, ii. 50. See also Biographia Literaria, ch. xxii, where C discusses the passage and objects to 'the frightful notion of lying awake in the grave'. See also DW's *Journal* entry 29 Apr. 1802 for the idea of lying in the grave 'to hear the *peaceful* sounds of the earth . . .'.

144 l. 144. See important anecdotal recollections *PW*, iv. 467.

145 '*I wandered lonely as a Cloud*'. Composed Mar. 1804–Apr. 1807. Published 1807. On 15 Apr. 1802 W and DW saw the daffodils along the western shore of Ullswater. DW records in her *Journal*: 'I never saw daffodils so beautiful, they grew among the mossy stones about and about them, some rested their heads upon these stones, as on a pillow, for weariness and the rest tossed and reeled and danced and seemed as if they verily laughed with the wind that blew upon them over the lake, they looked so gay ever glancing ever changing.' In the IF note W said: 'The two best lines in it [15–16] are by Mary.' W was particularly sensitive to misreading of this poem. See his letter of 4 Nov. 1807 and to Beaumont Feb. 1808.

146 l. 6/7. When the poem was published in 1815, W added another stanza at this point:

> Continuous as the stars that shine
> And twinkle on the milky way,
> They stretched in never-ending line
> Along the margin of a bay:
> Ten thousand saw I at a glance,
> Tossing their heads in sprightly dance.

Stepping Westward. Composed 3 June 1805. Published 1807. DW's *Recollections*, 11 Sept. 1803, describes the meeting rather as W does in the headnote and concludes: 'I cannot describe how affecting this simple expression was in that remote place, with the western sky in front, *yet* glowing with the departed sun.' In the MS of *Recollections* DW has written: 'The poem . . . was written this day while W and I and little Dorothy were walking in the green field, where we are used to walk, by the [river] Rothay. June 3 1805.'

147 *The Solitary Reaper*. Composed 5 Nov. 1805. Published 1807. DW's *Recollections* 13 Sept. 1803 record: 'It was harvest time, and the fields were quietly—might I be allowed to say pensively?— enlivened by small companies of reapers. It is not uncommon in the more lonely parts of the Highlands to see a single person so employed.' A note in 1807 identified the origin of the poem in a sentence from Thomas Wilkinson's *Tours to the British Mountains* (1824), which had been known to the Wordsworths in MS. It reads: 'Passed by a Female who was reaping alone: she sung in Erse as she bended over her sickle; the sweetest human Voice I ever heard: her strains were tenderly melancholy and felt delicious, long after they were heard no more' (p. 12). Both *Recollections* and the poem were, of course, written after the tour itself.

148 *Elegiac Stanzas*. Composed May–June 1806. Published 1807. In this poem, more than in any other save *The Prelude*, past and present, life and art interact. Peele Castle is off the southernmost coast of the Lake District, opposite Rampside, where W stayed in late summer 1794. John Wordsworth died 5–6 Feb. 1805. Sir George Beaumont's painting, 'A Storm: Peele Castle' was exhibited in 1806, and W probably saw it at the Royal Academy Private View 2 May 1806. The painting, which depicts a ship labouring past Peele Castle in very heavy seas, was engraved as the frontispiece for volume two of W's *Poems* (1815).

150 *A Complaint*. Composed *c.* Dec. 1806. Published 1807. W noted: 'Suggested by a change in the manner of a friend' (IF note). Almost certainly C, who stayed with the Wordsworths at Sir George Beaumont's Dec. 1806–Jan. 1807. His personal distress (C had decided finally to separate from his wife and family) deeply affected the Wordsworths. See Moorman, ii. 92–6.

151 *Gipsies*. Composed *c.* 26 Feb. 1807. Published 1807. W noted: 'I had observed them, as here described, near Castle Donnington, on my way to and from Derby' (IF note). In an essay called 'On Manner' of 27 Aug. 1815, later collected in *The Round Table* (1817). Hazlitt objected to what he called the 'Sunday-school philosophy' of the poem, an objection which elicited penetrating criticism from Keats: 'I think Hazlitt is right and yet I think Wordsworth is rightest. Wordsworth had not been idle he had not been without his task—nor had the Gipseys—they in the visible world had been as picturesque an object as he in the invisible. The Smoke of their fire—their attitudes—their Voices were all in harmony with the Evening—It is a bold thing to say and I would not say it in print—but it seems to me that if Wordsworth had thought a little deeper at that Moment he would not have written the Poem at all—I should judge it to have been written in one of the most comfortable Moods of his Life—it is a kind of sketchy intellectual landscape—not a search after Truth—nor is it fair to attack him on such a subject' (28–30 Oct. 1817).

St Paul's. Composed Apr.–early autumn 1808. Not published by W. See *PW*, iv. 374–5. The 'Friend', l. 2, is C, and W describes his experience after leaving him 3 Apr. 1808 in a letter of 8 Apr., which should be consulted.

152 '*Surprized by joy—impatient as the Wind*'. Composed 1813–Oct. 1814. Published 1815. W noted: 'This was in fact suggested by my daughter Catherine, long after her death' (IF note). See note above. Catherine was a much loved child, though 'the *arrantest* Mischief that ever lived' (MW, 1 Aug. 1810).

153 *Yew-Trees*. Composed 1811–14. Published 1815. W visited the Lorton

Vale yew-tree in late 1804 and composition may have begun then, but no MS evidence exists to support this attractive idea. In the IF note W said: 'Calculating upon what I have observed of the slow growth of this tree in rocky situations, and of its durability, I have often thought that the one I am describing must have been as old as the Christian era.' Clearly it was the yew's identity as a mute survivor which moved W's imagination to include in revision references to English warriors of the fourteenth century and to famous battles of the Hundred Years War. 'Yew-Trees' was one of the poems C chose to demonstrate that 'in imaginative power [W] stands nearest of all modern writers to Shakespeare and Milton; and yet in a kind perfectly unborrowed and his own' (*Biographia Literaria*, ch. xxii).

Lorton Vale and Borrowdale are in the western-central part of the Lake District, as is the mountain Glaramara.

154 *The River Duddon: Conclusion*. Composed 1818–20. Published 1820. The conclusion of 'The River Duddon' sonnet sequence. This sonnet has been selected as the finest of the sequence and the one best able to stand alone.

l. 5. Cf. C's description of a waterfall, 25 Aug. 1802: '. . . the continual *change* of the *Matter*, the perpetual *Sameness* of the *Form*—it is an awful Image and Shadow of God and the World'.

Airey-Force Valley. Composed Sept. 1835. Published 1842. Aira Force is on the western shore of Ullswater. 'Force' is the northern word for waterfall. In *A Guide Through the District of the Lakes* W declares Ullswater 'As being, perhaps, upon the whole, the happiest combination of beauty and grandeur, which any of the Lakes affords . . . Ara-force thunders down the Ghyll on the left . . .' (*Prose*, ii. 165–6).

155 *Extempore Effusion Upon the Death of James Hogg*. Composed Nov. 1835. Published 12 Dec. 1835 in the *Athenaeum* and 1836–7. W's very long IF note begins: 'These verses were written extempore, immediately after reading a notice of the Ettrick Shepherd's death . . . The persons lamented in these verses were all either of my friends or acquaintance.' The poem laments the following writers: James Hogg (1770–1835), called 'The Ettrick Shepherd', remembered now for his *Confessions of a Justified Sinner*, Sir Walter Scott (1771–1832), famous in his day as poet as well as novelist, 'The Lay of the Last Minstrel' being his best-known poem; Samuel Taylor Coleridge (1771–1834), the poet and thinker to whom W said he was most intellectually indebted (25 June 1832) and to whom *The Prelude* (1805) was addressed; Charles Lamb (1775–1834), best known for his *Essays of Elia*; George Crabbe (1754–1832), poet, author of 'The Village' and 'The Borough'; Felicia Hemans (1793–1835), a very popular poet, now largely forgotten.

ll. 1–5. Hogg was with W when they visited the Yarrow on 1 Sept. 1814. Scott was their companion when Yarrow was revisited on 20 Sept. 1831.

l. 10. Scott was buried in Dryburgh Abbey.

l. 12. Hogg was born in the Borders region of Ettrick Forest and was a shepherd in his early life.

l. 19. An allusion tying the poets together. Lamb is called 'gentle-hearted' in C's 'This Lime-Tree Bower my Prison', written in 1797 when C, W, and Lamb were all enjoying intense friendship. W presumably did not know that Lamb objected strongly—see his very funny letter of 14 Aug. 1800.

THE PRELUDE

157 Composed 1798–1850. A poem in two books was completed in 1799. The thirteen-book version was completed by 1805. The fourteen-book poem, published and given its title by W's widow and executors on his death in 1850, was essentially ready by 1839. For all three texts and a full account of the history of composition, see *The Prelude 1799, 1805, 1850*, ed. Jonathan Wordsworth, M. H. Abrams, and Stephen Gill (New York and London, 1979).

During the summer of 1798, towards the end of his period of greatest intimacy with C, W conceived the plan for *The Recluse*, the philosophical poem discussed in the notes to *Home at Grasmere*, p. 231. *The Prelude*, never so called by W, began as a work of self-analysis and intellectual and emotional stock-taking, addressed to C. In 1803, *The Recluse* languishing, W returned to his autobiographical poem and greatly enlarged its scope, including now a fuller treatment both of his own life and of Romantic aesthetics. The poem's structure underwent many changes, as W expanded it from a two to a five-book version and then further to the thirteen-book poem, but throughout its development it is clear that the ascent of Snowdon which opens Book xiii was designed as the climax of the whole.

The Prelude refers to W's own experiences, to historical events, to aesthetic and philosophic concepts, to other literature. For full annotation see Wordsworth, Abrams, Gill eds. cit. above and vol. ii of Raymond Dexter Havens, *The Mind of a Poet* (Baltimore, 1941). The notes below confine themselves to identifying people, places, and events and to giving only such textual information as contributes to an understanding of the growth of the poem's structure.

Book One

ll. 1–115. The opening celebrates W's sense of release and purposefulness when he went to Grasmere in late 1799. Allusions at ll. 6–7 and ll. 15–19 to Exod. 13:3 and the concluding lines of *Paradise Lost* establish the literary rather than the geographically specific nature of the passage and in particular of the 'city' of l. 7.

158 l. 271. The 1799 two-part *Prelude* began with this abrupt question.

l. 278. W was born at Cockermouth in the northern Lake District; 'sweet birthplace' alludes to C's 'Frost at Midnight', l. 28.

159 l. 309. W entered Hawkshead Grammar School in May 1779. The region around Hawkshead and the late, Esthwaite, is the setting for many of the childhood incidents described.

l. 317. *springes*. snares.

161 l. 376. *Patterdale*. the western side of Ullswater.

164 l. 497. *characters*. distinguishing marks, signs.

166 l. 570. *Bothnic main*. the northern Baltic.

168 l. 645. The first of many tributes to C in the poem.

l. 653. W has in mind the great task of writing *The Recluse*.

Book Two

169 l. 39. Hawkshead Town Hall, built in 1790.

170 l. 82. The Sabines were noted for frugality.

171 l. 96. *fountain*. spring.

l. 108. Furness Abbey in the south of the Lake District.

172 l. 141. *breathed*. allowed our horses to regain breath.

l. 151. W refers to the White Lion at Bowness and the still surviving house built on Belle Isle in the early 1780s.

173 l. 174. Robert Greenwood, later Senior Fellow of Trinity College, Cambridge. See *Wordsworth's Hawkshead*, 78–80.

174 l. 228. The image is of classifying objects or specimens as in a collection.

176 l. 314. W draws attention to an echo of *Paradise Lost*, ix. 249.

177 l. 349. School began at 6 a.m. in summer and 7 a.m. in winter. The friend was John Fleming.

178 l. 381. *plastic*. shaping.

179 l. 448. See C's letter of *c*. 10 Sept. 1799 in which he urgently entreats W to write a poem which might counter the tendency of the times towards reaction and depravity.

Book Three

182 l. 276. A reference to Chaucer's *Reeve's Tale* set in Trumpington.

l. 286. In tribute to Milton W echoes *Paradise Lost*, vii. 27.

183 l. 312. Cassandra repeatedly prophesied the fall of Troy, but was not listened to.

Book Five

185 l. 60. *Don Quixote* (1605), which W read as a child.

l. 71. The dream is a reworking of one experienced by Descartes in 1619. It is generally agreed that C drew W's attention to it.

188 l. 307. *notices*. remarks, observations.

l. 322. *terms of art*. technical language, jargon.

189 l. 332. *cunning*. arts, necessary knowledge.

l. 362. *pinfold*. pound, enclosure.

ll. 364–7. Reference to heroes of romance. Fortunatus's magical cap would take him wherever he wished. Jack the Giant-killer's coat made him invisible. Robin Hood led the band of outlaws who robbed the rich to give to the poor. Sabra was rescued from a dragon by St George and became his wife. See C's declaration, 16 Oct. 1797, of the importance of letting children read 'Romances, and Relations of Giants and Magicians, and Genii'.

190 l. 383. *engines*. machines.

l. 389. W interweaves memories of himself and a schoolfriend William Raincock. The episode was first cast in the first person, amongst the early drafts for the 1799 version of the poem, but put into the third person when published as 'There was a boy' in *Lyrical Ballads* (1800).

192 l. 470. The drowned man was James Jackson, schoolmaster, who died 18 June 1779.

Book Six

193 l. 339. *Fellow Student*. Robert Jones.

194 l. 357. *federal Day*. 13 July 1790. The eve of the anniversary of the Fall of the Bastille.

197 l. 572. Echoes Milton's description of God in *Paradise Lost*, v. 165: 'Him first, him last, him midst, and without end'.

Book Seven

198 l. 399. Shadrach, Meshach, and Abednego. See Dan. 3:23–6.

200 l. 651. St Bartholomew's Fair was held annually at Smithfield, where Protestants were martyred in Queen Mary's reign.

201 l. 675. *salt-box*. A rudimentary instrument, in which salt or similar substance was rattled.

l. 686. Madame Tussaud's wax-work collection opened in London in 1802.

l. 689. *Promethean*. inventive, creative. In Greek myth Prometheus fashioned man out of clay.

Book Eight

203 l. 75. *complacency*. without modern overtones, means tranquil satisfaction.

l. 86. *redounding*. eddying, swirling.

205 ll. 420–2. Corin and Phyllis are common names in pastoral poetry. '*Coronal*'. usually a circlet or crown, here a ring.

206 l. 681. An echo of 'Lycidas', 104–6.

207 l. 713. *Antiparos*. An island in the Aegean. *Yordas*. a cave in north-west Yorkshire, visited by W in May 1800.

Book Nine

208 l. 78. *Le Brun*. Charles le Brun (1619–90). His 'Magdalene' is now in the Louvre.

l. 294. Michael Beaupuy (1755–96). Though wounded in the Vendée, he did not die there, as W thought, but on the eastern front in 1796.

Book Ten

210 ll. 46–8. The Swiss Guard of the Palace of the Tuileries killed many insurgents before being themselves slaughtered. The corpses were burnt in the Place de Carrousel in front of the Tuileries.

211 l. 65. In Sept. 1792 many prisoners were executed after summary trial.

ll. 70–6. W echoes *As You Like It*, I. i. 13–16 and *Macbeth*, II. ii. 35–6.

l. 468. 'Moloch, horrid king besmeared with blood | Of human sacrifice', *Paradise Lost*, i. 392–3.

ll. 471–5. W was at Rampside on the south-west coast of the Lake District, near the estuary of the river Leven, Aug.–Sept. 1794.

212 l. 492. William Taylor (1754–86), headmaster of Hawkshead Grammar School, buried at Cartmel Priory.

213 l. 535. Robespierre was executed 28 July 1794.

l. 548. One of the labours of Hercules was the cleaning of the stables of King Augeas. He did it by diverting the rivers Alpheus and Peneus.

l. 549. *their own helper*. the guillotine.

214 ll. 559–66. A reference back to the boyhood episode of ii. 99–144.

l. 810. Almost certainly a reference to William Godwin's *Enquiry Concerning Political Justice* (1793). In this passage W selects only one aspect of Godwin's complex work, his emphasis on the power of human reason if fearlessly employed.

215 l. 905. W met C in Sept. 1795. They corresponded and by 13 May 1796 C could refer to W as 'A very dear friend of mine, who is in my opinion the best poet of the age'.

l. 908. DW lived with W at Racedown House in Dorset from Sept. 1795.

Book Eleven

216 l. 258. The two 'spots of time', 257–315, 344–88, were composed in early 1799 for the two-part version of *The Prelude*, where they appeared naturally amongst other memories of childhood. The lines which now make a transition between them were written in early 1804 and have clear links with the Ode ('There was a time'), completed then.

217 l. 305. *The Beacon*. A signal beacon on a hill above Penrith.

218 l. 317. *two dear Ones*. Mary Hutchinson and DW.

219 l. 366. W's father, John Wordsworth, died 30 Dec. 1783.

l. 367. *two Brothers*. Richard and John.

Book Thirteen

221 l. 5. W made a pedestrian tour of North Wales with Robert Jones in the summer of 1791. 'Bethkelet': Beddgelert.

l. 11. *glaring*: clammy.

223 l. 113. For the distinction see *Paradise Lost*, v. 487–90.

Further Reading

FULL citation for the authoritative editions of Wordsworth's letters, prose, and poems, and for DW's *Journals* will be found on p. 225. Scholarly works cited there are not mentioned again in the list below, in which the titles are given of further standard editions and recommended critical and scholarly studies.

EDITIONS

The Cornell Wordsworth is a multi-volume project which will be the authoritative edition of the poems when complete. Volumes published so far are:

The Salisbury Plain Poems, ed. Stephen Gill (Ithaca, 1975)
The Prelude, 1798–99, ed. Stephen Parrish (Ithaca, 1977)
Home at Grasmere, ed. Beth Darlington (Ithaca, 1977)
The Ruined Cottage and The Pedlar, ed. James Butler (Ithaca, 1979)
Benjamin the Waggoner, ed. Paul F. Betz (Ithaca, 1981)
The Borderers, ed. Robert Osborn (Ithaca, 1982)
Poems in Two Volumes, ed. Jared R. Curtis (Ithaca, 1983)
An Evening Walk, ed. James Averill (Ithaca, 1984)
Descriptive Sketches, ed. Eric Birdsall (Ithaca, 1984)
Peter Bell, ed. John E. Jordan (Ithaca, 1985)
The Fourteen-Book Prelude, ed. W. J. B. Owen (Ithaca, 1985)
The Tuft of Primroses with Other Late Poems for The Recluse, ed. Joseph Kishel (Ithaca, 1986)
The White Doe of Rylstone, ed. Kristine Dugas (Ithaca, 1988)
Shorter Poems, 1807–1820, ed. Carl H. Ketcham (Ithaca, 1990)
The Thirteen-Book Prelude, ed. Mark L. Reed (Ithaca, 1992)
Lyrical Ballads, and Other Poems, 1797–1800, eds. James Butler and Karen Green (Ithaca, 1993)

Other editions which will be of use are, in alphabetical order:

Samuel Taylor Coleridge, *Letters*, ed. E. L. Griggs (Oxford, 1956–71)
Sara Hutchinson, *Letters 1800–1835*, ed. Kathleen Coburn (London, 1954)
Henry Crabb Robinson, *Correspondence . . . with the Wordsworth Circle*, ed. E. J. Morley (Oxford, 1927)
Henry Crabb Robinson, *Henry Crabb Robinson on Books and Their Writers*, ed. E. J. Morley (London, 1938)
John Wordsworth, *Letters*, ed. Carl H. Ketcham (Ithaca, 1969)

William and Mary Wordsworth, *The Love Letters*, ed. Beth Darlington (Ithaca, 1981)

William Wordsworth, *The Critical Opinions of*, ed. Markham L. Peacock, Jr. (Baltimore, 1950)

William Wordsworth, *Literary Criticism*, ed. W. J. B. Owen (London, 1974)

William Wordsworth, *Literary Criticism*, ed. Paul M. Zall (Lincoln, Nebraska, 1966)

William Wordsworth, *Lyrical Ballads 1798*, ed. W. J. B. Owen (Oxford, 1967, 1969)

William Wordsworth, *Lyrical Ballads 1805*, ed. Derek Roper (London, 1968)

William Wordsworth, *The Prelude 1799, 1805, 1850*, eds. Jonathan Wordsworth, M. H. Abrams, Stephen Gill (New York and London, 1979)

William Wordsworth, *The Prose Works*, ed. Alexander B. Grosart (London, 1876)—includes Fenwick Notes.

CRITICISM, BIOGRAPHY, SCHOLARSHIP

M. H. Abrams, *Natural Supernaturalism* (New York, 1971)

M. H. Abrams, ed., *Wordsworth: A Collection of Critical Essays* (Englewood Cliffs, NJ, 1972)

Matthew Arnold, *Poems of Wordsworth* (London, 1879) and in *Essays in Criticism: Second Series* (London, 1888)

James Averill, *Wordsworth and Human Suffering* (Ithaca, 1980)

A. C. Bradley, *Oxford Lectures on Poetry* (London, 1909)

James K. Chandler, *Wordsworth's Second Nature: A Study of the Poetry and Politics* (Chicago, 1984)

C. C. Clarke, *Romantic Paradox* (London, 1962)

Jared R. Curtis, *Wordsworth's Experiments with Tradition: The Lyric Poems of 1802* (Ithaca, 1971)

Thomas De Quincey, essays collected in *Recollections of the Lakes and the Lake Poets*, ed. David Wright (Harmondsworth, 1970) and in *De Quincey as Critic*, ed. John E. Jordan (London, 1973)

David Ellis, *Wordsworth, Freud and the Spots of Time: Interpretation in the Prelude* (Cambridge, 1985)

Stephen Gill, *William Wordsworth: A Life* (Oxford, 1989)

Robert Gittings and Jo Manton, *Dorothy Wordsworth* (Oxford, 1985)

W. J. Harvey and R. Gravil, eds., *Wordsworth: The Prelude* (London, 1972)

Geoffrey H. Hartman, *Wordsworth's Poetry 1787–1814* (New Haven, 1964)

Donald E. Hayden, *Wordsworth's Walking Tour of 1790* (Tulsa, 1983)

Donald E. Hayden, *Wordworth's Travels in Wales and Ireland* (Tulsa, 1985)

Donald E. Hayden, *Wordsworth's Travels in Scotland* (Tulsa, 1985)

John O. Hayden, *The Romantic Reviewers 1802–1824* (London, 1969)

William Hazlitt, Essays in *Works*, ed. P. P. Howe (London, 1930–4): vols. xix. 9–25; iv. 111–25; v. 143–68; xvii. 106–22; xi. 86–95. For the essay from *The Spirit of the Age* see the edition by E. D. Mackerness (London, 1969)

Mary Jacobus, *Tradition and Experiment in Wordsworth's Lyrical Ballads 1798* (Oxford, 1976)

Kenneth R. Johnston, *Wordsworth and The Recluse* (New Haven, 1984)

J. Jones, *The Egotistical Sublime* (London, 1954)

Alec King, *Wordsworth and the Artist's Vision* (London, 1966)

Herbert Lindenberger, *On Wordsworth's Prelude* (Princeton, 1963)

W. J. B. Owen, *Wordsworth as Critic* (Oxford, 1969)

Thomas McFarland, *Romanticism and the Forms of Ruin* (Princeton, 1981)

Graham McMaster, ed., *William Wordsworth* (Harmondsworth, 1972)— Penguin Critical Anthologies Series.

James Maxwell and Stephen Gill, 'Wordsworth' in *English Poetry: Select Bibliographical Guides*, ed. A. E. Dyson (Oxford, 1971)

Mary Moorman, *William Wordsworth: A Biography. The Early Years* (Oxford, 1957); *The Later Years* (Oxford, 1965)

Richard J. Onorato, *The Character of the Poet: Wordsworth in The Prelude* (Princeton, 1971)

Stephen Maxfield Parrish, *The Art of the Lyrical Ballads* (Ithaca, 1973)

Robert Rehder, *Wordsworth and the Beginnings of Modern Poetry* (London, 1981)

Christopher Salvesen, *The Landscape of Memory* (London, 1965)

Ben Ross Schneider, Jr., *Wordsworth's Cambridge Education* (Cambridge, 1957)

Paul Sheats, *The Making of Wordsworth's Poetry 1785–98* (Cambridge, Mass., 1973)

Elsie Smith, *An Estimate of William Wordsworth by his Contemporaries 1793–1822* (Oxford, Basil Blackwell, 1932)

Leslie Stephen, 'Wordsworth's Ethics' (1876) in *Hours in a Library: Third Series* (London, 1879)

F. M. Todd, *Politics and the Poet* (London, 1957)

Jonathan Wordsworth, ed., *Bicentenary Wordsworth Studies* (Ithaca, 1970)

Jonathan Wordsworth, *The Music of Humanity* (London, 1969)

Jonathan Wordsworth, *William Wordsworth: The Borders of Vision* (Oxford, 1982)

Duncan Wu, *Wordsworth's Reading 1770–99* (Cambridge, 1993)

Duncan Wu, *Wordsworth's Reading 1800–15* (Cambridge, 1995)

INTELLECTUAL, POLITICAL, AND SOCIAL CONTEXT

M. H. Abrams, *The Mirror and the Lamp* (New York, 1953)

M. H. Abrams, 'English Romanticism: The Spirit of the Age', in *Romanticism Reconsidered*, ed. Northrop Frye (New York, 1962), 37–72

Marilyn Butler, *Romantics, Rebels and Reactionaries: English Literature and its Background 1760–1830* (Oxford, 1981)

Ian R. Christie, *Wars and Revolutions: Britain 1760–1815* (London, 1982)

James Engell, *The Creative Imagination: Enlightenment to Romanticism* (Cambridge, Mass., 1981)

E. J. Hobsbawn, *The Age of Revolution 1789–1848* (London, 1963)

Hugh Honour, *Romanticism* (London, 1982)

H. W. Piper, *The Active Universe: Pantheism and the Concept of the Imagination in the English Romantic Poets* (London, 1962)

Thomas McFarland, *Coleridge and the Pantheist Tradition* (Oxford, 1969)

Olivia Smith, *The Politics of Language 1791–1819* (Oxford, 1984)

Basil Willey, *The Eighteenth-Century Background* (London, 1940)

Carl Woodring, *Politics in English Romantic Poetry* (Cambridge, Mass., 1970)

Index of Titles and First Lines